Creative Economy

This book series covers research on creative economies based on humanity and spirituality to enhance the competitiveness, sustainability, peace, and fairness of international society. We define a creative economy as a socio-economic system that promotes those creative activities with a high market value and leads to the improvement of society's overall well-being.

As the global economy has developed, we have seen severe competition and polarization in income distribution. With this drastic change in the economic system, creativity with a high market value has come to be considered the main source of competiveness. But in addition to the improvement of competitiveness, we are required to work toward fairness in society.

In the process of developing a mature market, consumers come to understand that what they require most essentially is humanity and spirituality. This cannot be given or bought, but requires sharing with others across cultures and learning and developing further from their richness. Long-term sustainability of a company in this new age also requires building the same values of humanity and spirituality within its own internal organizational culture and practices.

Through this series, we intend to propose various policy recommendations that contribute to the prosperity of international society and improve the well-being of mankind by clarifying the concrete actions that are needed.

More information about this series at http://www.springer.com/series/13627

Nissim Otmazgin · Eyal Ben-Ari
Editors

Creative Context

Creativity and Innovation in the Media
and Cultural Industries

 Springer

Editors
Nissim Otmazgin
The Hebrew University of Jerusalem
Jerusalem, Israel

Eyal Ben-Ari
Center for Society, Security and Peace
Kinneret College on the Sea of Galilee
Galilee, Israel

ISSN 2364-9186 ISSN 2364-9445 (electronic)
Creative Economy
ISBN 978-981-15-3058-6 ISBN 978-981-15-3056-2 (eBook)
https://doi.org/10.1007/978-981-15-3056-2

This Springer imprint is published by the registered company Springer Nature Singapore Pte Ltd.
The registered company address is: 152 Beach Road, #21-01/04 Gateway East, Singapore 189721, Singapore

Preface

Creativity constituent lies at the heart of the media and cultural industries. These industries are directly dependent on a steady flow of creative ideas that must be tried and implemented if businesses are to succeed in turning them into marketable products and processes adopted by consumers. These businesses are also expected to provide working environments that adequately accommodate creative personnel and the processes by which creative ideas emerge. Musicians, animators, scriptwriters, craftsmen, designers, painters, architects, and many other artists often require a tailored working environment to stimulate, or at least to avoid stifling their creativity.

At the same time, however, creativity is a notion difficult to grasp or define and is sometimes a matter of feeling or implicit appreciation—"you know creativity when you see one." In this book, creativity is generally understood as the valorized production of culturally related artifacts and fashions undertaken by companies, entrepreneurs, promoters, and many other individuals who make their living out of the media business. Creativity is thus highly contextualized in the sense that it depends on the time and the place it is conceived. Hence, what is creative at a certain moment today might not be viewed so by tomorrow. And, accordingly, creativity cultivated in high-end fashioned designers' office in Shanghai might not be regarded as creative by an isolated community living in the Amazon rainforest.

Are there some communalities in the creative process that are common across time and space? What can we learn about the notion of creativity in different media and cultural fields? How is creativity cultivated and what are the social, cultural, and organizational conditions that accelerate or hamper creativity? Is creativity essentially an individual invention or is there such a thing as "corporate creativity" where organizations and companies are creative as collectives of individuals? These are some of the questions we address in this book through an analysis of different kinds of creativity generated in different cultural fields.

More broadly, this book is part of the attempt to set out an emerging agenda for the study of creativity in the cultural and media industries. The originality of this book lies in presenting a comparative and interdisciplinary perspective that develops a new framework and analytical concepts to understand the notion of creativity in the media and cultural industries, and in providing a series of fresh empirically based studies of the process of creativity in fields such as advertising, fashion, animation, and cinema. This comparative move is taken on in order to generate new insights about the particular features of the creative industries and new questions for future analysis. The constituent chapters provide substantial analysis for the way creativity is being conceived, cultivated, commodified, reproduced, marketed, and appropriated, emphasizing the role played by both individual creators and groups. While the focus of this volume is the media and cultural industries, they are investigated in the context of other groups and organizations connecting forms of creativity with an explicit emphasis on turning ideas into concrete practices and products.

The book is based on a workshop titled "Comparatively Speaking: Creativity and Innovation in the Media and Cultural Industries," which was held at the Center for the Study of the Creative Economy, the Faculty of Economics at Dōshisha University, Kyoto, in January 6–7, 2017, organized by Kawashima Nobuko and Nissim Otmazgin. We would like to thank the scholars and students who took part in the workshop and contributed their valuable input and knowledge. We also wish to thank Dōshisha University for hosting and supporting the workshop. Our utmost thanks go to Prof. Kawashima Nobuko. Without her help, this book would not have been published. We hope that this book will be of use to scholars and students of cultural and media industries, as well as to those interested in the wider phenomena which are positioned at the root of all cultural research: How is culture being produced, transferred, and accepted?

Jerusalem, Israel   Nissim Otmazgin
January 2020   Eyal Ben-Ari

Contents

Editors and Contributors

About the Editors

Nissim Otmazgin is a professor at the Department of Asian Studies, the director of the Institute for Asian and African Studies, The Hebrew University of Jerusalem, and a member of the Israeli Young Academy of Science and Humanities. A political scientist in training, his research interests include cultural diplomacy in Asia, popular culture and regionalization in East and Southeast Asia, and cultural industry and cultural policy in Japan and South Korea. His Ph.D. dissertation (Kyoto University, 2007), which examines the export of Japan's popular culture to Asia, won the Iue Asia Pacific Research Prize for outstanding dissertation on society and culture in Asia. As a part of this research, he conducted extensive fieldwork in Hong Kong, Singapore, Shanghai, Bangkok, and Seoul. He is the author of *Regionalizing Culture: The Political Economy of Japanese Popular Culture in Asia* (University of Hawaii Press, 2013) and coauthor (together with Michal Daliot Bul) of *The Anime Boom in the US: Lessons for Global Creative Industries* (Harvard University Asia Center Press, 2017).

Eyal Ben-Ari is a senior fellow of the Center for Society, Security and Peace at Kinneret College on the Sea of Galilee. He has carried out research in Israel, Japan, Singapore, and Hong Kong. His main areas of research are the sociology of the armed forces, early childhood education, and popular culture in Asia. Among his recent books are *Japanese Encounters* (2018), (with Zev Lehrer, Uzi Ben-Shalom and Ariel Vainer) *Rethinking the Sociology of Warfare* (2010), (with Nissim Otmazgin) *The State and Popular Culture in East Asia* (2012), and (with Jessica Glicken Turnley and Kobi Michael) (2017) *Social Science and Special Operations Forces*. He has published articles spanning a variety of disciplines including the

American Ethnologist, Cultural Anthropology, The Sociological Review, The Sociological Quarterly, Special Operations Journal, and the *Journal of Strategic Studies*.

Contributors

Eyal Ben-Ari Kinneret Academic College, Sea of Galilee, Israel

Karin Ling-Fung Chau King's College London, London, UK

Jennifer Coates The University of Sheffield, Sheffield, UK

Stan Erraught University of Leeds, Leeds, England, UK

Adam Johns Sophia University, Tokyo, Japan

Yael (yali) Nativ The Academic College for Society and Arts ASA, Netanya, Israel

Nissim Otmazgin The Hebrew University of Jerusalem, Jerusalem, Israel

Jimmyn Parc Sciences Po Paris, France;
Seoul National University, South Korea

Christopher Pokarier Waseda University, Tokyo, Japan

Jakob Thestrup The University of Tokyo, Tokyo, Japan

Heung Wah Wong The University of Hong Kong, Pok Fu Lam Road, Hong Kong

Part I
Introduction

Chapter 1
Creativity and Innovation in the Media and Cultural Industries: Setting an Agenda for the Social and Human Sciences

Eyal Ben-Ari and Nissim Otmazgin

The term "creativity"—and related expressions like originality, imagination, innovation or inspiration—has become a key word in today's media and cultural industries. Indeed, the term (frequently in concert with allied notions) is variously used as a guiding organizational principle, a marker of a peculiar form of production, a mobilizing and motivating slogan for employees in workplaces, or a motto differentiating them from other industries. Whatever the veracity of such claims, creativity has become a veritable watchword in media and cultural businesses.

In these industries, creativity is generally understood as the valorized production of culturally-related artifacts and fashions undertaken by companies, entrepreneurs, promoters and many other individuals who make their living out of the media business. The creative production may come in the form of developing new narratives, images, and commodities (a new dance choreography, a manga book, catchy advertisement campaign, or a new line of accessories), instigating change within the media organization (initiating transnational collaboration in marketing a new film, using anime technique and know-how in the video game industry, signing a tie-up agreement between a hit pop song and a trendy TV drama), and creating new market opportunities (turning K-pop into a global phenomenon, expanding the reach of Kyoto's traditional craft industry to contemporary consumers, Japanese and Western fashion brands entering East Asia's growing consumer markets).

At its most basic, creativity involves some kind of "play with form" or "playfulness"—a transformation of existing form (material or abstract) into something novel that is socially recognized and valued as such (Schwartzman 1978). Accordingly, it entails a dialogue with existing forms since it is only with reference to previous ideas or concrete artifacts that creativity can be identified. Creativity can take the most minute form (two dancers improvising) or a macro product (architectural marvels);

E. Ben-Ari
Kinneret Academic College, Sea of Galilee, Israel

N. Otmazgin (✉)
The Hebrew University of Jerusalem, Jerusalem, Israel
e-mail: nissim.otmazgin@mail.huji.ac.il

© Springer Nature Singapore Pte Ltd. 2020
N. Otmazgin and E. Ben-Ari (eds.), *Creative Context*, Creative Economy,
https://doi.org/10.1007/978-981-15-3056-2_1

it can be expressed in new markets (a move from a regional to wider marketplaces); or in novel processes (from hand-made to machine production, from small group creation to processes involving mass fan communities). Thus, as a number of papers (Wong and Chau, Otmazgin, Thestrup, Johns) underscore, innovation in processes are in themselves creative. And, these are related in that, for instance, a move to an international market as in "traditional Kyoto crafts" involves new materials and production and may entail different designs as well as a shift in branding what is considered to be "authentic". Moreover, while creativity involves a certain degree of uncertainty, its crucial feature is that upon entering a creative process the outcome is unknown. In more abstract terms then, while uncertainty is about classification—you don't know how to classify something—creativity is about indeterminacy—you cannot know the outcome of a process.

A review of the relevant scholarly literature reveals how different disciplines offer diverse but fruitful perspectives on creativity. Economists tend to look at the dynamics and markets for creative work and at the center of their work is uncertainty and the techniques for valorizing and managing it so that ventures (careers or businesses) are profitable (Flew 2004; Howkins 2001, 2013; Kawashima 2010; Kong and O'Connor 2009; Towse 2006). In addition, a closely related organizational and managerial literature has granted much attention to such issues as brokering in the cultural industries or the whole cultural production chain (DeFillippi et al. 2007; Jayne 2005; Pratt 2005). Long neglected in their discipline, sociologists have begun to analyze how key factors and mechanisms—institutional, cultural and interactional—in creative activity are socially based and developed. It has striven to focus on the agents or entrepreneurs who manipulate symbols, rules, technologies, and materials that create what is culturally acceptable and valued (Burns et al. 2015; Farrel 2001; Reuter 2015). And thus newer sociologically oriented studies emphasize how agents and entrepreneurs are socially embedded thereby facilitating or encouraging creativity (Burns et al. 2015). Psychologists, producing by far the most numerous studies, examine both the individual abilities and personalities facilitating creativity and the motivations impelling people to create by themselves or as part of small group dynamics (Wardle 2015). New areas include the cultural psychology of creativity emphasizing how creative products and processes are embedded within socio-cultural contexts. Here the emphasis is variously on how individuals transact with their own cultures (Glaveneau 2010, 2016; Niu and Sternberg 2008), pedagogical approaches linking creativity, imagination and learning (DeViney et al. 2010; Thomas and Brown 2007), or social psychology focusing on group structures facilitating creativity (De Vaan et al. 2015). Political economists examine the relationship between economic processes (such as the workings of markets) and political dynamics (such as the decisions of government agencies) in the media and cultural industries (Menger 2014; Seitz 2003; Otmazgin 2013) as well as how these industries are embedded in certain views of what labor and politics constitute (Lee 2017). Finally, cultural studies scholars focus on the dynamics involved in creative processes and analyze the cultural meanings of such processes, be they of elite or vernacular varieties, for their artistic qualities (Burgess 2006; Wu 2006).

Yet what does creativity in industry—of the traditional kind or the new cultural and media types—mean? What are the processes by which creativity is encouraged or limited in such contexts? What are the social, organizational or wider national and global conditions that encourage or limit creativity? Why has the concept of "creativity" proliferated in recent years? Or, to what uses is this term put? Our volume seeks to address these questions through offering a set of contributions based in different, but complementary, disciplines and a diversity of cases. In what follows in this introduction we sketch a tentative set of often overlapping clusters of issues that comprise the agenda for the study of creativity.

1.1   The Experiences and (Micro) Processes of Creativity

When being creative, individuals or small groups enter a time and space during which they playfully experiment with ideas, images or products (Ben-Ari 2018; Csikszentmihalyi 1996; Handelman 1998). Such experimentation is risky and (to differing degrees) uncertain since it always involves different types of resources, is frequently an active process within which narratives, representations or artifacts (such as commodities) emerge. This sort of creativity is very often situational in the sense that it involves an "eureka moment" after a longer (and sometimes frustrating) process. Sometimes it is the outcome of a non-productive process like "doing art for its own sake". Indeed, if we understand that the mark of creativity is that upon entering such a process the outcome is unknown then what kind of experience do participants undergo?

The emphasis on experience is important since it leads to three different questions. First, to experience creativity individuals and groups have to have expertise and discipline in a certain domain. Such mastery—a combination of skill and knowledge—seems to be a precondition for creativity and lies at the heart of improvisation in either situational or organizational creativity (Barret 1998; Fisher and Amabile 2009; Montuori 2003). This point can be seen in the contribution by Johns in Chap. 10 who emphasizes that only a thoroughly learned and internalized tradition (he focuses on long-established crafts) allows innovation. In this point, he echoes and develops a line of analysis that emphasizes how mastery of traditional arts is the basis for the invention of new processes and products.

Second, creative processes involve questions about shifting attention that participants experience. These shifts of attention from one thing to the next create spaces for insight (for example, lateral thinking comprises a set of techniques for deliberately shifting attention). In this sense, the "wandering mind" (or inattention) is crucial for creativity and innovation as is focused concentration (Zebelina 2018; Csikszentmihalyi 1996). Indeed, some research on creativity and attention (Carruthers 2016; Kasof 1997) has charted out how various types of attention, or better attentiveness, are related to a capacity for innovation. Pokarier's Chap. 2 (see also Erraught's Chap. 3) develops this scholarly literature in a fascinating direction by focusing on how creative agents operate within conditions of "attention scarcity" that characterizes many of the younger generations that are constantly monitoring and consuming multiple sources of information and entertainment. His essay charts out both the effects of this scarcity and how artists and certain consumers create communities of connoisseurship assuring the "quality" of products.

Third, and prefiguring the next section, the creative experience involves some kind of "letting-go" moment among individuals (dancers, artists, fashion designers or bureaucrats) in which new forms arise. These often involve a degree of freedom or autonomy from everyday restraints so that unpredictable outcomes may emerge (Sawyer 2000, 2007). This comes out most strongly in the contribution by Nativ (Chap. 4) who describes and analyzes how students improvising in free dance learn and experience a loosening of their bodies from the restraints of fixed motions and open up to new possibilities. The creativity involved centers on students entering a process whose outcome is unknown to them. Live show Jazz improvisations capture the creative moments this "letting-go" involves. Jazz improvisation is basically the making up of new melodic solo lines composed on the spot in which the singer or instrumentalist invents new melodies and lines over top of a chord progression played by rhythm section of instruments (piano, guitar, or drum for example). Here creativity is based on the previous skills and experience of the performer that are expressed almost subliminally, but also involves a necessary "letting-go" moment where new melodies are being composed (Blom and Chaplin 1988). In both dance and other forms of improvisation, as Nativ's chapter carefully underscores, creation is intimately related to execution.

1.2 The Social Conditions for/of Creativity

Creativity emerges within certain social and organizational conditions that can be arranged at the micro—(individual or small group), mezzo—(organizational or institutional), and macro—(societal and global) levels.

1.2.1 The Micro-level

Individual abilities, personalities and motivations are key factors that enhance or restrain creativity. Of especial importance is the willingness of people to enter "risky" situations whose results and effects are unknown (and perhaps unknowable). Nativ's chapter points to this crucial dimension of the individual and small group dynamics of dance creativity, that of trust, and in Chap. 6, Thestrup shows how the conjunction and often conflict between personal and professional identities among fashion and graphic designers is central to the process of creativity. Creativity at this level always involves an element of risk since any going beyond accepted ideas and boundaries may involve social sanctions such as censure, anger, ridicule or in extreme circumstances ostracism. Thus, one of the key features of creative environments is that they are non-judgmental. Within small groups of dancers, improvisation through bodily motions creates inter-subjective and inter-personal situations in which trust becomes both a private and a collective asset that balances risks and allows optimal conditions for creativity and innovation to arise (Molm et al. 2000).

It is for these reasons that small creative groups are distinguished by processes in which a *relative* egalitarianism exists between participants. In addition, they are characterized by a climate allowing participants to feel comfortable enough to experiment and take risks without too strong a fear of sanctions for failure (Paulus and Nijstad 2003; Paulus et al. 2003). The epitome of this kind of group is a brainstorming session in which members throw out ideas, even stupid ones, in an atmosphere allowing them to do so (Moreran 1996). The research by Sawyer (2000) and Sawyer and DeZutter (2009) echoes these conclusions not only for brainstorming or "bodystorming" (Stevens and Leach 2015) but more generally collaborative creation. From the perspective of the media and cultural industries it is interesting to note that newer research (Zittoun and Cerchia 2013) also shows that situations leading to creativity in small groups—and the rupture they bring about—can be intentionally designed.

1.2.2 The Mezzo-level

Structurally, empirical studies have shown that creativity very often emerges at the margins of networks and organizations or between them (Burt 2004; DeFillippi et al. 2007: 512; Levine et al. 2003; Perry-Smith 2006). Such emergence is explained in these studies in terms of the special viewpoints that peripheral members of groups bring with them or in terms of their social situatedness allowing these actors to link hitherto unconnected clusters.

Research on the dynamics of creativity argues that environments encouraging (or discouraging) creativity are characterized by a promotion or cultivation of certain times and places that are analytically separate from the everyday (think of art classes, high-tech hothouses, or the play of children). Organizationally, the question is what kind of readiness (translated into resources such as time and money) is there for experimentation, for allowing spaces and times apart from that of the everyday, or for failure (DeFillippi et al. 2007). Thus, fans' coproduction in Otmazgin's chapter may be means to create such spaces while minimizing risks and maximizing (potential) advantages. Similarly, one of the functions of *otaku*, popular culture's most avid fans, is to inhabit spaces for experimentation with minimal long-term risks regarding new products. The experimentation among amateur film-makers studied by Coates's study (Chap. 7) show how a separate space and time with low risk can be constructed at the periphery of an industry.

In a complementary manner, different contexts and organizations are characterized by different restraints or obstacles to creativity whether they be considerations of profitability, political sensitivity, or organizational inertia, Here the role of management is crucial because organizations and institutions distribute risk and creativity across space and time in different ways. Thus, in financially-led or market-led creativity individuals and groups receive incentives for coming up with new ideas and products but this often comes with the price of increased centralization of corporate power and these very incentives may form strict limits on the experimentation allowed (Hesmondhalgh 2019: 273–291; Pratt and Jeffcutt 2009). In this respect, key studies on the managerial literature (DeFillippi et al. 2007) tackle the processes, principles and methods by which organizations meet the challenges of both controlling and opening up avenues for creativity in the creative industries or what is called the "creative economy". Hence Catmull (2008) suggests three strategies to promote moves across limitations and hindrances: placing the creative authority firmly in the hands of project managers (and not senior executives), building local cultures that are egalitarian and supportive and purposely dismantle barriers between groups, disciplines and people.

Creative groups may be ad-hoc (a task force charged with finding solutions to a problem a business faces), permanent (a cluster of high-tech engineers or associations of craftsmen) or loosely enduring (artists' collectives or certain dance and theater troupes). What is important to all forms of organization, however, is that temporary autonomy is granted these groups for the duration of the creative process (Handelman 2004). These spaces and times for experimentation are temporarily autonomous from the goings-on of the organization and are crucial for creative processes to emerge. The contributions to this volume include examples of this point as advertisement companies that assign small teams to handle projects (Moeran 1996), creativity extracted at the interactive spaces between manga amateurs and the established industry (Otmazgin, Chap. 5), or groups of film-personnel deciding to make the movies they themselves want to see (Coates, Chap. 7).

Creativity in the media and cultural industries is the product of translating, commodifying, shaping, or managing the process by which new, different or innovative ideas, images or products are harnessed to the aims of the organization or business entity. The creative process may be self-managed or self-organized or directed by key actors (such as but not necessarily managers) so that its outcomes become part of corporate action. This dimension came out strongly in the division of labor in Kyoto's craft industry (Johns, Chap. 10), the extraction of creativity from fans (Otmazgin, Chap. 5) and the work of designers in an uncertain environment which requires them to both celebrate and suppress their individuality (Thestrup, Chap. 6). What is apparent is that there are a series of paradoxes (DeFillippi et al. 2007) or tensions in managing creativity: between the demands of markets and the leeway left for creativity, between the everyday routines and spaces set-apart for experimentation, or integrating creative and technical personnel in films or recordings for example.

1.2.3   The Macro-level

At this level, key values and cultural emphases shape and construct ideas about when creativity is considered an asset in certain society. For example, to what degree is individual thinking encouraged in schools? Or how risk-averse people are in a certain national context? Hence, where creative and interesting ideas get applauded there is a strong incentive to create. Furthermore, a certain level of affluence and garnering of cultural capital in a society are necessary for drawing people to culturally creative businesses and products. Sociologists and anthropologists would add that at this level cultural capital is crucial for it allows individuals the means to both discern what is innovative and to leverage their failures since their skill sets and mastery of a domain can be used to their advantage (Hooker and Nakamura 2003). Thus, for example the prevalence of anime and manga culture in Japan (appearing in Otmazgin's chapter) and the networks of people involved in them means that there is already a market in place with sophisticated consumers of such products and a marketing and sales system that allow new products to be quickly experimented with, decided upon and disseminated across places, organizations and individuals.

Here, state policies seem to be of importance (Mulcahy 2017; Otmazgin and Ben-Ari 2012). At one level, a strong and effective policy encouraging an industry to produce creative artifacts, designs or ideas may be more effective if it emphasizes investment in basic skills and expertise rather than in specific creations (funding particular films or exhibitions, for example), or supporting the infrastructure needed for industrial creativity (for example by ensuring widespread fast-internet). Given the tension between the logic of state bureaucracy and creativity, however, state intervention may stifle the very processes it sets out to promote. Thus, the state's role should not involve authoritative planning but rather facilitating, stimulating, and acting as a network hub.

1.3 Taking a Step Back: Creativity, Societies and Cultures

Taking a further step back from our analysis to an even more macro scale, we move to the level of societies and cultures and finally to some new global developments. To begin, members of different cultures valorize creativity somewhat differently. To put this point by way of dominant stereotypes, while in most Euro-American cultures creativity is often understood as creating something "original", "alternative", and "completely new", in many parts of East Asia (at least historically) creativity can *also* mean the modification of existing things or applications in ways that are not necessarily completely "new". And indeed, sustained research has shown that there are difference between individualistic and collectivistic societies (sometimes conflated into the Western and East Asian dichotomy) in terms of encouraging or discouraging creativity or in terms of defining what is creative (Bourdieu 1984; Chua et al. 2015; Lubart and Sternberg 1998; Niu and Robert 2008; Shau et al. 2019). Moreover, as studies of play and creativity have shown, societies also differ in terms of where and when to play and create (Daliot-Bul 2014; Kelly 2002). Fine (1988) also adds that who is allowed to be creative, as in children being encouraged to be so, is also important.

One important instance of this point is that it has been in Europe and America that the image of the creative genius working in solitude has emerged. Interestingly this view influenced much of the earlier psychological research on creativity that has by now moved to ideas of collective, collaborative or distributed creativity. Yet we should be careful in attributing the idea of solitary individuals at the apex of creativity only to Western cultures. While not valorized to the same extent as in many such cultures, in Japan there is nevertheless a recognition of the special gifts that some traditional artists have and this recognition has been formalized by the state via the label of "living national treasure". Here however, other research has shown that it may not only be cultural emphases that are important but the interaction between cultures as is evident in how societal diversity in immigrant societies contributes to creativity (Nijstad and Paulus 2003). However, we would do well to follow Simonton's (2003) caution that whatever the role of societies and cultures, psychological and social-psychological processes are important in understanding creativity.

Parc's study (Chap. 9) adds two more points to discussions at the macro, global level. First, ideas about the relations between creativity and copying are also histor-ically defined in terms of what is acceptable. While in the period before World War Two copying was considered perfectly normal as part of the creative process, today it is considered as a bad practice that is immoral (Schwartz 1996) and expresses a lack of respect for other artists. In other words, while in the past copying was not seen as a limit on creativity but a form of recognition of works, identifying with a certain group, a way to learn and master techniques, or as a basis for innovation and interpretation, in the contemporary world any copy is subject to limiting global legal regimes. Parc's second point is that creativity in the creative industries today cannot be understood apart from the juridification and judicialization of the globe (also Blichner and Molander 2008; Magnussen and Banasiak 2013; Magnussen and Nilssen 2013). Thus ideas codified in national and international legal regimes gov-ern any form of dissemination of copied products even if, from the producer's point of view, these products are innovative in terms of such criteria as style, process of creation, or use.

Finally, Erraught's study (Chap. 3) raises a fascinating issue centered on the future. He suggests that as music platforms like Spotify, Youtube or Amazon Music have emerged that today's music collections are vast assemblies that may be accessed anywhere and anytime thus granting consumers a breadth and depth of choice that is historically unique. But echoing Pokarier's contribution (Chap. 2), he goes on to propose that the curation of collections, and thus the recognition of creative products, have changed. To the older gatekeepers of recording companies, the press, radio and television producers and other entrepreneurs have been added electronic algorithms that now suggest to individual consumers songs to be listened to. These suggestions, in turn, are based on consumers' past consumption patterns and the choices of large communities of other listeners who have listened to these tunes. In this way electron-ically curated collections may actually limit consumers experimentation with novel tastes and developments.

References

Barret, F. J. (1998). Coda: Creativity and improvisation in jazz and organizations: Implication for organizational learning. *Organization Science, 95*, 605–622.

Ben-Ari, E. (2018). *Japanese encounters: The structure and dynamics of cultural frames*. London: Routledge.

Blichner, L. C., & Molander, A. (2008). Mapping juridification. *European Law Journal, 14*(1), 36–54.

Blom, L. A., & Chaplin, L. T. (1988). *The moment of movement: Dance improvisation*. Pittsburgh: University of Pittsburg Press.

Bourdieu, P. (1984). *Distinction: A social critique of the judgment of taste*. Cambridge, Massachusetts: Harvard University Press.

Burgess, J. (2006). Hearing ordinary voices; cultural studies, vernacular creativity and digital storytelling. *Continuum: Journal of Media and Cultural Studies 20*(2), 201–214.

Burns, T. B., Machado, N., & Corte, Ugo. (2015). The sociology of creativity: Part I: Theory: The social mechanisms of innovation and creative developments in selectivity environments. *Human Systems Management, 24*, 179–199.

Burt, R. S. (2004). Structural holes and good ideas. *American Journal of Sociology, 110*(2), 349–399.

Carruthers, L. (2016). *Creativity and attention: A multi-method investigation* (Doctoral Thesis, Edinburgh: Edinburgh Napier University).

Catmull, E. (2008). How pixar fosters collective creativity. *Harvard Business Review, 86*(9), 64–72.

Chua, R. Y., Roth, Y., & Lemoine, J. F. (2015). The impact of culture on creativity: How cultural tightness and cultural distance affect global innovation crowd sourcing work. *Administrative Science Quarterly, 60*, 189–227.

Csikszentmihalyi, M. (1996). *Creativity: Flow and the psychology of discovery and invention*.

Daliot-Bul, M. (2014). *License to play: The Ludic in Japanese culture*. Honolulu: Hawai'i University Press.

DeFillippi, R., Grabbner, G., & Jones, C. (2007). Introduction to paradoxes of creativity: Managerial and organizational changes in the cultural economy. *Journal of Organizational Behavior, 28*, 511–521.

De Vaan, M., Stark, D., & Balazs, V. (2015). Game changer: The typology of creativity. *American Journal of Sociology, 4*, 1144–1194.

DeViney, J., Duncan, S., Harris, S., Rody, M. A., & Rosenberry, L. (2010). *Inspiring space for young children*. Beltsville, Maryland: Gryphon.

Farrell, M. P. (2001). *Collaborative circles: Friendship dynamics and creative work*. Chicago: University of Chicago Press.

Fine, G. A. (1988). Good children and dirty play. *Play and Culture, 1*, 43–56.

Fisher, C. M., & Amabile, T. (2009). Creativity, improvisation and organizations. In T. Rickards, M. A. Runco, & S. Moger (Eds.), *Routledge companion to creativity* (pp. 13–24). Oxford, U.K.: Routledge.

Flew, T. (2004). Creativity, cultural studies and service industries. *Communication and Critical/Cultural Studies, 1*(2), 176–193.

Glaveneau, V. (2010). Paradigms in the study of creativity: Introducing the perspective of cultural psychology. *New Ideas in Psychology, 28*(1), 79–83.

Glaveneau, V.-P. (2016). From culture to creativity and the creative economy: A new agenda for cultural economics. *City, Culture and Society, 7*(2), 71–74.

Handelman, D. (1998). *Models and mirrors: Towards and anthropology of public events*. Oxford: Berghahn Books.

Handelman, D. (2004). Introduction: Why ritual in its own right? In D. Handelman & G. Lindquist (Eds.), *Ritual in its own right* (pp. 1–33). New York: Berghahn.

Hesmondhalgh, D. (2019). *The cultural industries* (4th ed.). London: SAGE.

Hooker, N. J., Czikszentmihalyi, M. (2003). The group as mentor: Social capital and the system model of creativity. In P. B. Paulus & B. Nijstad (Eds.), *Group creativity: Innovation through collaboration* (pp. 225–244). Oxford: Oxford University Press.

Howkins, J. (2001, 2013). *The creative economy* (2nd ed.). Penguin.

Jayne, M. (2005). Creative industries; The regional dimensions? *Environment and Planning C: Government and Policy, 23,* 537–556.

Kasof, J. (1997). Creativity and breadth of attention. *Creativity Research Journal, 10*(4), 303–315.

Kawashima, N. (2010). In T. Tachibanaki (Ed.), *Advances in happiness research* (pp. 311–324). Tokyo: Springer Japan.

Kelly, W. H. (2002). Training for leisure: *Karaoke* and the seriousness of play in Japan. In J. Hendry & Massimo Raveri (Eds.), *Japan at play* (pp. 152–168). London: Routledge.

Kong, L., & O'Connor, J. (Eds.). (2009). *Creative economies, creative cities: Asian-European perspectives*. Dordrecht: Springer.

Lee, H.-K. (2017). The political economy of "Creative Industries" media. *Culture and Society, 39*(7), 1078–1088.

Levine, J. M., Choi, H.-S., & Moreland, R. (2003) Newcomer innovation in work teams. In P. B. Paulus & B. Nijstad (Eds.), *Group creativity: Innovation through collaboration* (pp. 202–224). Oxford: Oxford University Press.

Lubart, T. I., & Sternberg, R. J. (1998). Creativity across time and place: Life span and cross-cultural perspectives. *High Ability Studies, 9,* 59–74.

Magnussen, A., & Banasiak, A. (2013). Juridification: Disrupting the relationship between law and politics? *European Law Journal, 19*(3), 325–339.

Magnussen, A. M., & Nilssen, E. (2013). Juridification and the construction of social citizenship. *Journal of Law and Society, 40*(2), 228–248.

Menger, P.-M. (2014). *The economics of creativity art and achievement under uncertainty*. Harvard, MA: Harvard University Press.

Moeran, B. (1996). *A Japanese advertizing agency*. London: Curzon.

Molm, L., Takahashi, N., & Peterson, G. (2000). Risk and trust in social exchange: An experimental test of a classical proposition. *American Journal of Sociology, 205*(5), 1396–1427.

Montuori, A. (2003). The complexity of improvisation and the improvisation of complexity: Social science. *Art and Creativity, Human Relations, 56*(2), 237–255.

Mulcahy, V. K. (2017). *Public culture, cultural identity, cultural policy: Comparative perspective*. New York: Palgrave-Macmillan.

Nijstad, B., & Paulus P. B. (2003). Group creativity: Common themes and future directions. In P. B. Paulus & B. Nijstad (Eds.), *Group creativity: Innovation through collaboration* (pp. 326–329). Oxford: Oxford University Press.

Niu, W., & Sternberg, R. J. (2008). Cultural influences on artistic creativity and its evaluation. *International Journal of Psychology, 36*(4), 225–241.

Otmazgin, N. (2013). *Regionalizing culture: The political economy of Japanese popular culture in Asia*. Honolulu: University of Hawai'i Press.

Otmazgin, N., & Ben-Ari, E. (Eds.). (2012). *Popular culture and the state in East and Southeast Asia, 2012*. London: Routledge.

Paulus, P. B., & Nijstad, B. (2003). Group creativity: An introduction. In P. B. Paulus & B. Nijstad (Eds.), *Group creativity: Innovation through collaboration* (pp. 3–14). Oxford: Oxford University Press.

Paulus, P. B., Vincent, R., & Nijstad, B. (2003). Enhancing ideational creativity in groups: Lessons from research. In P. B. Paulus & B. Nijstad (Eds.), *Group creativity: Innovation through collaboration* (pp. 110–136). Oxford: Oxford University Press.

Perry-Smith, J. E. (2006). Social yet creative: The role of social relationships in facilitating individual creativity. *Academy of Management Journal, 49,* 85–101.

Pratt, A. (2005). Cultural industries and public policy: An oxymoron? *International Journal of Cultural Policy, 11,* 29–44.

Pratt, A. C., & Jeffcutt, P. (Eds.). (2009). *Creativity, innovation and the cultural economy*. London: Routledge.

Reuter, M. E. (2015). A sociological model of creativity. In *Creativity —A sociological approach. Palgrave studies in creativity and culture*. London: Palgrave Pivot.

Sawyer, R. K. (2000). Improvisational cultures: Collaborative emergence and creativity in improvisation. *Mind, Culture, and Activity, 7*(3), 180–185.

Sawyer, R. K. (2007). *Group genius: The creative power of collaboration*. New York: Basic Books.

Sawyer, R. K., & DeZutter, S. (2009). Distributed creativity: How collective creations emerge from collaboration. *Psychology of Aesthetics, 3*(2), 81–92.

Schwartz, H. (1996). *The culture of the copy*. New York, USA: Zone Books.

Schwartzman, H. B. (1978). *Transformations: The anthropology of children's play*. New York: Plenum.

Seitz, J. A. (2003). The political economy of creativity. *Creativity Research Journal, 15*(4), 385–392.

Shao, Y., Zhang, C., Zhou, J., Gu, T., & Yuan, Y. (2019). How does culture shape creativity? A mini-review. *Frontiers in Psychology, 10*. Retrieved September 20, 2019 from https://www.frontiersin.org/articles/10.3389/fpsyg.2019.01219/full.

Simonton, D. K. (2003). Creative cultures, nations, and civilizations: Strategies and results. In P. B. Paulus & B. Nijstad (Eds.), *Group creativity: Innovation through collaboration* (pp. 304–325). Oxford: Oxford University Press.

Stevens, C. J., & Leach, James. (2015). Bodystorming: Effects of collaboration and familiarity on improvising contemporary dance. *Cognitive Process, 16*(1), 403–407.

Thomas, D., & Brown, J. S. (2007). The play of imagination: Extending the literary mind. *Games and Culture, 2*(2), 144–172.

Towse, R. (2006). Copyright and creativity: An application of cultural economics. *Review of Economic Research on Copyright Issues, 3*(2), 83–91.

Wardle, H. (2015). Afterword: An end to imagining? In M. Harris & N. Rapport (Eds.), *Reflections on imagination: Human capacity and ethnographic method* (pp. 275–294). London: Ashgate.

Wu, J. (2006). Nostalgia as content creativity: Cultural industries and popular sentiment. *International Journal of Cultural Studies, 9*(3), 359–368.

Zabelina, D. L. (2018). Attention and creativity. In N. R. E. Jung & O. Vartanian (Eds.), The Cambridge handbook of the neuroscience of creativity (pp. 161–179). New York, US: Cambridge University Press.

Zittoun, T., & Cerchia, F. (2013). Imagination as expansion of experience. *Integrative Psychological and Behavioral Sciences, 47*(3), 305–324.

Eyal Ben-Ari is senior fellow of the Center for Society, Security and Peace at Kinneret College on the Sea of Galilee. He has carried out research in Israel, Japan, Singapore and Hong Kong. His main areas of research are the sociology of the armed forces, early childhood education, and popular culture in Asia. Among his recent books are *Japanese Encounters* (2018), (with Zev Lehrer, Uzi Ben-Shalom and Ariel Vainer) *Rethinking the Sociology of Warfare* (2010), (with Nissim Otmazgin) *The State and Popular Culture in East Asia* (2012), and (with Jessica Glicken Turnley and Kobi Michael) (2017) *Social Science and Special Operations Forces*. He has published articles spanning a variety of disciplines including the *American Ethnologist, Cultural Anthropology, The Sociological Review, The Sociological Quarterly, Special Operations Journal*, and the *Journal of Strategic Studies*.

Nissim Otmazgin is a professor at the Department of Asian Studies the Director of the Institute for Asian and African Studies, The Hebrew University of Jerusalem, and a member of the Israeli Young Academy of Science and Humanities. A political scientist in training, his research interests include cultural diplomacy in Asia, popular culture and regionalization in East and Southeast Asia, and cultural industry and cultural policy in Japan and South Korea. His Ph.D. dissertation (Kyoto University, 2007), which examines the export of Japan's popular culture to Asia, won the Iue Asia Pacific Research Prize for outstanding dissertation on society and culture in Asia. As a part of this research, he conducted extensive fieldwork in Hong Kong, Singapore, Shanghai, Bangkok, and Seoul. He is the author of *Regionalizing Culture: the Political Economy of Japanese Popular Culture in Asia* (University of Hawaii Press, 2013) and (together with Miki Daliot Bul) of *The Anime Boom in the US: Lessons for Global Creative Industries* (Harvard University Asia Center Press, 2017).

Part II
The Experience of Creativity

Chapter 2
Creative Activity Under Attention Scarcity

Christopher Pokarier

Organisations, individuals, and the media apps themselves on our devices, vie constantly for our scarce attention. At the same time, digitisation has unleashed a flood of content, making cultural consumers dependent on new forms of intermediation, recommendation to navigate the plenitude. These are vulnerable both to commercial manipulation and quasi-random cascade effects, with no inherent bias to quality. Cultural experience is increasingly patterned by algorithmic assemblage, compounding the uncertainty that is a pervasive feature of the creative industries. For the dual developments of content digitisation and social media platforms accentuate four established concerns about evolving markets for cultural products, referred to here as *quality agnosticism, content deluge, balkanisation* and *dumbing down*. The suggested effects are inter-dependent, their scope and consequences disputed still. Yet, the issues they entail have become even more salient in the wake of clear recent evidence of similar, and adverse, effects on political discourse in the United States, Europe and beyond. This chapter speculates whether, in the cultural domain, virtual 'communities of connoisseurship', and new ecologies of curation, may attenuate the 'dumbing down' effects of attention scarcity, manipulation and cascade effects of quality-agnostic digital media platforms. A positive aspect of balkanisation may be shared discernment, with other attention-scarce consumers free-riding off such expertise, under certain conditions, which is conceptualised here through the notion of 'cultural consumption capital' (Caves 2000). Whether this counteracts other commercial drivers of dumbing down remains an open question; depending in part on collective social decisions about the algorithmic infrastructures of our virtual public spaces, and individual openness to diversity and aesthetic attainment.

The chapter then explores some of the challenges for creative work under such conditions of hyper-connectivity and content overload. As attention scarcity becomes more acute, the sensational may distract from the subtle, attention spans may shorten, and audience patience diminished with alternative entertainment always at hand.

C. Pokarier (✉)
Waseda University, Tokyo, Japan
e-mail: pokarier@gmail.com

© Springer Nature Singapore Pte Ltd. 2020
N. Otmazgin and E. Ben-Ari (eds.), *Creative Context*, Creative Economy,
https://doi.org/10.1007/978-981-15-3056-2_2

Enterprises and individuals in the creative industries then face profound dilemmas about the quality and mix of creative productive to bring to market, about promotion, and about engagement with potential audiences through social media. With the exception of the latter, such dilemmas are by no means new. 'Creatives' have always faced choices about what expectations to meet, to ignore, to seek to modify. Following Runco (1996), navigating this conundrum is conceptualised as involving creative 'discretion'. Creatives are understood to be making discretionary choices between ignoring certain expectations and potential influences, articulating one's own response in the hope of altering expectations in a favourable way, or conforming (by choice or subconsciously) to established expectations. *Creative discretion* amounts then to a judicious mix of choices about what expectations, often internalised through acculturation, training and exposure to market reactions, to *ignore*, to *articulate* a response to, or to *conform* to.

The hierarchical organisationally-situated creative—e.g. the employed designer—may have little individual discretion, with only the articulating and conforming options available in practice. For this reason, the *ignore* option may be likened to 'exit', while *articulate* relates to 'voice', and *conform* to 'loyalty', of Hirschman's (1970) influential 'exit, voice and loyalty' construct. Likewise, the 'free agent' creative (Pink 2001), may face 'exit' from commercial practice if unprepared to compromise one's creative concept or articulate it successfully. Some creatives, less immediately dependent on engaging clients as designers are, may be able to ignore commercial and other expectations in the short term, favouring personal creative authenticity. Artists, composers, writers, performers, may have some latitude if they have access to an alternative income stream, or can spare the time to earn one. Hence the 'ignore' expectations option is not synonymous with exit from the creative activity. It may bring immediate non-material gratification but represents a high-risk choice if social recognition and income from one's creative endeavours are sought. A resulting reputation for authenticity (see Guignon 2004) may help realise future rewards however, as we shall in the closing brief case study of artist Lucian Freud. It is a premise of this chapter that there are lessons to be learned from the practice of 'long lasting' artists for the contemporary exercise of creative discretion under conditions of attention and an apparent acceleration in cultural change. While social media possibly may have changed the pay-offs to creative immediacy from the situation prevailing in the early careers of recently celebrated but long-lived artists, its effects on the development of an individual's distinctive creative signature, portfolio of creative attainments, and perceived reputation, over time remain nascent and difficult to discern. Instead, mindful that the conundrums at the core of creative discretion are timeless ones, we look to several authoritative creative voices from the more or less recent past for tentative insights into how one might navigate the dilemmas of creative activity under attention scarcity.

This chapter take up the challenge, set by the editors of this volume, to engage with the experience of creativity in its contemporary context, both in the consumption and production of creative goods. A distinctive feature of contemporary life is an asymmetric tension between modern attention-scarce consumers and the intense creative attention embodied in fine cultural and aesthetic products. Highly resolved creative works look deceptively simple, revealing few traces of the struggle to realise them. The chapter first elaborates upon the modern condition of attention scarcity. It then explores consumption of creative goods under those conditions, through discussion of the aforementioned issues of *quality agnosticism, content deluge, balkanisation* and *dumbing down*. Whether counter-veiling pressures for quality might emanate from, what is termed here, 'communities of connoisseurship' is considered. We turn then to production of creative goods, with the locus of attention being the individual creative worker and the creative discretion they must exercise in navigating—choosing to *ignore, articulate* around, or *conform* to—contending expectations. The timeless conundrum of how to get original creative work done, balancing exposure to new influences and supportive creative communities with the solitude to develop one's own signature, is examined. Contemporary connectivity and mobility compounds these dilemmas, as does the arguably quickening pace of cultural exchange and change. The risks, personal, creative, and reputational, to forcing the pace of individual creative output are then discussed briefly. Following on from a cameo account of the effective creative habits of the late artist Lucian Freud, some final conclusions are drawn.

2.1 Issue: Attention Scarcity

Even before the rise of social media the notion of an attention economy was taking hold (Goldhaber 1997; Lanham 2006). Forster (2009: 12) notes that even in the inter-war period there were periodic discussions of attention scarcity. The powerful have always been able to command attention, and to consume fine products that embodied the creative attention and talents of those who laboured to create them. VIPs are marked out socially by the performative displays of attention they receive. Yet contemporary social media has effected a historical reverse: those with a talent for attracting attention—and few other material resources—can be made powerful. For in an era of attention scarcity, when even the privileged or well positioned gatekeepers of old media struggle to attract an audience, the digital limelight is highly saleable, giving rise to the phenomenon of the professional 'influencer'. Attention-attracting social media personas are for sale. Celebrity endorsements have been a feature of advertising since the rise of the mass media. Social media differs in its user-generated content, which brings an egalitarianism to the quest for attention. Social media platforms also make tangible the ability to attract attention: real time measures of friends, likes and shares. Robust metrics aid the monetisation of attention.

Individuals are drawn to social media by desire for social connection, and for the content, user-generated and shared from third party sources. Curiosity is a key driver of interest in content, while desires for self-affirmation, partly through the recognition of others, are factors in posting and monitoring reactions (Hardey 2013). Both impulses can make social media usage habit-forming, as evidenced in its extensive and intensive take-up; Facebook attracting 2.2 billion users in the twelve years since it shifted to an open platform model in 2006. Singer Shakira was the first person to gain 100 million 'likes' on Facebook, in July 2014, with footballer Ronaldo overtaking her soon after. Human curiosity is vulnerable to exploitation. Attention-grabbing headlines, 'clickbait', the dribbling out of content to keep audiences hanging on, are increasingly a purposive feature of the digital media platforms many use daily (Norman 2018). Silicon Valley pioneer Jaron Lanier (2018: 8) citing one of the founders of Facebook, notes that 'likes' and comments—a social validation feedback loop—give regular little dopamine hits that ultimately change one's relationship with society. And, fundamentally, with oneself.

The algorithms of social media, coupled with digital marketing, means no longer just advertising but "continuous behaviour modification on a titanic scale" (Lanier 2018: 6) It occurs at a micro-level though, through timely delivery of targeted content to match mood and moment, in ubiquitous efforts to nudge individuals to engage with the interests of those who will pay for it. The algorithms of social media platforms also incorporate an element of randomness deliberately—leaping mechanisms—to enhance adaptiveness (Lanier 2018: 15). Users are motivated to remain engaged, making sense of the mix of more and less familiar content, allowing 'discovery' of new interests that the platform then serves. Users may then propagate further those interests socially, across platforms that are content-agnostic but designed to ensnare users. Designed addiction, engineered habits (Eyal 2014: 2). There has been contention for some time about the impacts upon individuals of social media and smart phone addiction. More recent is pessimism about the impact of social media upon social and political fabric of our societies. Claims of Russian manipulation of American public opinion to favour the candidacy of Donald Trump, and social media as a factor in the Brexit vote, have made the digital connectivity of our daily lives ever more contentious. The content agnosticism of social media is now under critical scrutiny. What do these dynamic emergent properties potentially mean for demand for creative product, and for culture-at-large?

2.2 Consumption: Markets for Creative Goods Under Attention Scarcity

Within markets for creative goods, especially novel subjectively-experienced goods that are differentiated by aesthetic, cultural-symbolic, or emotion-laden attributes, uncertainty is always a given: the *nobody knows* effect of how consumers will react to new creative product (Caves 2000). However, with the spread of content digitisation and social media we can identity four additional issues. The first two compound uncertainty, the third centres on a perceived risk to quality, the fourth pertains to market fragmentation. The latter two do not axiomatically compound uncertainty, but do have implications for market structures and strategies. The four issues are *quality agnosticism*, *content deluge*, *balkanisation*, and *dumbing down*. All four phenomena have antecedents in analogue media markets but are potentially compounded by the scale and reach of content digitisation and social media, and have interdependent properties. Each phenomena is discussed briefly in turn below, but we first need to note an important analytical construct that may help us weight the overall impacts and probability of each.

Caves (2000: 176–178; 187) has provided a persuasive account of how the economics of the cultural and creative industries are influenced by the extent to which the accumulation of personal 'cultural consumption capital' enhances the utility individuals gain. In short, more intense engagement with a particular cultural product increases a capacity to appreciate the virtues of related cultural artefacts and experiences. Attentiveness is rewarding and begets further attentiveness. Marginal utility increases rather than diminishes with intensive consumption, upending a basic premise of earlier economic theory. Caves (2000: 175–178) posits that intense cultural consumption can be understood as a 'rational addiction'. At the same time, for the casual cultural consumer (indeed consumers in any segment in an era of online reviews and rankings), it becomes rational to free-ride off those literally invested in product knowledge. Such free-riding may lift overall standards if the free-riders can indeed reliably identify discerning cultural consumers who they can 'shadow trade'. As the first of our issues entails though, this is far from certain. The good taste of others is only obvious to those of good taste. Cowen (2002: 112) identified a potential collective action problem: with free-riding "...consumers tend to underinvest in the refinement of their tastes." He nonetheless identifies counter-veiling dynamics, which will return too.

2.2.1 Quality Agnosticism

This feared effect arises with the aforementioned architecture of social media platforms, where randomness and manipulation may lead content to 'trend' independent of its quality. The implications for creative work and enterprises are somewhat ominous: the success or failure of creative products may be rather more dependent on the vagaries of digitised information markets than the relative inherent properties of the product itself. This introduces a further element of radical uncertainty about the demand for creative work. This is in addition to the much-discussed challenges of adapting distribution and pricing strategies to the new realities of high definition streaming on demand, provided through new intermediaries and platforms that digital content providers face. Caves (2000: 8) recognised two temporal elements in creative industries, the first being *time flies*. One aspect of this is how some cultural product will date quickly, its meaningful references being to events of its time and/or its aesthetics bound to be superseded by changing tastes. Moreover, first-to-market (or to consumer attention) may trump quality if the stories or other attributes are similar and consumers are readily satiated. With the vagaries of social media as major information source, nobody knows if anybody will see the product, let alone how they will react to it.

Webster (2010: 601–608) explores the main mechanisms by which 'user information regimes' work: inbound link-based search, aggregating social networks, collaborative filtering, with varied (and contending) biases around user behaviour, personalisation preferences and popularity. Recommender systems are also never completely neutral (Webster 2014: 15–17). Social media platforms, as discussed, can operate by algorithms that are primarily designed to attract and retain users, without regard for content quality (Webster 2010; Webster and Ksiazek 2012: 52). Information cascades and contagions are inevitable (Sunstein 2006, 2007, 2009; Surowiecki 2004). Music download choices can be heavily influenced when users can see what other users, in aggregate or amongst friends, are downloading. Trend-forming consumption cascades can also arise through random copying of others' consumption decisions, as rigorously modelled by Bentley et al. (2007) and Acerbi and Bentley (2014). In Webster's words: "Under such circumstances, popularity is off less a function of quality than of luck." (Webster 2010: 607). The implications for polities and cultures of 'the algorithm as institution' (Napoli 2013), gives rise to discussions about an ethics of 'algorithmic assemblage' (Ananny 2016).

2.2.2 Content Deluge

Webster (2014: 1) wrote too of the countless digital content choices available, that "…almost without exception, their creators want attention. With it they hope to amuse, build social capital, make money, or change the course of human events…to find an audience, they must compete with one another in the marketplace of attention. It's a zero sum game that dooms most offerings to obscurity." In 2015 YouTube over four hundred hours of content uploaded to the site every minute. Some of this reflects the what has been referred to as the 'mass amateurisation' of content (Shirky, in Wu 2017: 269) A considerable part is also user uploads of professional third party content. While automated takedown notices increasingly enforce copyright, many rights holders have acquiesced in such uploads because of their promotional value, and because Youtube now also provides a partner program to share advertising revenues with contracting rights holders. Best-selling English singer Ed Sheeran had over 3.86 billion views on Youtube for his song The Shape of You in October 2018. Youtube, other sharing sites and major social media platforms—such as Facebook— are borderless in the scope; subject only to heavy-handed blocking of access, as in the case of China. Streaming services, and countless new media sites, along with old media turned digital, present yet more professional content. Caves' (2000: 9) second temporal element that distinguished the creative industries, *ars longa*, pertained to the varied longevity of creative products. While a music or dance performance completely depreciated with the end of the show, recordings of it, like reproducible compositions, texts or designs, could function as rent-generating artefacts for the duration of copyright protection. This potential inter-temporal value makes them an asset class for investment, their value being impacted by potential substitutes for

audience attention. Enterprises in the creative industries, and entertainment industries in particular, now face increased competition for attention from digitising of the
'back catalogue' of culture, further compounding uncertainty.

2.2.3 Balkanisation

To cope with the overwhelming choice audiences resort to what researchers have
long referred to 'repertoires', a limited number of channels, publications, websites,
apps etc., and heuristics, such as the judging a source by the aesthetic quality of
its webpages (Webster 2014: 36–7). Concerns about the potential fragmentation of
audiences for news and cultural product soon became salient with the rapid rise in
popularity of the internet (van Alstyne and Brynjolfsson 2005). The earlier spread of
cable television in the United States had concentrated the minds of media industry
analysts on the potential for such. With more choice, people might just watch more
of what they know they like, with less likelihood of serendipitous contacts with new
content. The individual and collective result might be an atrophying of tastes, and
pragmatic responses by media firms. More of the same, with diminishing demand for
creative endeavour. The edginess of HBO programming, for instance, has diminished
such concerns amongst media analysts; concluding that the channel subscription business models require innovative content to promote social buzz and high-commitment
viewers who will pay a fixed fee to access just a small part of overall programming.
This complements the common counter-argument to fears of balkanisation which
centres on the social currency that consuming a cultural product in common can
provide. A positive argument in favour of partial balkanisation is associated with
the 'long tail' associated with Anderson (2006). Digitisation, combined with search,
unlocked access to varied content that consumers had previously been denied because
of technical constraints in distribution, and vested-interest gatekeepers.

Webster and Ksiazek (2012) offered a qualified account of audience fragmentation, finding overlapping patterns of public attention rather than completely fragmented audiences. Helberger (2011) explored the case for regulatory interventions to
promote 'diversity by design' in digital content provision, though favours a user opt-in
model for 'exposure diversity'. She highlights the potential for built-in serendipity
to attenuate overwhelmed users' tendencies to resort to restrictive coping strategies and hide in 'information cocoons' (Helberger 2011: 454). Following Donald
Trump's presidential victory and the apparent influence of the so-called Alt-Right
right-wing new media, concerns about the impact of 'balkanisation' on the American polity have escalated. A seeming retreat from mainstream media, with conversations only amongst the like-minded in parallel virtual worlds, fast became a new
stylised-fact about contemporary American society. Regardless of the truth, or not,
of such accounts, we might note that cultural markets have rather different dynamics from political markets (Lindblom 2001). Indeed, Lindblom reminds us that a
strength of market systems is that they do not have the 'winner take all' property
of democratic polities. Much discussion of cyber-balkanisation is predicated on a

rather passive construct of audience exposure, by which happenstance (or manipulation) patterns consumption. By contrast, the cultural consumption capital model envisages increasing discernment with 'rational addiction' (Caves 2000: 175–178), with open questions about sharing behaviours amongst the culturally savvy. Could there be positive spillovers from the concentrated cultural consumption of the few to the many, through demonstration effects, or might the linkages with exclusive and contending social identities be too strong?

2.2.4 Dumbing Down

Lanier (2018: 20) argues that "social media is biased, not to the Right or Left, but downward...An unfortunate combination of biology and math favors degradation of the social world." Lanier, firmly in the 'dumbing down' camp owes much to his previously noted critical account of the dual effects algorithmic architecture of social media, and the addictive nature of the user experience. Attention scarcity itself also gives rise to dumbing down fears: impatient audiences, facing high opportunity costs in giving their close attention to any particular cultural product, will favour the concise, the readily-understood, the 'accessible'. New York Times bestsellers are getting rather shorter on average. Concerns about cultural dumbing down long predate the rise of social media, and were given impetus by debates over the ostensible cultural impacts of 'globalisation' from the late 1980s, as well as from within the growing literature on the cultural and creative industries. Cowen (2002), in exploring the impacts of increased cultural trade, offers a cogent account of how we all engage in both 'extensive' and 'intensive' cultural consumption. The judgements of those who are particularly attentive to the attributes of particular cultural products, and developments in the field, support the rather more lightly informed—indeed inattentive—consumption of many others (Cowen 2002: 102, 109). Contemporary social media further enables this, allowing the many to be rather inattentive to most product areas they only infrequently consume, while tapping the insights of the intensive consumers who are motivated also to share freely their knowledge. We may speculate that the 'intensive consumer' cognoscenti who actively share their knowledge, in addition to obvious intrinsic motivation, may also often have a positive self-identity as connoisseur that benefits from social affirmation through sharing.

2.2.5 Communities of Connoisseurship?

Digital connectivity may sustain what we might call communities of connoisseurship. Lively examples abound, from barista communities, to flower arrangement and a rich digital ecology of architectural commentary and news sites. Online communities of common interest—from illness support groups to fans/adherents of myriad cultural and 'high engagement' consumer products (think motorbikes)—were quick to form as uptake of the internet increased rapidly (Wu 2017: 269–271). Sometimes moderated, more often they are self-policed virtual communities of commentary, sharing and collaboration. The field of fragrance provides a striking example of a community of connoisseurship that is unequivocally dedicated to sharing knowledge and enjoyment of perfumes, fostering consumers' consumption capital and acting as a discipline upon the more cynical commercial practices of the notoriously opaque fragrance industry. There are several popular forums, most notably basenotes.net and fragrantica.com, and many participants post the same content to both. The quality of reviews is often very high, with expert professionals contributing, usually behind anonymous personas (the *nom de plume* effect) as well as numerous savvy amateurs. The most prolific reviewers on *Basenotes*, as of writing, had contributed over 2300 commentaries, and the most 'liked' reviewers typically had contributed at least half that number. Neither the exclusive network effect of a proprietary platform, nor negative behaviour of social media are seen. As in tech help sites—such as the several devoted to Apple Mac users' questions—much generosity of spirit is evidenced, and the collective preference for a forum animated by the better side of people's natures leads to quick censuring of unsociable conduct. We should be wary of an over-stylised dichotomy between digital communities of connoisseurship that lift standards, and social media platforms that lower them. For highly visual platforms such as Instagram can also be valuable to such communities—such as flower or interior designers, albeit with a lower level of engagement at times. As with all areas beyond the creative and cultural industries, the quality of social media is entirely a function of who one follows.

2.3 Production: Creative Endeavor Under Attention Scarcity

For those who engage in creative endeavors there are age-old dilemmas in how they stand in relation to their own visions, gatekeepers in their fields, their cultural inheritance, to wider audiences and market imperatives. Dilemmas too in how they let their curiosity roam, feeding their creativity, in engaging with fellow creatives, and in preserving sufficient personal space and time to create something substantial themselves. Artists cluster, and retreat, seeking optimal proximity to positive influences, buyers and sources of encouragement, and maximal distance from distractions. Our cultural histories reveal an ongoing tension between the celebration of solitude (e.g. Storr 1988) and even unsociability, in the creation of great works, and a focus on so-called 'creative cauldrons': unusual places and times where there was a critical mass of creatives and savvy audiences that would leave outsized cultural legacies. Italian cities of the Renaissance, the Bauhaus, the Bloomsbury set, Paris at several junctures in art and fashion, *fin de siecle* Vienna of Klimt, Schiele, the Werkbund and Freud. Budding creatives needed not only high intrinsic motivation, which numerous studies have found to be a necessary condition for sustained creative success, but also a judicious mix of personal openness to new influences, and an orientation to finding their distinctive creative signature.

2.3.1 Conceptualising Individual Creative Discretion

Runco offers a distinctive definition of creativity as "the construction of original and effective interpretations of experience" (2018: 247, 2017). The reference to 'construction' points to process; and also privileges personal constructions over socially-recognised creativity. Importantly, it removes the aspect of social certification of something as creative from its definition. Much literature on the psychology of creativity, somewhat oddly in this author's opinion, have conflated creative process and its social impact. For instance, Csikszentmihalyi (in Sawyer et al. 2003: 223) saw creativity as "...an original response that is socially valued and brought to fruition", holding that "...creativity does not exist until it produces a change in the culture". Was van Gogh not creative whilst painting, and only so once dead but recognised? For Runco (1996: 14) his notion of *discretion* in creative activity is "...partly heuristic cognition, and partly value judgement...", the latter necessary as the individual chooses "what to transform, what to attend to, and where to invest personal resources." A key aspect of this judgement is "about which *expectations* to abide by and which to ignore." (Runco 1996: 13). In the creative industries, these expectations can variously relate to anticipated critics' reactions, market demand, internal firm actors such as managers responsible for costs, senior designers policing an established signature style, and the like. The ability to *ignore* expectations becomes a key enabler of creativity; not only to engage in divergent thought but also to press on with an original idea in the face of resistance.

Sternberg (2018: 318) proposes recently an analytical construct of creativity, 'triangular theory', which understands creativity through acts of defiance: defying the crowd (people with more conventional beliefs), defying oneself, and defying the zeitgeist. Sternberg distinguishes the latter from the crowd in a similar way to how Czikszentmihalyi distinguished between the *field*—the identities and social organisation of a community of specialists, and the *domain* of knowledge. The discourse of crowd can be rather confusing for our purposes here, as it is important to distinguish between the old entrenched gatekeepers of the creative industries, and both the new opinion-shapers and the connected crowd of contemporary social media. The field/domain dichotomy is more helpful, but still hints at a bounded area of expert objective knowledge. Arguably, the boundaries of subjective (aesthetic) ways of knowing, to use Pable's (2009) distinction, are more ephemeral. Sternberg's schematic permits a plotting of creative acts that variously entail, for instance, personal creative growth that nonetheless does not defy the crowd or zeitgeist, high impact growth that involves all aspects of denying, and other variants. It offers a nuanced corrective to the aforementioned tendency of many psychologists of creativity to set a high threshold hurdle of social impact for something to constitute creativity. Yet it seems to retain a static focus on impact, leaving unclear how and when such creative acts of defying gain acceptance. Given our concern with attention scarcity, this is not trivial. These acts of defying may also be complex internal struggles, or not. Runco and Berghetto's (2019: 8) recent work recognises how "...'internalized' others serve as dialogic interlocutors and play an intra-psychological role in how an individual experiences, interprets, and engages with creative endeavours." Analytically, this brings professional identity to the fore, which this author explores elsewhere with a co-author (Thestrup and Pokarier 2019). Designers' professional identities may evolve such that they are more comfortable with the trade-offs between aesthetic and commercial imperatives, seeing creative resolution within such constraints to be fundamental to design work. This accords with Runco's (2018: 247, 256, 1996) sympathetic treatment of choices to *conform* to expectations; arguing that creativity requires people to be both originally divergent and conventional, as humans are social animals. Conformance at times is also appropriate, and so he emphasises 'discretion' in striking a balance. Moreover, as Thestrup[1] suggests—following the wise advice of a former professor—that creative propositions must also be imbued with a 'semiotic handle' to find resonance. Only from the familiar can the new be grasped.

The exercise of creative discretion will entail then both choices, conscious or otherwise, both to *ignore* and *conform* to expectations. We may postulate several mediating variables that will pattern individual creative discretion; factors such personality, identity, experience, pragmatics (especially immediate need for income). As noted in the outset, we may think also of a third discretionary act: to *articulate*, more or less proactively, one's creative proposition to targeted audiences. Plucker (2018: 176) currently proposes to develop a fresh conceptual angle on creative work through a focus on this function of articulation, "...to help explain how creators select potential audiences for their creative work and use communication and persuasion to maximise the value of that work in the eyes of those audiences." Sternberg's (2018: 318) notion of defying the zeitgeist is useful for thinking about how contemporary creatives may articulate their creative vision directly to consumers/audiences via social media. His schematic admits the possibility of changing the zeitgeist without persuading the existing field of experts. Social media may indeed be a means for bypassing established gatekeepers in the field. Parallels with the openness and democratising effect of the Salon des Refusés against the stiff conservative academicism of the Paris Salon in the 1860s–70s are readily imaginable. Yet there are also disconcerting contemporary parallels in the recent political influence of once-fringe populist rightwing media, such as the aforementioned Alt-Right phenomena of Breitbart and the like in the United States. The Trump and Brexit victories have sparked a flurry of studies in the rejection of expertise with anti-Establishment populism.

Runco (2018: 246) observes that "While biological evolution tends to be quite slow, cultural evolution is essentially immediate..." and "the problem is that humans may adapt to one state of affairs only to have the state abruptly change." Creativity allows humans to deal with such changes, and change is often a compelling impetus to creative initiative (as explored by Hirschman 1967). Creativity begets change, and in turn creates imperatives for creative responses to such change. As social media

---

[1]Personal correspondence, 27 October 2018.

arguably hastens cultural evolution, creatives face a stark dilemma in whether they seek to nudge the direction of change through frequent virtual social engagement, or retreat to concentrate on sustained distinctive creative work, in the hope that in an era of attention shortage, judiciously cultivated quality ultimately with have a more sustainable impact.

2.3.2 Distraction and Creative Habits

Samuel Taylor Coleridge should have ignored the knock at the door, if we believe his own account of how his epic poem Kublai Khan ended up in the form it did. A person from Porlock on business disturbed him whilst he hurriedly transcribed the work that had arrived to him fully formed during an afternoon reverie, with the result that some half of it was lost to the culture-at-large (Coleridge 2004/1816). In this account, distraction was an unbridled negative for Coleridge's ultimate creative legacy. Yet many have wondered in the two centuries since whether the person from Porlock was a fiction, a *deux et machina* that saved the author from the evident difficulties of bringing coherence and closure to the work, with an excuse that would resonate with any audience. For who does not feel that they could have accomplished more with their lives if only they had been spared from so many trivial quotidian distractions? Oscar Wilde (1963) left to posterity in *De Profundis*, written from Reading goal, probably the longest and most articulate complaint in history about the disruptions to his creative work by the selfishness of his former lover Lord Alfred 'Bosie' Douglas, who was also the catalyst for his incarceration. Distraction is not merely a curiosity in the history of past great minds. Recent research suggests that moves to open-plan office architectures, often thought to facilitate creative collaborations, may actually be counter-productive because of increased distractions (Kim and de Dear 2013; Liebl et al. 2012). One study showed people resorted to more, not less, electronic communications rather than face-to-face interaction (Bernstein and Turban 2018).

Intrinsic motivation, temperament and good work habits may help in the struggle against distraction, although contemporary ease of travel, cultural plentitude, and social media all threaten to keep the individual from creative endeavour. English novelist Kingsley Amis once remarked that "The art of writing is the art of applying the seat of one's trousers to the seat of one's chair." (BBC World Service, no date). Or 'arse glue', in the words of Australian maths whiz Geordie Williamson (Elliot 2018). Sitzfleisch—'sitting meat', one's butt—is a German metaphor for something akin to resilience or staying power needed to be productive and see a task through (Schultheis 2018). The creative must find their own good habits (see Eyal 2014), to make something new and valuable from plenitude. Lucian Freud admired the attribute of fastidiousness in an artist or other creative, but also too liveliness and imagination (Gayford 2010: 53). There will be arbitrary exclusions of possibly good influences: people, ideas, performances and exhibitions, theories, artefacts and traditions. British artists Gilbert and George have dined most evenings for over three decades at the same Kurdish restaurant, and have no kitchen in their home for they do not want the distraction (van Pragh 2009). Creative self-discipline may require long periods of digital and physical solitude. Most major religions depict the prophets having experiencing extensive and decisive periods of solitude. The poet Rainer Maria Rilke, in letters to an aspiring young poet who sought his advice, repeatedly stressed the importance of solitude to creative endeavour (e.g. Rilke 1986: 85–7). The temperamentally unsociable may have an advantage in some fields of creative endeavour where a capacity for solitary work is helpful, such as in the arts, but less so in scientific fields where sociability helps with collaboration (Bowker et al. 2017). Introverts come in for recent praise as less inclined to creativity-diminishing groupthink (Cain 2012).

2.3.3 Forcing the Pace?

For Rainer Maria Rilke, 'to live as an artist' requires "…deep humility and patience to wait for the hour when a new clarity is born.." which comes to its completion in the unconscious (Rilke 1986: 23–4). Yet creatives may be driven to force the pace of the creative process and the volume of outputs, despite Baumol's law dictating that creative endeavour and cultural performances are not amenable to some kinds of productivity enhancements that industrial processes are. Inherent personality factors, pragmatic imperatives such as a need for income, and a personal drive to validate one's creative self-identity with creative outcomes, may all lead to attempts to 'create in haste'. Projecting an active creative persona on social media may be a source of ongoing pressure, in an internalised variant of 'publish or perish', but with ambivalent implications for quality and creative sustainability. Sloterdijk (2016: 178) warns on the dangers of over-exposure, where art is reduced to mere spectacle.[2]

Being too eager to force the pace of creative endeavour may be risky not only to the quality of one's work but health as well. Modern pharmacology has provided the impatient, the distracted, or dispirited creative with means to force the pace. Many artists have been seduced by the potential of drugs to enhance creative attention, temporarily change mental states, or lift energy levels. Hallucinogenics such as LSD could offer a literal kaleidoscope of creative influences, without the artist ever leaving the studio (Carhart-Harris et al. 2018; Griffiths 2017; Iszáj et al. 2016). For many other creatives, certain drugs may help in 'cutting the Gordian knot', freeing them from their own anxieties, lethargies, distractions. It is long been speculated that Coleridge's Kublai Khan was conceived under the influence of opium. From Sigmund Freud's cocaine use (Oliver 2017), to postwar artists such as Andy Warhol, and Mark Rothko, musician Lou Reed, and fashion designer Mark Jacobs, drugs variously aided and bedevilled their creative endeavours (Deveney 2018). Artist Lucian Freud's habit was mild, merely heavy consumption of *Solpadeine* painkillers, codeine and paracetamol or ibuprofen, which he "…took addictively to maintain his energy and ease away

---

[2]I am grateful to Erez Golani Solomon for discussion around this point.

any aches or pains" (Greig 2013: 3). Lucian Freud once said that he avoided drugs as he wanted to the see the world more clearly as it was (Gayford 2010: 51).

Along with the attention economy has arisen a large-scale attention drug economy. Neuro-enhancement is now big business for the pharmaceutical industry, prompting ethical debates (Sahakian and Morein-Zamir 2007; Racine and Forlini 2010). A strong inclination to inattention, once seen as a particular personality trait, is now often associated with a diagnosis of ADHD (Attention Deficit Hyperactivity Disorder) and prescribing of stimulants such as methylphenidate (Ritalin). One recent estimate suggests nearly a fifth of all American tertiary students take such prescription drugs, with illicit use rising across a number of countries and even amongst researchers themselves (Maher 2008; Dietz et al. 2013; Maier et al. 2013). There is clearly strong market demand for new technological applications for cognitive enhancement, including low-cost brain stimulation devices, and the implications for competitive education environments and workplaces, and social justice, are still only being tentatively explored (Dresler et al. 2013; Maier et al. 2013; Sahakian 2014; Jane and Vincent 2015; Harari 2016). Amongst creative workers we can posit that the changing drugs of choice reflect a general shift from seeking inspiration to concentration. One recent study suggests that stimulants, even the ubiquitous caffeine, makes people slower and deeper thinkers (Franke et al. 2017), in Kahneman's terms (2013); rather contrary to the feared impacts of social media.

2.3.4 Creative Calling: Lessons from Lucian Freud

Rilke set the bar high with his exhortation to the committed writer to comprehensively habituate oneself to one's creative calling: "…build your life in accordance with this necessity; your whole life, even in its humblest and most indifferent hour, must become a sign and witness to this impulse." (Rilke 1986: 6). The late German-born British artist Lucian Freud seems to have taken that to heart, perhaps unsurprising as his architect father was a great admirer of Rilke in his youth and had met him. Freud's personality and self-identity were conducive to sustained and distinctive creative endeavour. Bearing the pedigree of being Sigmund Freud's grandson but the outsider experience of being a Jewish refugee from Nazism, from a young age he showed a passion for art and disregard for the expectations of school masters and others who would constrain him. Charming but self-absorbed, and capable of being rather cutting and cruel, he was nonetheless endlessly curious about other people (Hoban 2014: 34, 57). Lucian Freud showed an exceptionally patient attentiveness to his subjects, and determined indifference to critics, art world trends, public and private opinion during his more than six decades as a devout painter. Hoban (2014: 1) has described how Lucian Freud's gaze was insatiable, exemplifying 'the art of looking': "His omnivorous scrutiny bordered on the obsessive; his forensic curiosity was satisfied only through countless sittings, as if by minutely examining and recording the world in his studio, he could command it." His painterly work ethic was legendary: exhaustingly meticulous which made great claims on the resolve of his sitters. He could ignore their time and discomfort while honouring their bodily particularity with his creative attention. As the late US-based Australian art critic Robert Hughes wrote: "Every inch of the surface has to be won, must be argued through, bears the traces of curiosity and inquisition—above all, takes nothing for granted and demands active engagement from the viewer as its right." (quoted in Greig 2013: 19). Art critic Martin Gayford, who wrote a masterful account of his seven month experience of sitting for a portrait by Freud, described him as having the eye of a novelist, and his portraits as being powerfully imbued with 'the awkwardness of truth' (Gayford 2010: 58). Gayford (2010: 21) writes that Freud's "…peculiarity in the history of art is that he is aware of the individuality of absolutely everything…nothing is generalized, idealized or generic."

Lucian Freud showed always profound intrinsic motivation towards his art, working intently until the very last months before he passed away aged 88. Greig quotes him as saying that: "It is the only point of getting up every morning: to paint, to make something good, to make something even better than before, not to give up, to compete, to be ambitious." (Greig 2013: 10). While Freud painted mostly all day, every day, he also had a fondness for gambling on horses, had a prolific love life—fathering numerous children, dined well when he could afford it later in his career, and took a number of baths each day (in common with fashion designer Tom Ford). Lucian Freud liked company, but as regular breakfast companion Greig (2013: 3) recalled, "…often it was arranged on the spur of the moment. He hated being pinned down, having to see anybody." Freud hated intrusion so gave his phone number to very few people. Lucian Freud's assistant during his last two decades, David Dawson, said that: "Having his privacy made his freedom. I wasn't a gatekeeper, but I did help take some of the interruptions away from him." (Field 2013). A journalist noted Dawson "..is softly spoken, but has an air of toughness about him that Freud clearly relied on." (Field 2013). Freud was committed to the practice of figurative art, ignored art trends, "…certain that prolonged and intense observation of the human figure was the core of an artist's purpose." (Greig 2013: 10). For decades this was financially very costly to him, as there was little interest in portraiture at a time of conceptual and pop art. Pragmatics did not prevail. Yet Freud's self belief was ultimately rewarded with recognition later in life, and considerable wealth. He certainly exemplified Runco's (2018: 247) definition of creativity as "the construction of original and effective interpretations of experience"; the experience being his intense seeing of the individual physicality and personality of each of his patient subjects. A reclusive figure to whom social media use would have been anathema, his oeuvre is valued more than ever today.

2.4 Conclusion

As consumers, citizens are confronted with a deluge of information, ubiquitous demands upon their attention, with marketers, digital entertainment firms and social media platforms deploying ever more innovative communications design and manipulative distributive practices (Williams 2018). Social media platforms are predicated on monetising the attention that shared content attracts, and are evidently designed for addiction. All the while, an ever larger part of the 'back catalogue' of culture is digitised, available on demand, while cultural content flows across porous borders in greater volume, at increasingly speed. Just as affluent individuals have been shown to pay relatively less attention to others (Kraus et al. 2010; Dietze and Knowles 2016), will the spoiled-for-choice consumer became deadened to the hallmarks of quality, of embodied creative and artisanal attention, in the myriad products and services at hand? We may hope that digitally-enabled communities of connoisseurship, coupled with self-curating, discerning self-identities active on social media, may in time raise consumer/audience standards in many fields (Cowen 2002: 116). Certainly creative professionals are already supported through such communities, even if the content generated is not often shared more widely. Although firms in the 'sensibility business', especially those positioned in luxury goods, once tended to haughty and closed demeanours towards both clientale and critics, many are now leaning more towards more transparency, less 'blackboxing', of the creative process. Hermes allowed a journalist to the observe the development of a new fragrance, from the initial work by in-house perfumer Jean-Claude Ellena until the product went to market (Burr 2007). Around the same time Louis Vuitton opened themselves up to a substantial documentary on designer Marc Jacobs' work as creative director for the brand (Prigent 2007), and some years later Dior permitted a documentary around designer Raf Simon's first collection for the brand (Tcheng 2015). The resulting fashion and fragrance media content attracted large audiences within the devoted consumer communities. All these major luxe brands have developed active social media strategies but remain meticulous in managing their brand personas via digital media. Individual creatives may embrace social media to engage with potential audiences for their work but run the risk of being trapped in a reactive short-term posture. Over-exposure may diminish the market cache of a creative identity, while distracting from serious creative work.

An intermediate position may be for creatives to adopt a semi-distant stance, concentrating on doing distinctive quality work in a well-conceptualised problem space. Reiter-Palmon (2018: 188) has found that "when problem construction is more effortful or deliberate, the resulting solution tends also to be more creative." Creative discretion should be more effectively realised that way; in particular, it will aid the selective *articulation* of one's creative vision to discerning and influential, yet evolving, niche audiences. There are vibrant ecologies of new attention intermediaries, from countless blogs and influencer social media feeds, to full-scale new media that were born digital—such the website 'business of fashion'—which have grown out of the initiatives of 'intensive' consumers of a particular creative domain (Cowen 2002: 113–119). One of the major developments in the art world in recent decades is the rise of a cadre of curators, who are increasingly celebrities in their own right. They offer not merely expert selection and recommendation but also about effective contextualisation, meaning-making[3] (O'Neill 2012; Balzer 2014; Obrist 2014; Synder 2015; Bhaskar 2016). The successful curator effectively is an agent of attention

---

[3]From a conversation with Ayelet Zohar, 2nd July 2018, Tokyo.

to a bundled array of otherwise disparate art objects and experiences. Curation has gained such cultural currency that all manner of individuals and marketers embrace the discourse, to the unease of some in the professional art curation world. Miller (2016) was prompted to write an influential commentary asking whether we really are all curators now? The association of the faddy 'curatorial turn' (O'Neill 2007) with 'hipster culture', and richly parodied, nonetheless prompts the observation that cosmopolitan consumer cultures has embraced the artisanal. This orientation is very much about connoisseurship, resistant to calculative commercial dumbing down. It represents perhaps a new egalitarianism, respect for a labour of love, for the craft of creation.

Alfred North Whitehead famously stated that "civilization advances by extending the number of important operations which we can perform without thinking of them." (1911: 61; cited in Langlois 2001). Bertrand Russell (1984) hoped that technological advancements could liberate people from drudgery for more creative and intellectual pursuits. Czikszentmihalyi (1997: 351–358) explored the ways that our daily routines could be simplified to leave attention for creative endeavour. Yet, many people seem harried and distracted, despite being profoundly enabled by technology. Wu (2017: 352) ponders "… what are the costs to a society of an entire population conditioned to spend so much of their waking lives not in concentration and focus but rather in fragmentary awareness and subject to constant interruption? In this respect our lives have become the very opposite of those cultivated by the monastics, whether in the East or West, whose aim was precisely to reap the fruits of deep and concentrated attention." If we adhere to Viennese Secession's dictum '*der zeit ihre kunst: der kunst ihre freiheit*' (to each age its art: to art its freedom), then perhaps we will see an art of hasty distracted connectivity. Perhaps we can all learn instead from New York street photographer Saul Leiter who, after a period of early prominence, happily worked in obscurity for decades, only to be celebrated in his 80s. Leiter said: "I'm a person who likes to postpone things. I see no reason for being in a rush." (Leach 2013). The editors of this volume surely wish though that I had not taken Leiter's outlook to heart.

References

Acerbi, A., & Bentley, R. A. (2014). Biases in cultural transmission shape the turnover of popular traits. *Evolution and Human Behavior, 35,* 228–236.

Ananny, M. (2016). Towards an ethics of algorithms: Convening, observation, probability and timeliness. *Science, Technology and Human Values, 41*(1), 93–117.

Anderson, C. (2006). *The long tail: How endless choice is creating unlimited demand.* London: Random House.

Balzer, D. (2014). *Curationism: How curating took over the art world and everything else.* Ontario: Coach House Books.

BBC World Service (no date) *How to write a novel.* http://www.bbc.co.uk/worldservice/arts/features/howtowrite/novel.shtml. Accessed 25 May 2018.

Bentley, R. A., Lipo, C. P., Herzog, H. A., & Hahn, M. W. (2007). Regular rates of popular culture change reflect random copying. *Evolution and Human Behavior, 28,* 151–158.

Bernstein, E. S., & Turban, S. (2018). *The impact of the 'open' workspace on human collaboration* (p. 373). Philosophical Transactions B: Royal Society.

Bhaskar, M. (2016). *Curation: The power of selection in a world of excess.* London: Piatkus.

Bowker, J. C., Stotsky, M. T., & Etkin, R. G. (2017). How BIS/BAS and psycho-behavioral variables distinguish between social withdrawal subtypes during emerging adulthood. *Personality and Individual Differences, 119,* 283–288.

Burr, C. (2007). *The perfect scent: A year inside the perfect industry in Paris and New York.* New York: Picador.

Cain, S. (2012). *Quiet the power of introverts in a world that can't stop talking.* New York: Crown Random House.

Carhart-Harris, R. L., Erritzoe, D., Haijen, E., Kaelen, M., & Watts, R. (2018). Psychedelics and connectedness. *Psychopharmacology (Berl), 235*(2), 547–550.

Caves, R. E. (2000). *Creative industries: Contracts between art and commerce, Cambridge.* Mass: Harvard University Press.

Coleridge, S. T. (2004). The complete poems. In K. William (Ed.), *Christabel, Kubla Khan, and the pains of sleep, 1816* (2nd ed.). London: William Bulmer.

Cowen, T. (2002). *Creative destruction: How globalization is changing the world's cultures.* New Jersey: Princeton University Press.

Czikszentmihalyi, M. (1997). *Creativity: The psychology of discovery and invention.* New York: Harper Collins.

Deveney, R. (2018). *5 Word-famous artists and their drugs of choice.* www.therecoveryvillage.com. Accessed 29 July 2018.

Dietze, P., & Knowles, E. D. (2016). Social class and the motivational relevance of other human beings: Evidence from visual attention. *Psychological Science, 27*(11), 1517–1527.

Dietz, O., Striegel, H., Franke, A. G., Lieb, K., Simon, P., & Ulrich, R. (2013). Randomized response estimates for the 12-month prevalence of cognitive-enhancing drug use in university students. *Pharmacotherapy, 33*(1), 44–50.

Dresler, M., Sandberg, A., Ohla, K., Bublitz, C., Trenado, C., Mroczko-Wasowicz, A., et al. (2013). Non-pharmacological cognitive enhancement. *Neuropharmacology, 64,* 529–543.

Elliott, T. (2018). *Maths prodigy comes home to establish $5 million world-class maths centre.* New South Wales: The Sydney Morning Herald.

Eyal, N. (2014). *Hooked: How to build habit-forming products.* New York: Penguin Random House.

Field, M. (2013). *Freud in Austria: Why did Lucian finally relent and allow his paintings to be shown in Austria? The Independent,* 10 Nov.

Forster, J. J. H. (2009). Digital technologies and the intensification of economic and organisational mechanisms in commercial sport. In N. K. Pope, K. A. L. Kuhn, & J. J. H. Forster (Eds.), *Digital sport for performance enhancement and competitive evolution: Intelligent gaming technologies.* New York: Hershey, PA: Information Science Reference.

Franke, A. G., Gränsmark, Patrik, Agricola, A., Schühle, K., Rommel, T., Sebastian, A., et al. (2017). Methylphenidate, modafinil, and caffeine for cognitive enhancement in chess: A double-blind, randomised controlled trial. *European Neuropsychopharmacology, 27,* 248–260.

Gayford, M. (2010). *Man with a blue scarf: On sitting for a portrait by Lucian Freud.* London: Thames & Hudson.

Goldhaber, M. H. (1997). The attention economy and the net. *First Monday 2*(4), 7 April. Internet journal @ firstmonday.org, no page numbers.

Greig, G. (2013). *Breakfast with Lucian: The astounding life and outrageous times of Britain's great modern painter.* London: Jonathan Cape.

Griffiths, M. D. (2017). Drug use and creativity: Can psychoactive substance use enhance creativity? *Psychology Today,* 21 Feb, psychologytoday.com.

Guignon, C. (2004). *On being authentic.* New York, London: Routledge.

Harari, Y. N. (2016). *Homo deus: A brief history of tomorrow.* London: Harvill Secker.

Hardey, M. (2013). Note to selfie: You're more than just a narcissist's plaything. *The Conversation,* 21 Nov.

Helberger, N. (2011). Diversity by design. *Journal of Information Policy, 1,* 441–469.

Hirschman, A. O. (1967). *The principle of the hiding hand* (pp. 10–23). Winter: The Public Interest.

Hirschman, A. O. (1970). *Exit, voice and loyalty: Responses to decline in firms, organizations, and states, Cambridge.* Mass: Harvard University Press.

Hoban, P. (2014). *Lucian Freud: Eyes wide open.* Icons, Seattle: Amazon Publishing.

Iszáj, F., Griffiths, M. D., & Demetrovics, Z. (2016). Creativity and psychoactive substance use: A systematic review. *International Journal of Mental Health and Addiction, 15*(5), 1135–1149.

Jane, E. A., & Vincent, N. A. (2015). *The rise of cognitive enhancers is a mass social experiment.* www.theconversation.com. 15 June.

Kahneman, D. (2013). *Thinking fast and slow.* New York: Farrar, Straus & Giroux.

Kim, J., & de Dear, R. (2013). Workspace satisfaction: The privacy-communication trade-off in open-plan offices. *Journal of Environmental Psychology, 36,* 18–26.

Kraus, M. W., Côté, S., & Keltner, D. (2010). Social class, contextualism, and empathic accuracy. *Psychological Science, 21*(11), 1716–1723.

Langlois, R. (2001). Knowledge, consumption and endogenous growth. In U. Witt (Ed.), *Escaping satiation: The demand side of economic growth* (pp. 97–114). Berlin: Springer.

Lanham, R. A. (2006). *The economics of attention: Style and substance in the age of information.* Chicago: The University of Chicago Press.

Lanier, J. (2018). *Ten arguments for deleting your social media accounts right now.* New York: Henry Holt.

Leach, T. (2013). *In no great hurry: 13 lessons in life with Saul Leiter,* documentary film, directed by Tomas Leach, co-produced with Margit Erb.

Liebl, A., Haller, J., Jödicke, B., Baumgartner, H., Schlittmeier, S., & Hellbrück, J. (2012). Combined effects of acoustic and visual distraction on cognitive performance and well-being. *Applied Ergonomics, 43,* 424–434.

Lindblom, C. (2001). *The market system.* New Haven: Yale University Press.

Maher, B. (2008). Poll results: Look who's doping. *Nature, 452*(7188), 674–675.

Maier, L. J., Liechti, M. E., Herzig, F., & Schaub, M. P. (2013). To dope or not to dope: Neuroenhancement with prescription drugs and drugs of abuse among swiss university students. *PLoS ONE, 8*(11), e77967.

Miller, A. (2016). Are we really all curators now? *The Spectator* 9 July.

Napoli, P. M. (2013). *The algorithm as institution: Toward a theoretical framework for automated media production and consumption.* Fordham University Schools of Business Research Paper. Available at SSRN.

Norman, D. (2018). *Why bad technology dominates our lives,* according to Don Norman. Fast Company, 17 July. Accessed at www.fastcompany.com.

O'Neill, P. (2007). The curatorial turn: from practice to discourse. In J. Rugg & M. Sedgewick (Eds.), *Issues in curating contemporary art and performance* (pp. 13–28). Intellect: Bristol.

O'Neill, P. (2012). *The culture of curating and the curating of cultures.* Cambridge, MA: The MIT Press.

Obrist, H. U. (2014). *Ways of curating.* London: Penguin.

Oliver, S. (2017). *A brief history of Freud's love affair with cocaine: The founder of psychoanalysis had a serious blow habit.* vice.com, 24 June.

Pable, J. (2009). Interior design identity in the crossfire: A call for renewed balance in subjective and objective ways of knowing. *Journal of Interior Design, 34*(2), v–xx.

Pink, D. H. (2001). *Free agent nation.* New York: Warner.

Plucker, J. A. (2018). It all makes sense now that I think about it: A quarter century of studying creativity. In R. J. Sternberg & J. C. Kaufman (Eds.), *The nature of human creativity.* Cambridge: Cambridge University Press.

Prigent, L. (2007). *Marc Jacobs and Louis Vuitton,* documentary by Ande Media and Arte France.

Racine, E., & Forlini, C. (2010). Cognitive enhancement, lifestyle choice, or misuse of prescription drugs: Ethics blind spots in current debates. *Neuroethics, 3,* 1–4.

Reiter-Palmon, R. (2018). Creative cognition at the individual and team levels: What happens before and after idea generation. In R. J. Sternberg & J. C. Kaufman (Eds.), *The Nature of Human Creativity* (pp. 184–208). Cambridge: Cambridge University Press.

Rilke, R. M. (1986). *Letters to a young poet* (Stephen M., Trans.). New York: Vintage Books.

Runco, M. A. (1996). Personal creativity: Definition and developmental issues. *New Directions for Child Development, 72,* 3–30.

Runco, M. A. (2018). Authentic creativity. In R. J. Sternberg & J. C. Kaufman (Eds.), *The Nature of Human Creativity* (pp. 246–263). Cambridge: Cambridge University Press.

Runco, M. A., & Beghetto, R. A. (2019). Primary and secondary creativity. *Current Opinion in Behavioural Sciences, 27,* 7–10.

Russell, B. (1984). *In praise of idleness and other essays.* London: Urwin Paperbacks.

Sahakian, B. (2014). *Record seizure of smart drugs including one untested in humans shows growing market.* www.theconversation.com. 31 Oct.

Sahakian, B., & Morein-Zamir, S. (2007). Professor's little helper. *Nature, 450,* 1157–1159.

Sawyer, R. K., et al. (2003). *Creativity and development.* Oxford: Oxford University Press.

Schultheis, E. (2018). *Sitzfleisch: The German concept to get more work done.* bbc.com, 4 Sept.

Sloterdijk, P. (2016). *Selected exaggerations: Conversations and interviews, 1993–2012.* Cambridge: Polity Press, German original published in.

Sternberg, R. (2018). The triangle of creativity. In R. J. Sternberg & J. C. Kaufman (Eds.), *The nature of human creativity* (pp. 318–334). Cambridge: Cambridge University Press.

Storr, A. (1988). *Solitude: A return to the self.* New York: Free Press.

Sunstein, C. R. (2006). *Infotopia: How many minds produce knowledge.* New York: Oxford University Press.

Sunstein, C. R. (2007). *Republic.com 2.0.* New Jersey: Princeton University Press.

Sunstein, C. R. (2009). *Going to extremes: How like minds unite and divide.* Oxford: Oxford University Press.

Surowiecki, J. (2004). *The wisdom of crowds.* New York: Doubleday.

Synder, I. (2015). Discourses of 'curation' in digital times. In R. H. Harris, A. Chik, & C. Hafner (Eds.), *Discourse and digital practices: Doing discourse analysis in the digital age* (pp. 209–225). Oxford: Routledge.

Tcheng, F. (2015). *Dior and I,* documentary film, produced by Guillaume de Roquemaurel.

Thestrup, J., & Pokarier, C. (2019). *Designing under uncertainty: Professional identity and market discipline in creative industries.* Japan: Waseda Global Forum.

van Alstyne, M., & Brynjolfsson, E. (2005). Global village or cyberbalkans: Modelling and measuring the integration of electronic communities. *Management Science, 51,* 851–868.

van Pragh, A. (2009). Eccentric duo wear their obsessive art on patriotic sleeves. *Sydney Morning Herald,* July 14. Syndicated from *The Telegraph,* London.

Webster, J. G. (2010). User information regimes: How social media shape patterns of consumption. *Northwestern University Law Review, 104*(2), 593–612.

Webster, J. G. (2014). *The Marketplace of Attention: How audiences take shape in a digital age.* Cambridge: MIT Press.

Webster, J. G., & Ksiazek, T. B. (2012). The dynamics of audience fragmentation: Public attention in the age of digital media. *Journal of Communication, 62*(1), 39–56.

Wilde, O. (1963). *The works of oscar wilde.* In G. John (Ed.), London: Spring Books.

Williams, J. (2018). *Stand out of our light: Freedom and resistance in the attention economy.* Cambridge: Cambridge University Press.

Wu, T. (2017). *The attention merchants: The epic scramble to get in our heads.* New York: Vintage.

Christopher Pokarier is professor in the School of International Liberal Studies, Waseda University, teaching creative industries, communication design, and comparative enterprise. He has undergraduate and masters degrees, in journalism and government, from the University of Queensland, and completed his Ph.D at the Australian National University. Before joining Waseda in

2004 he was senior lecturer in international business at Queensland University of Technology, Brisbane, Australia. His current research interests encompass the creative industries in place branding, higher education marketization, and the future of the university campus.

Chapter 3
Outsourcing Taste; Are Algorithms Doing All the Work?

Stan Erraught

It is a truism that is nevertheless true that creativity does not come into existence in a vacuum. Creative endeavour, whether individual or collective, requires a material and social context within which it can practice. This context includes, but is not limited to, the existence of an audience that might be expected to understand the work produced, the means by which the work can reach that audience and at least the possibility—within capitalism—that the single creative practitioner or collective enterprise can profit from such work.

Popular music, by which, for the purpose of this essay, I take to refer to—for the most part—music produced from within the post- Rock and Roll, Anglo-American cultural space, has always had a specific and necessary entanglement with the technology by which it is disseminated and consumed. An alternative definition to the one offered above might simply state that popular music is recorded music: not music that *is* recorded, but music that is made *as* recordings. In other words, the primary object is not the song, or the score, but the record. Over more than 60 year history of this form of popular music, the physical—and later 'virtual'—form that recordings have taken has changed many times: I imagine it would be possible to listen to the same Elvis Presley recording of 'Blue Suede Shoes' as a 78 rpm disc, a 45 rpm single, on a 33 1/3 LP compilation, on cassette tape, on 8-track tape, on a CD, as a digital download and as streamed content from a platform such as Spotify—and, of course, on the radio. It is even possible that the same listener might have purchased or consumed the same or similar content in all these formats.

Each of these formats brings with it specific affordances: the car radio, the high-end stereo system, the smartphone, all permit differing modes of attention and demand specific social contexts. The argument I wish to pursue here is that the technological and social context in which popular music, and the associated industry, reached its commercial—and some would argue, artistic—apotheosis in the roughly

S. Erraught (✉)
University of Leeds, Leeds, England, UK
e-mail: S.Erraught@leeds.ac.uk

© Springer Nature Singapore Pte Ltd. 2020
N. Otmazgin and E. Ben-Ari (eds.), *Creative Context*, Creative Economy,
https://doi.org/10.1007/978-981-15-3056-2_3

two and a half decades between the mid-sixties and the late nineties of the 20th century was supported by a notion of taste that had its roots in 'high' modernism, albeit misconstrued, and that as listening habits and industry structures have been transformed since the start of this century, so have the ways in which taste is understood and mobilised by the industry. The first section will look at how notions of taste and judgement, rooted in Kantian aesthetics, were smuggled into the commercial music industry, even as the inheritors of that tradition—the Frankfurt school—railed against it. The second section will examine how the technological changes and consequent shifts in listening practices wrought by the move to digital means of production and dissemination have disrupted this 'ideology of rock' and the final section will posit some possible outcomes.

3.1 Notions of Taste and Judgement

The notion of taste as judgement, as an act that affirms and confirms a common humanity and that is independent of 'interest' in the sense of something that we might profit by, or that might have emotional associations, is fundamental to the construction of the European, and later the American bourgeoisies, and their understanding of themselves.

The view of culture, which, in much of Europe certainly, involved music as the pinnacle of disinterested artistic endeavour, as something separated from the cultic and from aristocratic privilege, was the necessary alibi for a rising class, one that did not inherit a sense of itself as the measure of all things. By insisting on the universality and necessity of the judgment of taste, it was able to lay claim to a common humanity, to mechanism of judgement that rested not on revelation or on tradition, but, as with the 'facts' of science, on a deduction, albeit a complex and reflexive one.

Music was central to this, although Kant, from whom this notion of taste stems, was indifferent to its charms, considering a 'minor art' and one that interrupted the discourse of gentlemen at dinner (*Anthropology* 2006, 7: 281).[1] Music, particularly in the German tradition that shadowed the idealism that provided its philosophical clothing, most nearly approximated the ideal of the vanishing aesthetic object, the thing that was not a thing that underwrote the harmony of the faculties that, in turn, affirmed the *sensus communis,* the common sense that grounded our humanity and our social being (*Critique of Judgement* 1987, 5: 240).

Art, and the taste for it, affirmed a notion of value that was supposed to be opaque to the market, even as the artist—and in particular the composer and/or musician— became entirely the creature of that market, as patronage from church and court withdrew. This value absolved the class that most benefitted from its construction from the charge of vulgarity, and effectively replaced—or at least supplemented— religion as the site of detachment from the struggles of a fallen world.

---

[1]References to Kant given according to *Akademie* pagination, as is conventional.

Popular culture, of course, lay outside this articulation of taste completely, just as it was considered beneath the considerations of copyright (see Attali 1985, p. 54).

Since the end of the second world war we have seen the displacement of the old hierarchies of taste with either an eclecticism that permits the subject to strategize her engagement with culture according to occasion or a simple, and wholesale, replacement of 'high' culture by popular culture (see Huyssen 1988; Kellner 1989; Harvey 1989 etc.). This replacement has, of course, been extensively theorised within the literature of cultural studies but, as much of this work has emerged from disciplinary discourses that tend to bracket the idea of value, in favour of description, there remains, I think, much work to be done to say how the idea of value functions within this new terrain.

The culture industry critique, originating from first generation Critical Theory, most particularly from the work of Adorno and Horkheimer (1979 and also Adorno 1991), remains unavoidable as a theoretical resource. They understood that the transformation of the products of culture into mass produced artefacts brought culture under the logic of the commodity, and the discourse of alienation and reification, rooted in Marx, via Lukacs (1967). The logic that informed artistic and cultural practices could no longer be plausibly upheld as protected by the membrane of disinterest and notions of value outside the market. This had the effect, as Adorno noted, of created a tear, a diremption, between the popular and the shrinking and threatened arena in which the autonomous artwork might operate: they became two halves of a torn unity, to which however 'they did not add up' (Adorno in Adorno et al. 1977, p. 126)—because, in the trauma that separated them, each was deformed. The popular lost its connection to the nourishing stream of innovation and adventure provided by autonomous art and that art lost its access to the demotic, and to a language able to communicate more generally. Art became incomprehensible in order to avoid co-option by the market and popular culture submitted to the logic of the commodity that denuded it of all access to spirit. This diremption meant that each was defined against the other: to be a person of 'high' culture meant to be the enemy of the popular, and to be a devotee of the popular required the construction of an aesthetic, however makeshift, that countered the scorn of highbrow.

There was a time—perhaps—when popular music was innocent of the claims of taste, and of the aesthetic. However, and perhaps beginning in the 1920s when Jazz began to be written about seriously, first in Europe and later in its homeland, an argument that could be taken into the territory of the highbrow was needed. With Western pop music, by which I mean, for the moment the music created, for the most part in the US and in Europe that was rooted in the eruption of rock and roll in the mid-1950s, the field was untroubled by this anxiety until the sixties: by which time, when music rooted in these forms began to understand itself in ways that were not completely indexed to the market, what Simon Frith (1983) has called 'an ideology of rock' was developed, one that, while attempting to counter the condescension of the highbrow, managed, perhaps less than consciously, to import—as Alison Stone (2016) has perceptively detailed—the categories by which this condescension was upheld into its own discourse. The oppositions between pop and rock, indie and mainstream, 'commercial' and not, by which much of the conversation around popular music distinguishes the worthy from the unworthy repeats the same distinction in a minor key that conservative critics such as Roger Scruton deprecate popular music as whole. Often this is taken to refute Adorno—special pleading on behalf of some treasured cases rescued from the vulgar mass that, under certain circumstances, this music can, after all be art. Here, the identification of exceptions really does prove the rule.

This particular aesthetic ideology was one of the engines that helped drive the huge expansion of the popular music industry from the sixties until it fell off the cliff in the early years of this century. The shift from pop to rock heralded the move from the single to the album and the construction of a canon of rock music that was informed by an array of gatekeepers (or cultural intermediaries)—press, radio, promoters, and, of course, record company A&R—that constituted an ideological apparatus of taste, not, to be sure, one that was uniform, but one that occupied a field where all the actors had, for the most part, enough common ground and a language in which and by which judgements of value that fed into articulations of the market might be constructed.

Much of this language was permeated with notions of value and distinction centred around the idea of genre and, separately, but connectedly, that of authenticity. Genre had a dual function: it identified music and identified likely audiences. It was thus constructed in two, sometimes overlapping, sometimes conflicting ways. The first one was as a way record companies used to match audience and artist (see Negus 1999). The second was, often, a more organic process whereby a scene identified itself, often in explicit opposition to the first process, around a group of artists and venues, built networks of communication and reinforcement and would—as in the paradigmatic, and perhaps overdetermined case of punk—negotiate its entry to the marketplace on (some of) its own terms. This differing modulations of genre meant that each genre had its own specific gravity: some, such as jazz, and in particular, its sub-genres, such as fusion, afro-jazz, jazz-funk etc. had specific musical markers, necessary and usually sufficient conditions, relatively free of additional scene-specific markers. You could play jazz-funk just about anywhere, and while there was a certain racial coding involved, your success at being a jazz-funk artist or ensemble was more or less dependent on musical skills and attributes. At the other extreme, a genre such as Northern Soul was retrospective, DJ and audience driven. No one ever set out to make a 'Northern Soul' record until the scene was well established: until then, and eclectic and unconnected selection of tunes, assembled by the taste of a few DJs in a few clubs in the north of England and driven by success on the dancefloor, determined what Northern Soul would be.

What these differently weighted distinctions meant though was that 'your' scene or genre felt not simply like a market segment, but brought with it all kinds of consequences regarding ones particular social position, and the articulation of this location. 'Your' genre was the ideal to which all others aspired, but fell short: it expressed its time and identity was intimately bound up with this: 'our' music intrinsically and unavoidably tied to other commitments—social, political, and representational.

Arguments about some notion of aesthetically demarcated 'truth', often parsed as 'authenticity' or in similar terms, has been central to both the distinctions between genres within popular music and as ways of understanding and evaluating works within particular genres. Certain specific qualities become constitutively evaluative—rootsy-ness in certain kinds of country music, flow in rap, heaviness in metal etc. The more a tune embodies the defining quality of the genre, the better it will be—and not all of these qualities will translate across genre.

Nevertheless, in the heyday of the recording business as the purveyor of physical product, in a media landscape that was constituted hierarchically and where influence was negotiated at arms' length between producers of cultural product and the evaluative critical apparatus that played a key role in disseminating and articulating the qualities of such works, there was a sense that all popular music was part of a singular field, and that popularity, sales, and critical approval—and eventually canonicity and sustainable careers—were up for grabs under the same conditions for all. Even at genre level, taste was a matter of public negotiation—you heard music on the radio, you read about it in a magazine, and while this was one-way traffic, it was something you knew other were listening to, and reading. The act of commitment as what would now be called an advocate-consumer to a particular record involved a public act—buying that record. For most of us, our purchases were matter for debate and *dissensus* within our social group—in much of the world, and for the audience that consumed pop and rock, buying a record was a relatively substantial investment, both of money, and of aesthetic 'risk' capital. Music, then, not simply as an active practice, but, as fandom, was social.

3.2 'Ideology of Rock'

The changes wrought on the recording industry by successive transformations in the means of production and distribution since the CD era have been well rehearsed in the literature, and there is a growing literature that examines the ways in which consumers now engage with music, and how transformations in the ways in which music is channelled has effected changes in the ways in which its users value it.

In the rest of this paper, I wish to look at how taste, and the ways in which listeners understand what they are doing in the act of judging, and the consequences and entailments of those acts, has changed as a consequence of the shift from music understood as something instantiated as a physical-and scarce—commodity, to something understood as 'ubiquitous' and effectively free, or at least, without a unit price. The shift to streaming has radically undermined the traditional sites of gatekeeping, of endorsement, critique and recommendation—where once we heard—or heard/read about—a piece of music, and went through successive stages of growing engagement leading to the eventual purchase of a relatively high value object, this process will now occur in seconds—and likely as not, guided by an algorithm.

As noted above, the changes in the patterns of distribution and consumption of recorded music have been extensively covered in the literature. Does this represent a shift comparable to the shift to mechanical reproduction of music at the turn of the 20th century, and is a continuation of these technologies by other means?

We can consider music to exist in different regimes of commodification, all of which are still with us, though some are residual, some dominant, some emergent: music as published score, music as live sound at a public concert, and music as recorded sound in the form of player piano rolls or audio recordings in many other formats, analog or digital. (Taylor 2016, p. 21)

Or, is it that, as Fleischer insists, the shift to a subscription service, whereby the consumer pays a monthly tariff for unlimited access to a vast database of tracks, rather than paying for individual tracks, or pre-selected bundles—albums—represents more than simply a practical change

The decommodification of individual recordings (at the consumer's side), now coincides with the recommodification of music as an experience. (Fleischer 2017, p. 158)

How do consumers understand what they are doing as they stream? Before looking at this more closely, however, I wish to examine a slightly different aspect of this change, one that, I think, has been overlooked. This is the way in which the temporal order of the pop process has shifted in quite complex ways and in different directions over the past two decades.

The first aspect is that pop careers have become longer, and the time between events, and phases of those careers longer also. The shifts in David Bowie's sound, personae and audience between 1972 and 1979 would be unimaginable now for a comparable pop star—three years between albums has become the norm, songs stay on the charts—themselves a metric that has altered beyond the scale of comparison—for comparative aeons.

Connected to this, the past has become much longer, available in much greater depth and more present. There was a time when back catalogue didn't stay on the shelves for very long, and 5 years ago was pre-history. Anyone who remembers trying to buy Velvet Underground records in the early 1970s will concur. Now, people born this century are familiar with music recorded 30 years before they were born, and, because they generally consume it on the same platforms as music recorded yesterday, some—I would argue—of its historical specificity, the sense of its connection to its time is lost. Nor, however, does the vinyl fetish do anything to resolve this—a newly pressed copy of *Forever Changes* is still a 21st century artefact. The past recedes the more we try to approach it. This flattening, the recuperation of history that also denies its historicity, while allowing access to a wealth of previously available—and sometimes historical recordings that were never available—also stifles innovation in what we might call an infinite context. We know too much for innocent experimentation.

Conversely, the time taken to hear about a band, hear them and either decide to investigate further or dismiss them can all happen within minutes. Once, you might, if you were the sort of music fan who wished to keep up, or even be ahead of the curve, you might see a mention of a band in an article in the music press, after which months might elapse before you heard them. Radio in your country might not be interested, if you lived outside any of the major music business centres records might take a long time to reach you etc. The effect was of a slow priming of one's interest, and, given the level of investment buying an LP entailed, the commitment was—compared to clicking on a YouTube or Soundcloud link—quite substantial.

One effect of all this is that, while we all live in the now, we no longer share a public now. Once, knowing what was Number One was at least as culturally central as knowing at least something about sport—now it is perfectly possible to be hugely invested in popular music and have no idea what is in the charts. It was always, of course, possible to pretend that one didn't care—but you knew. Equally, as noted above with regard to genre, whereas once it was possible to be devoted to metal, or punk, or whatever, and pretend to avoid all other genres, in order to stay current with your chosen genre, you would forced into at least semi-public realms occupied by other musics. You would, by a process of osmosis, absorb something about the many others of your field, and, since arguing the superiority of one genre and its associated subculture was a large part of participation therein, you needed to pay attention to what was going one elsewhere, if only to hone your weapons. The other possible effect of this was that you would, occasionally—and this was the gift of radio and record shops—hear something outside your normal zone of appreciation that would captivate, and relativize any fixed sense of yourself as a fan, and as a connoisseur. The charts could do this too—quite often, and this was perhaps more true of Britain than the US, utterly strange music would emerge into public view via specialist shops and audiences.

This aspect of popular culture, the sense of it as a counter-public sphere, where music functions as a placeholder for a view of the world that encompassed politics, fashion, other art forms and patterns of socialisation, is, I think, much more muted now. There is less to argue about.

Genre has moved from being something that functioned as a signifier for a world view, a form of life at least to some extent, to being simply a tag, a trace, a sliver of code. More to the point, one's individual taste becomes understood, by the market, as truly individual, a fingerprint, rather than a 'type'.

So if music means less, what does this mean for the recording industry?

Genre has moved from being a complex and weighted system of distinctions to being more simply a map of a terrain: one of the problems being that the terrain is unimaginably vast. One particular trope of the discourse of choice that permeates much of the language of the market in cultural commodities these days is that of scale—Spotify/Netflix/Amazon like to tell you how much is in there, suggest infinite resources. This is both comforting—you'll always be able to find what you want, and obscurely troubling—how will you know what you want, and what might you be missing out on?

The old maps, if we thought of it at all topographically, at least had familiar hills and a horizon: the new ones find us adrift in deep space, without an up or a down, or a direction home. Which is where the algorithms come in.

In order to try and understand how listeners navigate this new territory, it might be useful to look at the languages people use in order to describe their listening habits. Hagen (2016), following Markham (1998) and White and LeCornu (2016), has suggested that the metaphors that allow us to understand what we do may be divided into the following categories: we either see the internet, or parts of it, as a *tool*, as a *place*, or as *way of being*. One distinction that Nylund Hagen noted was that older consumers, those for whom streaming has taken the place, partially or completely, of the ways of listening they grew up with it, tend to cleave to the 'tool' repertoire of metaphorical descriptions. Streaming is something that allows them access to a convenient copy of the 'real' thing—their record collection, whether still existing, or the collection they once had. For such consumers, the experience is something like fast food: it fulfils an immediate need, but is not to be compared to a proper meal, and is, in the end, unsatisfying, for, even if they no longer sit down and play a CD or LP very often anymore, that mode remains imaginatively primary. For such listeners, songs are still organised according to their original order as albums: such listeners remain aware of the chronology of an artist's career, and genre switching can have the same slightly transgressive feel that wandering into another section of the record shop would have had. Playlists, if used at all, are not imaginatively possessed— while, for a certain generation, they might recall the mix-tape, the lovingly compiled cassette of personal favourites assemble for a friend or lover—for this cohort, that level of affective engagement with something that is, after all, just a list on a screen, remains impossible.

The metaphor of place applied to streaming, as Nylund Hagen describes, is almost always a personal, private place—albeit one that can be shared, in a curated and carefully managed way by making playlist available to others. To some extent this reflects the way in which listeners interact with the wider internet, and more particularly social media. Occasionally accounts are shared with siblings, friends, or partners, becoming a shared space that, in some way mimics a 'real' place in which music is heard.

For many listeners, and particularly those for whom streaming represents their primary mode, both in the sense of being the first mode of listening they adopted for themselves and in being the mode in which they more or less exclusively engage, music, generally listened to on headphones via a phone, becomes so intimately bound up with all aspects of life as to almost recede into a kind of taken-for-granted-ness, or, in phenomenological speak, ready-to-handedness. It is described in terms of affect, of feelings: music interacts with the lifeworld to heighten or transform the affective tenor of the everyday. Music consumption becomes close to frictionless, and choice, mediated by habit augmented by algorithmic prosthesis, ensures that little that would disrupt this continuum is able to intrude.

As will be seen, this is radically different from the kind of singular, if contested, social space that was constituted by the 'ideology of rock' as described above. If no one can hear what you are listening to, then no one can call your taste into question: and if you're not even sure what it is you are listening to in the first place, then you cannot even doubt your own judgement.

The notion of various internet companies as 'platforms' suggests neutrality: the provider is there to allow the consumer and the provider to meet in a safely negotiated space. This supposed neutrality is belied by certain consequences of streaming, and more particularly, of Spotify. Firstly, and most obviously, the platform does not simply supplement other methods of distribution and engagement: it aims to, and largely does, replace them. The effect of this on the income of musicians has been perhaps the most remarked and deprecated effect of Spotification. The platform radically restructures the market.

A second effect, not entirely exclusive to streaming, but certainly one that it has greatly enabled, is the shift from listening on speakers, in a static location, to listening on headphones, and to files that contain significantly less sonic information than a CD or a record. Not unnaturally, musicians and producers tailor the content and form of their recordings to these: shorter intros to avoid the skip reflex, sparser, and often slower songs to avoid aural exhaustion. Liz Pelly, in a recent article in *The Baffler*, identifies a genre that 'has practically become synonymous with the [Spotify] platform' a kind of 'muted, midtempo, melancholy pop', usually female fronted, that perfectly fits the mood and affect-oriented type of listening the service affords: or 'Spotify-core'.

She continues:

> Music trends produced in the streaming era are inherently connected to attention, whether it is hard-and-fast attention grabbing hooks, pop drops and chorus-loops engineered for the pleasure centre of our brains, or music that strategically requires no attention at all—the background music, the emotional wallpaper, the chill-pop-sad-vibe playlist fodder..... all this caters to an economy [....] where the most precious commodity is polarized human attention .... And where success is determined, almost in advance, by data. (Pelly 2018)

3.3 Possible Outcomes

It is, of course, not the first time that technological innovation has caused a shift in the sound of music—recording methods and limitations have always dictated not only how music gets made, but how it sounds, its form, and mode of address to the listener. Adorno, as often prescient, noted that the gramophone would have the effect of making all music chamber music (Adorno and Levin 1990). On a similar note, Compton Mackenzie, writing in *Gramophone* on the introduction of the LP bemoaned the laziness and inattention that would ensue once the serious listener did not have to leap up periodically to change the record, as with 78 s, with their playing time in the region of three minutes (Hamm 1985, p. 25).

It would be tempting to enlist the evidence above into a jeremiad about a lost moment of cultural heft, when popular music 'meant something' and to mourn the drift of pop into the shallows. This is not my intention: there are many positive features to the shift away from the 'ideology of rock'. More women than ever are involved in the production of popular music and the casual misogyny, in both content and business practices, that gave to lie to its progressive credentials is fast disappearing. More popular music from outside Europe and the North America and in languages other than English is reaching a global audience: Korean pop, Afrobeats (mostly from Nigeria) and various Latin forms, most notably reggaeton, have all made large inroads into a previously homogenous Anglo-American sphere. The purpose of this essay has been to argue that the notions of taste that grounded that ideology and thus the business that boomed on the back of the perceived cultural value of certain kinds of popular music have been undermined by changes in practices of distribution and consumption. Further, I would argue that this tells us something interesting about the ways in which technological shifts in production and distribution can affect the meanings ascribed to cultural products—and, indeed, the nature and intentions of those products.

References

Adorno, T. & Horkhemier, M. (1979). *The dialectic of enlightenment*. Cumming (Trans.). London: Verso.

Adorno, T. (1991). *The culture industry: Selected essays on mass culture*. In Bernstein (Ed.), London, New York: Routledge.

Adorno, T. W. & Levin, T. Y. (1990). *The curve of the needle*. In October (Vol. 55, pp. 48–55), Winter.

Adorno, T., Benjamin, & Bloch, E. et al. (1977). *Aesthetics and Politics*. London: Verso.

Attali, J. (1985). *Noise: The political economy of music*. Massumi (Trans.). Minneapolis: University of Minnesota Press.

Fleischer, R. (2017). If the song has no price, is it still a commodity? Rethinking the commodification of digital music. *Culture Unbound, 9*(2), 146–162.

Frith, S. (1983). *Sound effects: Youth, leisure and the politics of rock*. London: Constable.

Hagen, A. N. (2016). The metaphors we stream by: Making sense of music streaming. *First Monday, 21*(3–7).

Hamm, C. (1985). *Putting popular music in its place*. Cambridge: Cambridge University Press.

Harvey, D. (1989). *The condition of postmodernity*. Oxford: Blackwell.

Huyssen, A. (1988). *After the great divide*. London: Macmillan.

Kant, I. (1987). *Critique of judgement*. Pluhar (Ed.), (Trans.). Indianapolis: Hackett.

Kant, I. (2006). *Anthropology from a pragmatic point of view*. Louden (Trans.). Cambridge: Cambridge University Press.

Kellner, D. (1989). *Critical theory, marxism, and modernity*. Baltimore: Johns Hopkins University Press.

Lukacs, G. (1967). *History and class consciousness*. In Livingstone (Trans.). London: Merlin.

Markham, A. (1998). *Life online: Researching real life experience in virtual space*. Lanham MD: Altamira.

Negus, K. (1999). *Music genres and corporate cultures*. Oxford: Routledge.

Pelly, L. (2018). Streambait pop. In *The baffler*, Dec 2018.

Stone, A. (2016). *The value of popular music: An approach from post-kantian aesthetics*. London: Palgrave-Macmillan.

Taylor, T. D. (2016). *Music and capitalism*. Chicago: University of Chicago Press.

White, D., & LeCornu, A. (2016). Visitors and Residents. In *First Monday, 16*(9).

Stan Erraught is from Dublin and had a long career as a guitar player, songwriter, performing and touring musician and producer with various bands based there before moving into stage and production management in the festival and live music area. He combined this with a belated return to academia; an MA (Essex) and then a Ph.D. (NUI/UCD) in philosophy, specialising in Critical Theory and Kantian and post Kantian Idealism with particular reference to the relation between politics and aesthetics. His Ph.D. thesis (2010) was entitled Kant's Political Aesthetic: Time, Space and Judgement. He was an adjunct and associate lecturer at UCD and at Trinity College Dublin between 2010 and 2012, teaching at UG and PG level in Critical Theory and Political Philosophy more generally. He moved sideways into a music related role at Bucks New University in High Wycombe, where he was, first Senior Lecturer and then Principal Lecturer in Music and Event Management (2013–2017). He joined the School of Music in Leeds in September 2018. He has given numerous conference papers and presentations in all the above areas. In early 2018 he published a monograph on Music, Value and Utopia: Nostalgia for an Age Yet to Come? (Rowman and Littlefield).

Chapter 4
Embodied Social Dimensions in the Creative Process: Improvisation, Ethics and Gender in Choreography Classes in Israeli High-School Dance Programs

Yael (yali) Nativ

Improvisation is a common practice in choreography and creative process classes in dance programs in Israeli high schools. The Israeli Ministry of Education's Dance Curriculum states that the goal of teaching improvisation "is to develop creativity, self-movement study, self-awareness, solving problem skills and decision-making".[1] Dance teachers in the field add that improvisation allows young dancers to find their own movement language, which goes beyond specific instructions given in traditional technique classes such as Ballet and Contemporary dance. While these important skills focus on the individual, I illuminate a different dimension of improvisation, looking at the social conditions of the creative process, as an interactive and collective practice by exploring the linkage between risk and trust as an essential mechanism. Based on observations in dance improvisation and choreography classes and interviews with students and teachers, I show how improvisation and the dynamic of risk and trust produce unique embodied reciprocity-based interactions. This issue of an active body constructing relationships of trust is at the heart of this article. Hence, I argue, in improvisational conditions of uncertainty and risk, the dancing body produces a strong sense of solidarity within a group. Furthermore, I show how the improvising body creates inter-subjective and inter-personal situations in which trust becomes both a private and a collective asset that balances risks and competition and allows optimal conditions for creativity and innovation to arise. In the last part of the chapter, I move from dance and connect the concept of risk and trust as social elements in improvisation to the larger field of the creative industries and to the notion of innovation production in the creative process.

The discussion of trust offers at least four interesting perspectives: The first looks at the dancing body, trying to understand how embodied practices articulate social

---

[1] Dance Curriculum for Dance Programs in High Schools, Israeli Ministry of Education 2006.

Y. Nativ (✉)
The Academic College for Society and Arts ASA, Netanya, Israel
e-mail: yalinativ@gmail.com

© Springer Nature Singapore Pte Ltd. 2020
N. Otmazgin and E. Ben-Ari (eds.), *Creative Context*, Creative Economy,
https://doi.org/10.1007/978-981-15-3056-2_4

51

environments. The next couple perspectives look at how risk, trust and intimacy take root in the bodies of adolescent girls; and how dance improvisation becomes part of educational schooling of young girls, emphasizing management of creativity as a unique platform for learning social skills in formal education. The fourth offers a brief look at the potential dynamics of improvisation and the linkage between risk and trust as a structure beyond dance discussing its possible scenarios and advantages in other fields of the creative industries.

Theatrical dance is considered a common practice among adolescent girls in Western society (Stinson 1997; Thomas 1993). In Israel today (population approximately 9 million), there are more than 100 dance programs both is middle schools and high schools. About 1500 students, most of them girls, are active in them. All programs are designated for matriculation exams and follow a national curriculum including Ballet, Contemporary Dance, Improvisation, and Choreography classes, as well as theoretical courses. Most of the dance programs in Israel were initiated during the 80s and 90s. Many of them are in "regular high schools".[2] In my research, I was interested in the "regular" girl, the one that did not necessarily have clear ambitions to become a professional dancer and yet, decided to engage herself in a demanding, time consuming, and physically and mentally difficult dance program in her busy 3 years of high school.

4.1 Body, Improvisation, Risk and Trust—Theoretical Aspects

In recent years, bodies have been seen as far more involved in world forming and world making. The concept of "group" (Latimer 2008) and the idea of bodies that create the-world or a-world through everyday interaction has been suggested in limited terms already by Bourdieu (1984, 1990) through the notion of Habitus and by Goffman (1959) who looked at face and its social work and by others. From another (and later) angle, Deleuze and Guattari (1988) suggest the perception of a possible embodied social order through the concept of "assemblage". The assemblage body is situated within a multitude of other bodies it relates to and its action depends on them. Such a notion of a connected "body of bodies" argues for a body that its actions and reactions produce constant flow and a permanent state of becoming. For Deleuze and Guattari, the body exists only through external connections and affects: "We know nothing about a body, until we know what it can do, in other words, what its affects are, how they can or cannot get into composition with other affects, with the affects of another body" (Deleuze and Guattari 1988: 257). Yet, bodies come to play in different ways, and variations in body formations create significant differences in both the degree and kind of involvement to which bodies react and work with, hence producing various qualities of social embodied experiences and textures.

---

[2]To differentiate them from high schools for the arts, in which the orientation of teaching and training is semiprofessional, aiming at a career in dance.

The notions of assemblage, flow and becoming can be easily related to the practice of improvisation and the creative process. Improvisation exists in variety of Western and non-Western performing arts such as jazz music, theater and dance. The literature describes it as a playful activity, which is embedded in an existential experience in the "here and now" and is based on the ability to spontaneously respond without preplanning from one moment to the next (Nachmanovich 1990). Others explain improvisation as a real time process, grounded in a collaborative action (Duby 2017; Sawyer 2000).

In relation to dance, improvisation is described conjointly as a fusion of creation and execution of movement. Dancers simultaneously originate and perform movement without preplanning, responding to various stimuli (Blom and Chaplin 1988, 1992; Zaporah 1995; Foster 2003).

Synthia Novack (1990), one of the founders of the American Contact Improvisation Movement shows how improvisation, which entails touch, physical sensations and transformation of body weight to another body, requires a constant reorientation in changing environments. She describes improvisation as an active situation, in which two moving bodies are searching compatibility and result in an ongoing production of innovation:

> […] contact improvisers use momentum to move in concert with a partner's weight, rolling, suspending, lurching together. They often yield rather than resist, using their arms to assist and support but seldom to manipulate. Interest lies in the ongoing flow of energy rather than on producing still pictures as in ballet; consequently, […] dancers improvise their movements, inventing or choosing it in the moment of performance (ibid., p. 8).

Philosopher Sheets-Johnstone (1999) explains that the emerging relationship between thinking, acting, time and space in movement improvisation produce social and reflexive interaction. According to her, and in contrast to traditional Cartesian Western logic, the activity of improvisation unites body and mind, action and thought. The body in improvisation she adds, is not a symbol of meaning nor is it mediated by language, but it is a non-representational embodied moving entity which creates its' own dynamics and constructs its own social relations. Hence, improvisational movements do not necessarily reflect ideas or thoughts, nor do they represent the feelings of the dancers, but they are a physical presence, which organize its relational world.

Lack of preplanning or being in the "unknown" in improvisation creates by definition a situation of risk and uncertainty. The scholarly literature suggests (Li 2012) that trust between people tends to arise in conditions of uncertainty, complexity and ambiguity, when vulnerability is high, when the stakes of unmet expectations are high as well and when a long term inter-dependence and reciprocal relationship exist. And indeed, one of the definitions of trust is presented as "a behavioral decision to accept (and even appreciate) vulnerability (i.e. trust-as-choice)" (Li ibid.: 101).

In that respect the literature on social organization argues for example, that chances for greater trust between workers grow in relationships that are based on reciprocity in conditions of uncertainty. Scholars Molm et al. (2000), and Yamagishi et al. (1998) thus argue that trust is one aspect of a broader connection of feelings towards a partner, which include affective commitment, and that reciprocal exchange will achieve higher levels of trust, attachment and commitment.

Similarly, Seligman (1998) differentiates between confidence and trust, with confidence that is based on knowledge, control of known systems of regulations, sanctions and formal conditions. He claims that an alternative interpretation of the word confidence is the word secret, and indeed, in confidence embedded an essence of clear structures and established social consents. On the other hand, trust will arise when there is lack of preconceived affirmations and only on circumstances of uncertainty of outcomes:

> Trust is needed when there is no basis for confidence, for example, when behavior cannot be predicted or when strangers are part of the interaction. Trust is necessary when the other is unknowable, when behavior cannot be imputed or predicted [...] (ibid.: 393).

And Giddens (1991) in his book Modernity and Self-Identity argues that intimate trustful relationships are possible when there is an exchange of self and reciprocal and vulnerable reflexivity.

In reference to dance, Israeli anthropologist Cohavi (2007) talks about the linkage between trust and risk in her research on one dance company in Israel. Cohavi discusses the physical and existential risk that the dancers are required to face when dancing choreographer Rami Be'er's works. Be'er is known for architecturally transforming the stage by means of tilted props creating a physical experience of structured unbalance for the dancers. Hence, Cohavi argues that dancing in these circumstances demands a collective responsibility from the dancers. Moreover, she claims that the practice of dance is characterized with a systematic tension between "stretching the body to its limits and self-preservation and safety" (ibid.: 222) that forces the dancers to totally rely on each other. Cohavi's analysis adds to the tight connection between physical operations and the production of trust and risk relationships. I argue in this context, that dance improvisation, which indeed challenges body limits and the sense of safety, intensifies the bond between uncertainty, risk and trust, and maximizes the potential of trust formation as a social construct within creative environments.

4.2 Learning to Trust—Improvising Dancing Bodies

Choreography teachers said in interviews that teaching dance improvisation is based on deliberately ambiguous instructions. The goal, they say, is to give some information but in such a way that will allow on the part of the students space for creative and innovative interpretation and revelation of new ideas and movement materials.

> Instructions are ambiguous in class, said Michal. "it's not that they are not clear, but you do want to create some mystery... in the beginning, the girls would get nervous about it, edgy [...] but when we succeed embracing this mystery in live improvisation, they suddenly were so excited! [...] they watched each other in the group from inside and out, and suddenly things happened, situations were created. They could really transform to that place where trust relationships were starting to form. Until then, they did not want to work. It was hard".

From Michal's words, we learn that the young improvising dancers experience constant tensions between the known and the unknown, concern and trust. However, there is a demand to be at risk and exercise it but yet in a supportive environment. The beginning is fearful and resistant but when students do succeed to get into the flow of improvisation, they are excited. Risk and the sense of discovery are linked and 'diving' into the unknown turns out to be an enjoyable creative activity that carries a profit of something new.

Sharon, another teacher uses improvisation in every choreography class. She says about trust:

> It is built-in into the process of the class. It is obvious. Without creating a supportive environment, intimate... choreography process creates this by nature. Without it, we would not have the openness that the creative process demands. It is a place where one may allow herself to be confused hoping to find new things. It is always the group element, the togetherness, and the continuing collective development. There are witnesses to how you and others act and grow.

According to Sharon, trust is an essential "natural" element in the practice of improvisation and the creative process, so much so that it becomes an integral part of the life of the group. The risk-trust mechanism not only produces new discoveries but also constructs relationships of reciprocity and a texture of intimate and ethical social environment of interdependency and commitment.

The next observation from my field nots, taken in choreography class for 10th graders deepens our understanding of the activity of dance improvisation and demonstrates how trust and risk work:

> The girls are asked to find a partner. Some of them are sitting close to each other on the floor; others are standing in pairs. Some parts of their bodies (hand, leg, back) touch each other. There is no other explicit instruction as to how to sit or stand; nor to how to move or where to. It is quiet. No music. The next instruction is to shift their body parts to each other. "Let go," says the teacher. The girls touch each other gently; sometimes they shake their partners' hand, head, or shoulders. Next, they are asked to transfer their full body weight on to each other while in motion. Again, it is not explained how to do it. The girls are leaning on each other, moving at the same time from one position to the next. A couple is moving down to the floor; rolling on and against each other, they pose fully stretched stomach to stomach breathing; from there they are rolling somehow to sitting position sited back to back, resting both their heads backwards on each other's shoulder, eyes closed. Then they separate to individual movement and find a new partner.

During this improvisation, the girls are free to choose their place in the room and to find their partner. In order to perform what they are asked to do, they need to stand physically very close one to each other. The instructions such as "give your body parts", "transfer your body weight to the other body", or "surrender to gravity", are open and obscure a bit as Michal explained earlier. They contain no specific explanations as for which parts of the body to use, for how long or in what way. This approach allows the movement to be revealed, as the partners are moving together. Unlike traditional dance technique class, where exercises are structured and demonstrated in extreme accuracy, in improvisation the path of the movement is unknown and the accuracy is shifted to the attention that is being given to the process. The couple who work together learn to commit their bodies to each other while searching the next step or phase of their joint movement. Where will they be in the next moment? None of them knows. Sometimes they do not even see each other and still they are asked to fully physically support each other in this unexpected continuous reciprocal motion. Trust can be constructed in this situation only upon the consent of both participants to engage in a collaborative relationship in conditions of an extreme vulnerability. This demands a mutual undiscussed contract to take responsibility each one on herself and on the other. The physical embodied relationships that come out of such a joint act are foundational for trust building as it involves surrendering control to someone else. Since this action is happening also in synchronization, both dancers let go and receive their bodies' weight at the same time, creating a mutual power in motion. It is the actual physical act that allows them to put faith in each other's body, producing in fact a third entity. One that creates dynamics of exchange and constructs its own social relations. This demonstrates Deleuze and Guattari's (1988) concept of "assemblage" of bodies and Sheets-Johnstone's (1999) idea of a non-representational body that produces a joint social environment.

Another observation from choreography class with 11th graders illuminate other aspects of trust:

> The girls are in the studio working in couples on devising their own duets. They practice momentum in movement, catching and jumping. At this early stage, they are still improvising, seeking new materials. Some of them are showing the other what they have found or how to do such and such movement. It is noisy in the room and the teacher works with them in turns, listening, looking and suggesting ideas. I focus on one couple, Noa, quite a small petit size girl who is working today with Liat who is just the opposite – large and massive. Noa situates herself as far as possible from Liat. Then she is running towards her, very fast. She is jumping into Liat's arms while turning herself tilting to the side in the air bringing her belly to meet Liat's, her legs rapping her around her lower back. Liat is struggling to hold Noa's body weight and jumping momentum. Her legs and arms are shaking from the effort. I find myself breathing deeply. This was a scary leap. Liat is still shaking and turning around struggling to hold on. Eventually Noa is sliding to the floor laying down laughing, "let's try again" she says. They do it again and again, trying to figure out the best way their bodies can work together.

Noa throws herself on Liat's body. They both know how this begins but they never know how it ends, where and in what condition they will find themselves in. During this repetitive procedure, they train not only on their movement and body skills but also on their ability to unconditionally trust and support each other in a risky physical situation. In addition, one has to remember that even and once they figure out through these endless tryouts the "right way" to perform this jump, in real time performance they will still might be faced with an unknown situation.

According to philosopher Merleau-Ponty (1945), the body investigates, learns and knows itself and reality via its actions in the world. It practices cultural schemes through repetitions but not in a mechanical or automatic manner but in a way, that produces motorized meaning (Crossley 1995). Training in dance improvisation may be suggested as a practice that produces such social meaning in developing relationships of trust, responsibility and intimacy in conditions of uncertainty and instability. Furthermore says Merleau-Ponty, living in our bodies, means sharing embodied space with others and exercising notions of inter-corporeality. These notions are commonly produced into a joint space in which feelings, sensations, thoughts and intentions work together kinesthetically. Therefore, it is the physical body, which organizes in its action the social environment and its ethical order. Thus, the ability of the young dancers to deposit trust in their own bodies and in other bodies strives from their accumulative embodied and sensual knowledge.

The issue of trust comes up often when the girls talk about their experience in improvisation. For example, Na'ama (11th grade) said: "I think it developed in me abilities to listen to others and somehow to compromise with them. Because in Composition classes it's about giving space to others". Dana (from the same class) said that working on dance improvisation and the creative process in a supportive environment opens possibilities to deeply get to know each other through the body: "it's like there is a true legitimacy to get to know the people I work with. To create a dance with them, to see them express themselves in a supportive space without competition"; and Keren (11th grade) talks about the role of the body: "it creates a different kind of openness. Because it is in a group… because the whole thing with the dance is the body. Your body is a personal thing. If you are working with it close to others, it creates closeness. There is something right in it. And true. It is something, yes, more free". Galit, one of the teachers supports these notions and says: "Look, there is something physical that is very strong in dance improvisation classes. Defiantly. Something emotional that reconnects people".

Social qualities of attentiveness, reconnection, embracing vulnerability, openness, and closeness are produced in dance improvisation classes. They are all profits that arise from learning to trust in risk situations and are at the foundational construct of an evolving embodied sociability. Moreover, trust that is created between the young dancers is transformed to a powerful social value that configures the relationship within the group beyond the improvisational moments. In this sense trust designs a framework of values and ideological discourse that may address other social group issues such as competitiveness as we will see next.

Ambitiousness and competition exist at high school dance programs as they are immanent to the professional dance world and. The young dancers face a robust demand to challenge themselves and improve their performance from one class to the next, from one day to another. Although the teachers voice such high standard of achievement and push the girls to do more and better, they put a lot of effort in an intentional regulation and moderation of competition and potential jealousy. Yet, unlike the professional world, where competition is a legitimate individual goal, in the dance programs competition is presented as an educational situation and discussed profoundly in terms of values of collectivity and solidarity. This is possible, I claim, due to the relationships of embodied trust formed between the girls in improvisation classes and during working on the creative process. Embodied trust consequently works as a structural construct that mediates implicit and explicit competition and forms a socially protected space in which the girls feel comfortable in various risk situations of vulnerability, weakness and exposure. Trust, therefore, works as a powerful social element transforming and preserving the ethical structure of the group. For example, when Galit (teacher) says: "It is extremely important to me that the girls will develop constructive positive relationships" she seeks to affirm the values of collectivity, solidarity and interdependency that are already embodied and familiar to the group as a social system. Hence, this specific ideological and ethical discourse becomes a common one and is accepted among the girls who are well experienced and trained physically in practicing and producing relations of trust in their bodies.

The practice of trust seems to function as a collective moral merit within the dance groups. The teachers use it to soften and moderate signs of individual ambitiousness and to create an ethos of group collectivity. By maximizing the potential embodied trust built in improvisation classes, they produce an ideological discourse that creates a social structure where the dancing body serves both as a private and a collective territory on which this valuable element grows.

The improvising dancing body trains and practices risk and trust situations that support powerful actions of potential innovation production and creativity. Alongside the artistic and aesthetic discoveries of movement materials, the body recreates intimate and moral relationships that assist building a safe environment.

I will add shortly, that from a gender point of view this separate feminine group of girls students and their women teachers within the high school, conduct a creative independent social group that maintains a subversive alternative option to the standard schooling and to the traditional Cartesian Western logic. By practicing management of risk and trust in their bodies, they unit body and mind, action and thought and represent an ethical collective embodied educational model that promotes both skills of artistic improvisation and creativity as well fresh social skills of creative collaboration. They in fact succeed to *unlearn*, as Bell Hooks suggests (1984) traditional paradigms of schooling and learning formations and replace them with an innovative educational approach.

4.3   In Lieu of a Conclusion: Improvisation, Risk and Trust in the Creative Industries

In the last few decades innovation, creativity and the ability to collectively improvise becomes more and more popular in literature on the creative industries, the work place and education. Governments foster innovative collaborations and creativity is named within the school curriculum (Prus et al. 2017; Craft 2003). The creative skills, they say, are important for surviving the economy and society of the twenty-first Century.

In this last section, I briefly explore the potential role and dynamics of improvisation and the linkage between risk and trust in relation to the discourse and practices in the creative industries. I suggest the possible advantages of scholarly research in this direction and argue that it is possible and even needed to draw upon the concept of risk and trust as a social construct as it is analyzed in processes of dance improvisation and to implement it into relevant and various situations of improvisation in the creative industries. These may be either looking at a macro level at how organizations work, define and redefine themselves and collaborate; or at a micro level, exploring the interactive mechanisms of the creative process and innovation production between people.

For example, a study that was done in Manchester's Institute for Popular Culture in Banks et al. (2000), presents the ways by which risk and trust are relevant to the management of the cultural industries of local fashion, music and design. The authors suggest that both risk management and trust negotiations are characteristic to the unique working practices in these fields, which are similar, I find, to the conditions of improvisation. All of them, they argue, work through a changing dynamics of (dis) and (re) organization of their entities as creative industries which means they operate in permanent conditions of uncertainty and instability. In addition, claim the writers, cultural industries articulate their operations in subjective, intimate and informal contexts producing micro level creative and social processes of innovation initiatives and collaborations. These are formed, I would suggest based on the sense of closeness and solidarity that is produced as a direct result from improvising and the need to collaboratively reorganize themselves in vulnerable situations.

A different approach comes from Montuori (2003) who claims that the concept of improvisation becomes increasingly popular in the creative industries. He discusses innovation as an emergent property of the relationship between order and disorder and suggests that the study of improvisation should include exploration of inter-subjectivity, emotions, performance and social creativity; all may be looked at through the relationship that are developed between people improvising in risk and trust situations, as I have shown. Furthermore, Montuori turns to the arts and argues that in order to understand the lived phenomenon of improvisation and the ways it challenges traditional ways of thinking, it is imperative to draw from artistic, performative and subjective experience. In other words, he might be suggesting that looking at improvisation such as in dance may educate the cultural industries with new skills and social and understandings of how to manage creative processes and the dynamics of risk and trust.

Last example comes from Edwin Cutmull who is currently the President of Pixar Animation Studios and Walt Disney Animated Studios in the U.S. In a piece, he published in the Harvard Business Review (2008) titled "How Pixar Fosters Collective Creativity" he connects risk and trust situations to micro level and interactive elements. Responsibility, a sense of community building, solidarity, collectivity, collaboration, intimacy and informality, he says, all which appear as social principles in dance improvisation as we have seen, are the goal of a good management and leadership of the creative process:

> Management's job is not to prevent risk but to build the capability to recover when failures occur. ..... What's equally tough, of course, is getting talented people to work effectively with one another. That takes trust and respect, which we, as managers can't mandate; they must be earned over time. What we can do is construct an environment that nurtures trusting and respectful relationships and unleashes everyone's creativity. If we get that right, the result is a vibrant community where talented people are loyal to one another and their collective work, everyone feels that they are part of something extraordinary, and their passion and accomplishments make the community a magnet for talented people coming out of schools or working at other places.

In view of these examples and the discourse they present, I offer my suggestions for further research and investigation, referring to the structured linkage between risk, trust and improvisation and its connection to production of creativity and innovation. The first would be the issue of looking into symmetrical/equal informal social power relations as a system that encourages improvisation, taking risks and the production of creativity. The second suggest looking at micro level interactions in specific collaborative situations, in order to understand strategies and mechanisms of risk and trust building. The third is practical in nature and follows Montuori's idea, calling for implementing artistic improvisational processes in non-artistic environments such as businesses, start-ups, education or other initiatives, to create an experiential training environment of the conduct of risk-trust management towards innovation. As it is now quite clear that people will dare to play only with the ones they trust.

References

Blom, L. A., & Chaplin, L. T. (1988). *The moment of movement: Dance improvisation*. Pittsburgh: University of Pittsburg Press.

Blom, L. A., & Chaplin, L. T. (1992). *The intimate act of choreography*. Pittsburgh: University of Pittsburg Press.

Bourdieu, P. (1984). *Distinction: A social critique of the judgment of taste*. Cambridge, MA: Harvard University Press.

Bourdieu, P. (1990). *The logic of practice*. Palo Alto, CA: Stanford University Press.

Cohavi, T. (2007). Between dance and anthropology [in Hebrew]. Dissertation submitted for the degree of "Doctor in Philosophy", Hebrew University of Jerusalem.

Craft, A. (2003). The limits of creativity in education: Dilemmas for the educator. *British Journal of Educational Studies, 55*(2), 113–127.

Crossley, N. (1995). Merleau-Ponty, the elusive body and carnal sociology. *Body & Society, 1,* 43–63.

Cutmull, E. (2008). How Pixar fosters collective creativity. *Harvard Business Review, 86*(9), 64–72.

Deleuze, G., & Guattari, F. (1988). *A thousand plateaus: Capitalism and Schizophrenia*. London: The Athlone Press.

Duby, M. (2017). Improvisation unfolding: Process, pattern and prediction. *World Futures, The Journal of New Paradigm Research, 74*(3), 187–198.

Foster, S. (2003). Improvisation in dance and mind. In A. Albright & D. Gere (Eds.), *Taken by surprise: A dance improvisation reader* (pp. 3–14). Middletown, CT: Wesleyan University Press.

Giddens, A. (1991). *Modernity and self-identity: Self and society in the late modern age*. Stanford, CA: Stanford University Press.

Goffman, E. (1959). *The presentation of self in everyday life*. University of Edinburgh.

Hooks, B. (1984). *Feminist theory: From margin to center*. Cambridge: South End Press.

Latimer, J. (2008). Introduction: Body, knowledge, worlds. *The Sociological Review, 56*(2), 1–22.

Li, P. (2012). Exploring the unique roles of trust and play in private Creativity: From the complexity-ambiguity-metaphor Link to the trust-play-creativity Link. *Journal of Trust Research, 2*(1), 71–97.

Lovatt, A., O'connor, J., & Raffo, C. (2000). Risk and trust in the creative industries. *Geoforum, 31*(4), 453–464.

Merleau-Ponty, M. (1945). *Phenomenology of perception*. London & New York.

Molm, L., Takahashi, N., & Peterson, G. (2000). Risk and trust in social exchange: An experimental test of a classical proposition. *American Journal of Sociology, 205*(5), 1396–1427.

Montuori, A. (2003). The complexity of improvisation and the improvisation of complexity: Social science, art and creativity. *Human Relations, 56*(2), 237–255.

Nachmanovich, S. (1990). *Free play: Improvisation in life and art*. New York: Penguin Putnam Inc.

Novack, C. (1990). *Sharing the dance: Contact improvisation and American culture*. Madison: University of Wisconsin Press North Atlantic Books.

Prus, I., Nacamulli, R., & Lazzazara, A. (2017). Disentangling work place innovation: A systematic literature review. *Personnel Review, 46*(7), 1254–1279.

Sawyer, R. K. (2000). Improvisational cultures: Collaborative emergence and creativity in improvisation. *Mind, Culture, and Activity, 7*(3), 180–185.

Seligman, A. (1998). Trust and sociability: Oh the limits of confidence and role expectations. *American Journal of Economics and Sociology, 57*(4), 391–404.

Sheets-Johnstone, M. (1999). *The primacy of movement*. Amsterdam and Philadelphia: John Benjamins.

Stinson, S. W. (1997). A question of fun: Adolescent engagement in dance education. *Dance Research Journal, 29*(2), 49–69.

Thomas, H. (1993). *Dance, gender and culture*. London: Palgrave, Macmillan.

Yamagishi, T., Cook, K., & Watabe, M. (1998). Uncertainty, trust, and commitment formation in the United States and Japan. *American Journal of Sociology, 104*(1), 165–194.

Zaporah, R. (1995). *Action theater: The improvisation of presence*. Berkeley, CA: Basic Books.

Yael (yali) Nativ is a dance scholar with sociological and anthropological orientations. She is a Senior Lecturer at The Academic College for Society and Arts, and a lecturer at Levinsky College for Education in Israel. In addition she teaches at Masson Gross School of the Arts Online at Rutgers, State University of New Jersey. In her writing and research, she explores social and cultural issues looking at the linkage between dance, body, culture, education, gender and creativity. Her book Fractured Freedom: Body, Gender and Ideology, which she co-wrote with Dr. Hodel Ophir, was published in 2016 (in Hebrew). Currently she is engaged in an ethnographic research, looking at the experience of the body among professional ageing dancers who still perform on stage.

Part III
Processes of Creativity

Chapter 5
Creative Masses: Amateur Participation and Corporate Success in Japan's Media Industries

Nissim Otmazgin

Massive commodification and marketing of media culture is not, of course, unique to Japan. Many countries have commodified and industrialized culture to some degree, whether for purposes of entertainment or propaganda (Mulcahy 2006), to boost the economy (Holroyd and Coates 2015), brand their achievements (Schwak 2016), or attain "soft power" (Otmazgin 2013). Japan, though, is an extreme case in which various forms of media productions have evolved and a wide variety of entertainment and fandom are highly commercialized. As Richie (2003, 10–31), one of the most prolific writers on Japanese society and culture, once noted, Japan is an "image factory," with an impressive capacity for inventing and commercializing cultural innovations and fashion trends, both native and imported. Other media scholars (e.g. Condry 2013; Lamarre 2019; Ueno 2002) have emphasized Japan's media industries' close synergy between different media fields, especially anime, manga, and video games, which blend into a powerful synthesis of text, image and sound—a process known as "media-mix" (Steinberg 2012)

Indeed, over the postwar years, the Japanese media industries have developed their own sophisticated and highly efficient way of translating artistic innovations into accessible consumer products and marketing them to designated audiences at home. Essentially, this way is an industry-driven process that entails extracting and indigenizing creativity, images, fashion trends, material pleasures, and fads, and then producing, standardizing, and marketing a related line of products. Although artistic innovations are at the heart of these creations, they are commercially worthless unless they are packaged in a way that marries cultural ideas with consumerist logic.

This chapter looks closely at the link between creativity and cultural production by focusing on certain types of commodification mechanisms, which are beneficial to the debate over the notion of creativity and its social and cultural underpinning (Caves 2000; Hartley 2005). Specifically, this chapter analyzes amateur-professional

N. Otmazgin (✉)
The Hebrew University of Jerusalem, Jerusalem, Israel
e-mail: nissim.otmazgin@mail.huji.ac.il

© Springer Nature Singapore Pte Ltd. 2020
N. Otmazgin and E. Ben-Ari (eds.), *Creative Context*, Creative Economy,
https://doi.org/10.1007/978-981-15-3056-2_5

collaborations in Japan's manga, anime, and television industries to describe a synergetic cultural production mechanism that is based not only on individual creativity per se but on the interactive relationship between the industry and the fans. Referring to the post-Fordist literature on new modes of collaboration in the organization of work (Tomaney 1994), this study suggests that "creativity" in the cultural and media industries is not only based on adjusting production to immediate market needs and, thus, shortening the distance between producers and consumers, but also on the intimate incorporation of consumers into the production process. This partnership between professionals and amateurs constitutes an effective mechanism for diversifying, commodifying, and commercializing various forms of art and culture. The result is the delineation of boundaries between the producer and the consumer, and in practice a hybridized system of production that is much more attuned to creativity and voices coming up from below.

Focusing on manga, anime, TV and idol-related industries in Japan, this chapter emphasizes the notion that creativity is being facilitated not within the studio but through close reciprocal relations between the industry and its audience. The creative stage is often taken by amateurs, but the development of creativity into commercial products and its translation into commodities is undertaken by an agent or mediator assigned by the established industry. Thus, the media industries need to have constant interaction with the relevant communities of amateurs. These relationships, between the established industry on the one side, and the audience on the other, many of whom are creative amateurs, are characterized by continuous social and cultural engagement and constant redefinition of the partnership they constitute. For the media industries, these relations are vital to the thrust of their work, that is, utilizing and valorizing individual creativity and turning it into a commercialized set of products as part of the corporate success. For the audience, the relationship with the industry presents an opportunity to take part in the creative process and have a say in the final design of the product. For successful amateurs, these relationships provide some chance to exhibit their talents and even become a professional. Put simply, these are circular relationships: (1) fans consume cultural products and make their voice heard; (2) some become amateur artists and conceive new products and ideas; (3) through close communication with the industry new commercialized products are created and popularized; (4) successful amateurs become professionals.

The type of cultural production this chapter describes is very different from the so-called Hollywood model of cultural production, which is typically carried out by small teams of professional creators, including experienced creative personnel and managers, technical experts, and producers, sometimes assisted by large-scale subcontracting (Aksoy and Robins 1992; Elsbach and Kramer 2003). To be sure, the Hollywood model has changed over the years, gradually loosening the tight control the industry used to exert over the production of popular culture before the 1970s. Although Hollywood productions are now carried out by multiple professionals led by project teams (Ryan 1992, 124–134; Storper 1994, 200–216), and American animators have been deeply influenced by the "anime boom" of the 1990s and 2000s (Daliot-Bul and Otmazgin 2017), American productions are still much more centralized and more professionally-driven than their Japanese counterparts.

Moreover, the sort of creative ecosystem that this chapter describes is not simply a case of collaboration. In the media industries, collaboration is generally defined as any activity that entails working jointly with others in the making and marketing of musical and visual cultural commodities such as television dramas, music, animation, and movies and their derivative products (such as video games, food, culinary utensils, magazines, toys, accessories, or stationery) and spin-offs such as DVDs or video-on-demand (Otmazgin and Ben-Ari 2013: 1–2). Here, however, the chapter describes a new hybrid type of partnership between professionals and non-professionals. The unforeseen potential (or affordances) of this union are much greater. While any sort of collaboration naturally involves risk, here the experimental aspect is much greater and the results are much less foreseen. Second, the mode of communication within this system of production is less systematic and less target-driven than in media collaborations involving groups of professionals. This is because the expectations and the contract created between members of the organization—professionals and non-professionals—are implicit and negotiated. As this chapter later shows, this flexibility is a pivot for the utilization of the amateurs' creative labor.

In what follows, this chapter discusses the structure of Japan's manga and anime industries, emphasizing their overall decentralized and heterogeneous nature, which allows the sort of professional-amateur intimacy that exists in Japan. The chapter then examines closely four features which demonstrate the aforementioned flexibility of cultural production: the *dōjinshi* community, the *otaku* market, music-television shows, and the newly created virtual idols. Some of these cases have been the object of vast academic investigation, especially in the fields of cultural anthropology and cultural studies (Allison 2006; Azuma 2009; Brienza 2016; LaMarre 2009; Otmazgin 2013: 53–64; Pellitteri 2012). Here, however, the focus is on their relationships with Japan's established media industry, in a way that is relevant to the discussion on the process of cultural creativity. In the conclusion, the chapter draws a few theoretical insights emanating from Japan's audience-driven production system.

5.1 Japan's Decentralized Media Marketplace

One of the noticeable characteristics of Japan's media industries, especiallythe anime and manga industries, is that they are structurally decentralized. Although there are a few mammoth enterprises, the creative process involves a large number of comparative players including thousands of small companies, venture start-ups, and consulting firms. There are five key TV stations in addition to 127 terrestrial TV stations and 547 cable TV companies, almost all involved in television production to one degree or another. There are approximately forty record companies, of which the eight largest account for the majority of sales. In the early 2000s, there were seventy-three music production companies, eighty-five major recording studios, and approximately 2400 other registered companies engaged in various stages of commodifying and commercializing music—in addition to the thousands of so-called "indie" (independent) companies involved in alternative, small-scale productions of music and visual images. In addition, there are about ten major publishers and three main movie companies, while the video game industry is made up of 146 mainly small companies that together employ a creative population of some 18,500 (JETRO 2006; Dentsū Communication Institute 2009; Media Innovation Lab 2017).

The anime industry, with 2.2 trillion yen in sales in 2016, comprises approximately 620 production and post-production companies that employ about 5000 animators. The manga industry, with almost 450 billion yen in sales in the same year, employs about 6000 professional cartoonists and 26,000 assistants, working with 1670 publishers (Association of Japanese Animations 2016, 2017; APJEA 2017). While major anime production houses handle everything related to the production of anime series and movies, from planning to production, the process is decentralized and much of the work of the production houses centers on coordination. The anime production houses subcontract much of the work to smaller studios in both Japan and abroad, especially in Asia, which specialize in drawing, background art, and shooting, collaborate with voice and music studios, and outsource much of the in-between stage—tracing errors and finalizing the images (Morisawa 2013: 258).

Tokyo is the nucleus of Japan's cultural industries. It is where many of the products are initially conceived, produced, and marketed. Tokyo's "pop culture triangle" includes the Akihabara, Shibuya, and Harajuku districts, where artists and agents interact to explore new production possibilities. Shibuya, Shimokitazawa, and Kichijoji are the most prolific locales for the making of contemporary Japanese pop music. In anime, approximately 90% of Japan's animation companies operate inside the city of Tokyo (542 of the 622 studios), together with all the major newspapers and publishers, and all the major TV stations (Association of Japanese Animations 2016).

Another decentralizing feature in Japan's media marketplace, especially in anime, is the funding of productions. This sort of cooperative financing is relevant to our discussion since it demonstrates the heterogeneity of the actors involved and the decentralized nature of their operations. Until Netflix recently started financing anime, about 80% of Japan's anime productions were produced with funding provided by "production committees" (*anime seisaku iinkai*). This system first emerged in the 1980s but came to prominence in the late 1990s and early 2000s (Steinberg 2012: 172). Television networks or advertising agencies organize a group of possible sponsors—record companies, toy makers, publishers, etc.—who agree to participate in sponsoring a certain anime production. In return for their investment, once the production is finished, the members of the production committee share the copyrights of the final product and earn from television advertising, overseas sales, and derivative products such as game software (Daliot-Bul and Otmazgin 2017: 62–64).

These sponsors may include, for example, publishers such as Shueisha and Shogakukan, DVD makers such as Bandai Visual and King Record, makers of game software such as Sony Computer Entertainment, Sega, and Konami, makers of toys such as Takara-Tomi and Bandai, record companies such as Victor Entertainment and Sony Music Entertainment Japan, television channels such as Fuji Television and NHK, and advertising agencies such as ADK and Dentsu. There is no guarantee that the anime production will be successful, but the production committees' participatory funding system allows the members to share the risk in case a certain production fails. The downside is that production committees prefer risk-averse plans, which result in a proliferation of sequels, prequels, spin-offs, and franchise reboots.[1]

While the existing literature emphasizes the heterogeneity of Japan's media marketplace, very little is known about the relationship between the companies that make up Japan's media industry and the fans who purchase the products made by the industry. It is known that fans create demands for products and that the practice of fandom serves as a form of marketing (Kelts 2007; Leonard 2004; Shiraishi 2013), but less is known about how exactly fans impact the creative process. It is assumed that the media industry targets fans' interest and it is a known fact that many of Japan's manga and anime established artists started as amateurs before working their way up. But very little is known about the sort of communication and negotiation taking place before the final product is available for sale. In other words, there is a lacuna in understanding and conceptualizing the sort of relationships between companies and their representatives and amateur-fans in Japan's media marketplace.

5.2 *Dōjinshi*'s Creative Input

The manga industry provides a good example of how corporate production efforts coincide with fans' consumption practices. Japan's manga industry is an enormous business with nearly 450 billion yen in sales (for 2016). In 2015, about 400 million manga books were sold in Japan, in addition to 350 million manga magazines. In 2016, the online manga sales increased by 27% compared to the year before, totaling 150 billion yen (APJEA 2017; Media Innovation Lab 2017: 20). While the manga industry employs about 6000 professional cartoonists and 26,000 assistants, amateur manga artists and fans of their self-published works, known as *dōjinshi*, have become an integral part of the industry.

Dōjinshi started to appear in Japan in the mid-1970s, when manga fans and amateur manga artists gathered to trade and share the latter's work. Nowadays, *dōjinshi* events draw tens of thousands of amateur artists selling their homemade comic books and animation. Special manga markets held in Tokyo each August and December draw half a million visitors, and in 2016, *dōjinshi*-made manga sales totaled 795 million yen (Yano Research Institute 2017, 2). *Dōjinshi* borrows liberally from existing works. Many times, the characters are indistinguishable from the originals on which they are based, although the stories usually include a lot more parody, sexual escapades, and violent scenes. This is enabled thanks to the loose copyright enforcement on the part of the industry. To be sure, some Japanese media industries are aggressively protective over their copyright (one example is Sanrio, the owner

---

[1]In recent years, however, Netflix has emerged as an important player as it is willing to fund expensive anime productions. This potentially reduces the need to rely on production committees for funding. Netflix's long-term influence on anime production is yet to be seen.

of the Hello Kitty copyrights). In fact, Japanese copyright protection law is just as restrictive as American copyright protection. But there is an unspoken understanding between the established manga industry and the *dōjinshi* community that allows fans and amateur creators to issue small-scale editions of manga that parody characters and story lines already in the market without being sued for copyright violation. In some manga and anime productions the industry overlooks copyright infringement in exchange for cultivating bottom-up creativity.

Dōjinshi operations can reach quite a large scale. Between 2007 and 2017, there were between 140 and 200 *dōjinshi* events every year, were thousands of *dōjinshi* introduced their work, met with publishers, and sold parts of their work or related merchandize.[2] At the Super Comic City events in Tokyo and Osaka hundreds of thousands of books are sold ever year in cash transactions totaling billions of JPY. Despite the growth in scale, the established industry continues to tolerate these activities in the belief that they serve to maintain fresh interest in buying mainstream manga and cultivate a pool of talented manga artists—some of whom will later be recruited by the established industry (Norris 2009; Pink 2007). Takeda Keiji, one of the organizers of Japan's largest *dōjinshi* gathering, explains:

> *Dōjinshi* create a market base, and that market base is naturally drawn to the original work.... *Dōjinshi* conventions are also where we're finding the next generation of authors. Publishers understand the value of not destroying this arrangement... and *dōjinshi* creators honor their part of this silent pact. They tacitly agree not to go too far—to produce work only in limited editions and to avoid selling so many copies that they risk eating into the market for original works. (quoted in Pink 2007)

One of the biggest problems of manga publishers in Japan is that they need to constantly extract new talents and develop new stories, but they cannot take too big a risk. A series of bad decisions regarding which manga to publish may result in severe financial losses. By scouting and approaching an amateur artist who has to prove himself/herself in the highly competitive *dōjinshi* world, the level of risk is significantly reduced. Put differently, these special relationships between amateurs, fans, and the major manga producers allow established companies to tap into the creative process of gifted amateurs, gauge and develop new products, and recruit new talent—without being heavily involved in commissioning polls, conducting surveys or carrying out other forms of formal market research among focus groups. Talent scouts from large and small manga producers frequent the major *dōjinshi* conventions in order to seek out new talent and ideas, and they sometimes contact the artists they find there with job offers. Among the famous professional manga artists who got their start in the *dōjinshi* arena are Takahashi Rumiko, Fujishima Kōsuke, CLAMP, and Akamatsu Ken (Kinsella 2000, 134; Shimoku 2008, 120–129).

The emergence of Webtoons *dōjinshi* in recent years makes the symbiotic relations between the established industry and creative amateurs even closer (Oh and Koo 2010). Here, the industry set up online platforms to extract and cultivate creativity from ground level, utilizing the participatory power of social media. Comico, run by

---

[2]Based on data obtained from http://ketto.com, a website that specializes in documenting dōjinshi events. Accessed September 20, 2018.

Korea's NHN Corporation, is a good example of such a platform.[3] At Comico, an amateur who registers on the forum can upload his/her manga and anyone can read and give feedback on it. Groups of fans sometimes endorse a certain amateur artist by supporting his/her progress and making constructive comments. If the amateur artist gets enough points, his/her work will be moved to another forum where only selected works are uploaded. If, in this new forum, the amateur artist receives a good reaction, he/she may become an official artist, signed up to a contract, with his/her work being moved to the official Comico site. Similar to other amateur platforms such Shōnen Jump Rookies (https://rookie.shonenjump.com) and Manga Park Rookies (https://manga-park.com/rookie), at Comico the amateur is paid for his/her work only after he/she gets a contract. Prior to this, he/she is just challenged to become the official artist and his/her labor is not compensated in terms of direct payment.

Comico is not so different from other fan communities and forums, such as DeviantArt, pixiv, Instagram or even Facebook, where people upload their work for the sake of sharing their talent and perhaps becoming known. After uploading their work, they are able to see in real time how many reactions they get, what kind of comments are left, and what kind of people view their work. For amateur artists, this kind of feedback may provide motivation to continue, with a chance of being recruited by an official company and turning professional. For the established industry, these sorts of forums enable a gauging of new ideas and approaching creative personnel. The amateurs themselves serve as both creative labor and the supportive/critical voice that helps shape the final product.

The publisher-*dōjinshi* relationship demonstrates that Japan's media industry is not only decentralized in the sense that a large number of players are invested, but also maintains various implicit production contracts with a great number of individual amateurs. In other words, fans of manga are not only consumers, but also actively contribute to the creative process and eventually to the production. In this sense, they constitute an unavoidable pressure group that the industry must take into account and eventually view as an integral part of the production cycle.

5.3 *Otaku*-Driven Production

Another feature that exemplifies the interactive relationship between the established industry and the fans as part of the creative process can be called "the *otaku* system." *Otaku* is a Japanese slang term coined in the 1980s, which refers to people, usually socially inept young men with an obsessive interest in, usually, video games, anime, or manga. Initially, *otaku* was a pejorative term that was synonymous with social misfit, nerd, or maniac. However, the term *otaku* has experienced a transformation of meaning in the past two decades, from initially referring to youngsters obsessed with anime to describing groups of consumer-oriented fans of a variety of popular

---

[3]For Comico participation, see guidelines in http://www.comico.jp/guide/official.nhn. Accessed May 1, 2018. I thank Bonwon Koo for the insightful information about Comico.

culture products and trends. Nowadays, it has become more accepted and can be used in a more or less positive sense (Azuma 2009: 3–18). The term is now generally used to describe youngsters driven by a strong interest in contemporary culture and lifestyle, or to those who choose to facilitate social connections through specific, non-mainstream cultural practices such as cosplay. *Otaku* are also heavy users of information technology.

From an economic point of view, otaku constitutes a community of ardent consumers who spend much of their disposable income on media-related items. Nowadays, young Japanese who live with their parents no longer spend the bulk of their income on basic food, shelter, and clothing, but devote much of it to the acquisition of consumer goods, such as communication and other electronic devices, popular culture products, and fashion. A survey conducted by *Nikkei Shinbun*,[4] Japan's leading daily economic newspaper, estimated that in the early 2000s, teenagers in Japan spent more than 75% of their disposable income on cultural consumption in the form of video games (both hardware and software), anime, music, books, and movies, while people in their twenties spent approximately 40%, and people in their thirties and forties less than 30%.

A report by Nomura Sōgō Kenkyūsho (Nomura Research Institute 2005) has estimated that in 2004 there were approximately 1.31 million Japanese *otaku* who obsessively consumed comics, anime, accessories (such as posters and pictures), fashion, and various game and visual software as well as hardware parts worth 2720 billion yen. This figure does not include consumption by "ordinary people," excluded from the research, which focused solely on *otaku*. A more recent study by Yano Research Institute (2017), found that in 2016 there were approximately 1.42 million Japanese defined as *otaku*, mostly teenagers and people in their twenties, who consume popular-culture related merchandise worth approximately 5.5 billion yen. Their favorite consumer items include manga, animated figures, plastic models, dolls, cosplay, and games. Here, too, the figures refer only to what they recognize as *otaku* consumers and not to other "ordinary" consumers.

Aside from representing a sizable portion of the consumer market, *otaku* members function as a "safety net" when new products are launched and a seismograph for the creative process. *Otaku* are likely to be first in line to purchase new products prior to commercial marketing in the wider market. The *otaku* are considered to be very creative people and old or uncool productions will not have a positive response. The success of a new product, especially short-lived products prevalent in popular culture, depends heavily on the immediate reaction of consumers. Positive input (for example, reports of long lines of people waiting to buy the newest video game console) can stimulate further demand in the wider market.

The existence of *otaku* as a large creative fandom base is closely linked to Japan's social context. Many of these youngsters—either *otaku* or *dōjinshi*—are able to dedicate their energy and time to creating things they like because they live in Japan— a country with solid social networks like medical insurance and plenty of part-time job (*arbaito*) options. Dedicating much of their income to anime and manga will

---

[4]A survey by *Nikkei Shinbun*, January 24, 2005, 25.

not allow them to save much, but at least they can survive and do the things they like. In other words, Japanese who grew up amid the wealth of postwar Japan Inc., such as *otaku*, have been infused with huge amounts of creative energy without the sense of obligation to save and sacrifice for the nation's postwar reconstruction which their parents had (Kelts 2007: 180). Their decision to opt out of Japan's mainstream "salary-man" employment system has provided them with time to engage in artistic and cultural creativity.

The *otaku* market's role in the launch of a new media product is illustrated in Table 5.1. When a new product is launched, it is only after it has won the *otaku*'s approval that the product is introduced to a wider group of consumers. In the third stage, a successful product becomes a commercial goldmine not only in itself, but also in the form of a host of spin-off products. A successful manga character, for example, can amplify the development and sales of other inspired products, such as video games and animated television series. After a certain period, the products experience a natural decline in popularity and are replaced by new ones.

Because they are so preoccupied with media culture, *otaku* possess unique knowledge of the latest cultural trends and innovations and serve to filter or herald the diffusion of new popular culture products and trends to the market. In fact, *otaku* are the biggest experts in the field, often more knowledgeable than the producing companies themselves. They cherish creativity and their input to the established industry serve as a kind of proof against boring productions. Figure 5.1 illustrates the relationship between the established industry (often a venture company), *otaku*, and the wider

Table 5.1 *Otaku* and stages of diffusion of new products into the market

1. The *Otaku* Stage	2. Popularization 1	3. Popularization 2	4. Declining Stage
Initial consumption and assessment of new products entering the market	The consumption of products by a wider circle of consumers	Mass consumption of products, diversification of the products and marketing of related products and accessories	A gradual reduction in the consumption of products and the appearance of new products

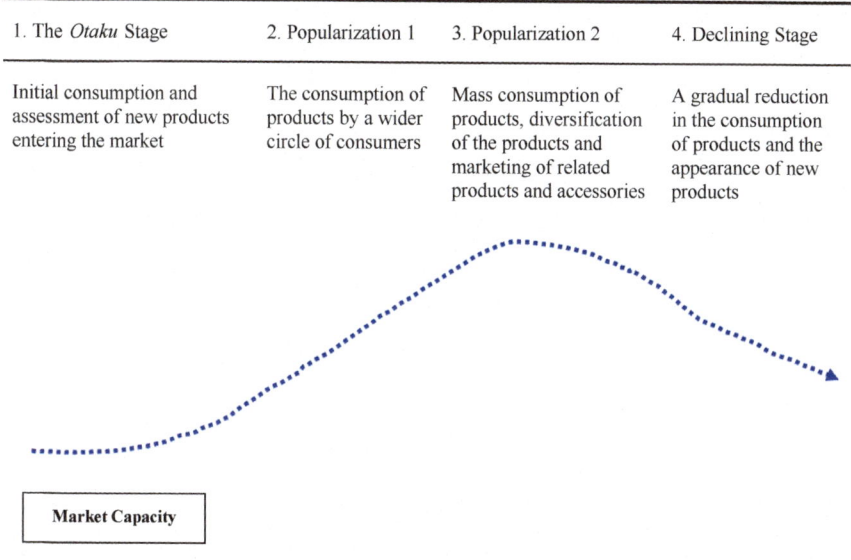

Market Capacity

Source Nomura Sōgō Kenkyūsho (2005: 47). The dotted line indicates the increase/decrease in sales

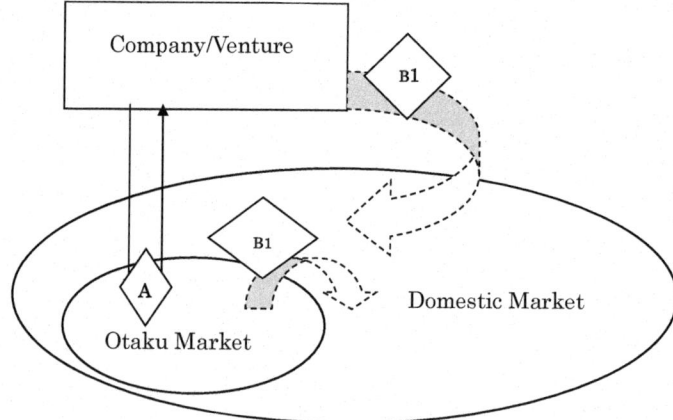

Fig. 5.1 The role of *Otaku* in fostering the diffusion of new products into the market

domestic market. Stage B represents the launch of products directly to the market. In Stage A, the company/venture is in constant communication with the *otaku* market while launching new products to the wider market (Stage B1).

For the purpose of this chapter, the *otaku* market is an illuminating example of professional-amateur creativity for a number of reasons. First, similar to *dōjinshi*, *otaku*-driven production demonstrates how cultural production in Japan involves intensive interaction with the audience to the point that it constitutes a complete cooperative system of creative media production. Second, the *otaku* market suggests that we should replace the distinctions between "industry," "producer," and "consumer" in favor of a more hybrid notion of cultural coproduction. Third, the *otaku*, in fact, create a pressure group within the industry and have an impact on its decisions. Lastly, the *otaku* market proves that creativity in the media industries does not rest in the hands of a small group of professionals but involves masses of active fans, which constitute an important part of Japan's media marketplace.

5.4   Televised Music Shows

Studies of popular televised music shows in Japan provide another evidence for the continuous interaction between the established industry and amateur participation. These TV shows are professionally choreographed competitive music performances by amateur singers. The audience judges the performances and ultimately selects one winner, giving them the satisfaction of active participation in the show. These amateur shows are part of a broader entertainment trend based on interaction between producers and consumers, who both contribute to the final product. In order to achieve optimal exposure for these relatively inexpensive and versatile productions, amateur music shows are highly structured in terms of performer roles and show themes.

For our discussion on creativity, these shows demonstrate the close extraction and cultivation of amateurish creativity being part of corporate success. Since the dependency on audience participation constitutes the essence of the whole production, the industry must interact with the audience and with amateur singers, induce excitement among everyone, and develop ways to cultivate talent from ground level. However, unlike the previous two cases discussed earlier, *dōjinshi* and *otaku*, in televised music shows the production is highly orchestrated and its borders are well-defined by the industry. Unlike the *dōjinshi*, who are given a vast degree of creative freedom and the industry does not really know what the outcome will be, in TV shows the interaction with fans tends to be much more controlled and even manipulated by the industry.

Nowadays, talent shows like "American Idol" and "America's Got Talent" are popular worldwide; but these were already very popular in Japan in the 1970s and 1980s, achieving audience ratings of more than 40% for most of the period. The best-known example of this genre is *Sutā Tanjo* (A Star Is Born), a popular star-search program developed in Japan in the 1970s (Iwabuchi 2002). The program was produced by NTV—one of Japan's biggest television stations—in close collaboration with recording companies and talent agencies. The production of the program featured close cooperation between the industry (the television station, recording companies, and talent agencies), and between the studio audience and the amateur singers. The program auditioned amateur singers by holding singing competitions that were broadcast live from public halls. The adolescent winners of these competitions, having been selected by executives of top record companies and management agencies in attendance at the competitions, were then turned into professional music artists and star-idols. Famous performers who got their start on the show include Yamaguchi Momoe, Mori Masako, Sakurada Junko, Iwasaki Hiromi, Nakamori Akina, Koizumi Kyoko, and Pink Lady. In the 1980s, other successful music programs included The Best Ten (TBS, 1978–1989), Top Ten (NTV), Music Station (Asahi), *Heisei Meibutsu Ikasu Bando Tengoku* (Paradise for Cool Bands) (TBS, 1989–1991), and *Yuyake Nyan Nyan* (Fuji TV, 1968–1988).

Talent music shows in the 1970s and 1980s were a good solution for Japan's media industries, who were looking for new productions without taking a high risk. Unlike investing in finding and training new musical talents from the very beginning, these shows brought the talent into the studio and made the audience both the judge and the marketer of successful singers. These shows have since evolved into a new genre of television programming that combines music, comedy, and dance performances with active audience participation. Meanwhile, they have also modified the structure of music production by eliminating some of the boundaries between the creative work of the professionals and that of the amateurs and consumers. In fact, music has become more dependent on television exposure, and new trends in multifaceted televised music production have emerged (Stevens and Hosokawa 2001: 227–230). Up to the 1970s, there were clear divisions of labor in the Japanese music industry between lyricists, composers, and arrangers, all of whom had exclusive contracts with record companies. Indie music artists, especially those representing rock music, were excluded from mainstream production channels. Amateur programs on television, however, have now given these bands a stage on which to debut and become popular, bypassing the established industry and facilitating a shift in the position of music artists vis-à-vis the industry. By giving the audience the power to choose winners, these productions broadened the industry's search for talent and created new production opportunities. In other words, a new partnership has been formed, made up of the industry, the amateur performers, and the audience who get to judge and rate them according to flexible guidelines and with some degree of uncertainty.

5.5   Virtual Animated Idols: Integration of Technology and Fandom

The world of animated characters which are created by fans, known as "Virtual YouTubers", or "VTubers," provides a very recent example of the utilization of amateur talent for the production of commercial media genres and goods. The ability to use new technologies to create new virtual characters and turn them into "live" idols allows fans to not only "consume" these artists' music and visuals but also to participate in the production process and to have an impact on their career. What is glaring in this case, compared to the previous three cases already discussed (*dōjinshi*, *otaku*, televised music shows), is the strong lineage between amateur creativity and new media technology and the ability of this technology, which becomes more and more accessible, to almost dismiss the boundaries between the producers and the consumers. The result is a "hybrid reality" that merges the real world with the virtual and makes amateurs and the industry interact in real time to produce new entertaining entities.

The "VTubers" is an almost exclusively Japanese phenomenon. These are virtual characters who, similar to human idols, sing, dance, play video games, try new applications, and live stream their chats with viewers. Some are 3D characters capable of smooth gestures and changing facial expressions that emulate emotions. Their main appearance is on YouTube, but some have gained enough popularity that they now hold live events in the real word, appear as guests on TV shows and anime series, and even collaborate with real human idols. Unlike "usual" anime characters, VTubers communicate freely with fans in real time. Although they are manipulated by humans, they convincingly give the impression that they are behaving on their own free will. Thus, according to Hiroata Minoru, a journalist specializing in virtual-reality news, "fans are seeing these characters almost as humans."[5]

Hatsune Miku is the pioneer of Japan's animated virtual characters. Miku is a game-embedded anime-like character that can also be made to sing and dance. Miku

---

[5]Quoted in Kazuaki Nagata, *Japan Times*, "Japan's Latest Big Thing: 'Virtual YouTubers'," July 17, 2018. Available at: https://www.japantimes.co.jp/news/2018/07/17/national/japans-latest-big-thing-virtual-youtubers. Accessed August 24, 2018; see also Jennifer Sherman, "Virtual YouTuber Trend Expands with Talent Agencies, TV Appearances," *Anime News Network*, April 4, 2018. Available at: https://www.animenewsnetwork.com/interest/2018-04-15/virtual-youtuber-trend-expands-with-talent-agencies-tv-appearances/.130149. Accessed August 24, 2018.

combines music, visual anime, and game software, and is based on the active participation of the audience who is expected to "feed" it with new songs. Miku was initially conceived as a Vocaloid program by a group of Spanish amateurs. Yamaha, which recognized the potential of Miku and wanted to venture into new media fields, provided the financial support to develop Miku's software, and finally bought the rights for the entire program. Rather than maintain strict control over Miku's copyright and make consumers pay, Yamaha actually encouraged consumers to develop the software and take an active part in animating and marketing Miku. Fans were asked to create their own Vocaloid video clips and upload them to an internet platform such as YouTube. New streaming technologies, such as Twitch.tv and Niconico, enabled fans to watch and react together to Miku's Vocaloid videos in real time. Later on, new MMD (multimedia domain) technologies enabled the creation of anime-like 3D avatars that move according to the dancing movement of real fans. These days, there are also real-life events and live performances by Miku, projected as a hologram in front of a live audience, sometimes together with human celebrities. In this sense, through the active participation of amateur fans, Miku has received a life of its own and is continuing to develop and venture into new media fields.

Likewise, Kizuna Ai is considered the world's first virtual YouTuber. Kizuna, who looks like a teenage girl, became an internet phenomenon in 2016, thanks to two popular YouTube channels. Kizuna is thought to have been created by an anonymous animation voice actor and she not only functions as an idol-like animated character that creates Vocaloid, but she also answers fans questions almost instantly, thus creating a sense of "real" intimacy. Due to its popularity, in 2018, Kizuna appeared in an anime series called Magical Girl Site, received her own television program that premiered in April the same year, and was even appointed as an ambassador to promote tourism by the Japan National Tourism Association. Building on Kizuna's success, merchandize companies started to create and sell Kizuna-related products.

The number of VTubers have proliferated rapidly over the past two years. The Tokyo-based data research firm User Local Inc. estimated that the number of VTubers has doubled from 2000 to 4000 in only two and a half months.[6] According to this report, the character Kizuna Ai has a fan base of more than two million followers. Kaguya Luna and Mirai Akari, two other virtual characters, were ranked second and third with 750,000 and 625,000 followers respectively. Nekomiya Hinata and Siro, VTubers who debuted in early 2018, reached almost 500,000 followers each in just six months. These figures outnumber the followers of many famous Japanese live YouTubers.

In this emerging field of VTubers, the established industry soon followed. A few game developers, merchandize sellers, and talent management agencies have become active, seeking business expansion opportunities and gauging new talent. Japanese internet media company GREE, known for its social network services and smartphone games, announced in April 2018 that it is establishing a new venture that will invest ten billion yen in the emerging VTuber business. Wright Flyer Live, a subsidiary of GREE, plans to cultivate and manage new VTubers, as well as produce

---

[6]Nagata, "Japan's Latest Big Thing: 'Virtual YouTubers'."

its related video program projects. Duo Inc., a Nagoya-based startup, launched a management agency called ENTUM to cultivate new talent and develop the VTuber business. According to Daichi Tsukamoto, the company's CEO, "We've had some auditions and realized that there are really creative people in this world.... If someone helps them out a little bit, they could become extraordinary talents. [The VTuber trend] sort of shows that it's possible to live as someone else through a virtual avatar."[7] The company has since become involved in collaborating with fan-talent, making new videos, producing events and merchandize, and managing business discussions with clients. By summer 2018, ENTUM's clients included such famous VTubers as Mirai Akari, Nekomiya Hinata, Yomemi, Todoki Yuka, and Mochi Hiyoko. Some of these companies use *pixiv*, a specialized internet forum which ranks people who create animated characters. Some of the game and anime companies use forums such as pixiv to announce job opportunities on new projects.

In summary, the production of these animated virtual characters almost diminishes the boundaries between producer and consumer in both the production and marketing stages. The virtual reality enabled by streaming technology does not only encourage fans' participation, but is actually based on fans' creative input. In this case, the industry (game and software developers, internet infrastructure companies, merchandize manufacturers, etc.) plays only a secondary role in the production, following and accommodating amateur-driven creations. This, eventually, blurs the boundaries not only between professionals and non-professionals, but also between reality and virtual reality.

5.6   Conclusion

What connects the four forms of entertainment discussed in this chapter (*dōjinshi*, *otaku*, music talent shows, virtual idols) to the issue of creativity is that they involve a sort of creativity which is being cultivated through the interaction between the industry and the audience. In this sense, the notion of creativity in these media industries is, most basically, the collaborative extraction and valorization of new ideas, images, sounds, and imagination from the audience. Although the established industry provides the managerial, financial, and technical resources needed for wide-scale culture production, the industry stays attuned to bottom-up creativity as well as to changing market needs, and encourages the audience to take an active role in both the creative and marketing stages.

From an organizational point of view, the established media industry in Japan has used the huge amount of creative energy available in the marketplace for its own purpose, and has succeeded in fostering a close proximity between professionals and amateurs. Rather than underplaying private initiatives and making unilateral decisions about what sort of media culture consumers want, the media industries have supported, recruited, co-opted, and sometimes followed them to their advantage.

[7]Sherman, "Virtual YouTuber Trend Expands With Yalent Agencies, TV Appearances."

Because private and individual initiatives are seen as opportunities rather than threats, there is room for close reciprocity between amateur creators, culture production companies, and consumers. At the same time, it should be noted, however, that individuals who are not part of the established industry, such as fans, amateurs, temporary workers, and students, carry out a lot of the creative work. Their work is sponsored, guided, and packaged by industry representatives, often for no or very little compensation, and only a small number of them rise to fame.

The question is, do these industry-amateur relationships in Japan constitute a new model of coproduction? According to Piore and Sabel's (1984) seminal work on "flexible specialization", our advanced industrial society has been going through vast changes brought about by the dynamism of the market and the need to adjust production to the constant changes being demanded. Based on their research on shoe producers in northern Italy, they describe a proactive system where both skilled and semi-skilled workers are incorporated into the production cycle. Criticizing the Fordist literature, which describes an ecosystem where skilled workers convert all input into the production system in the most rational and standardized way without much autonomy, post-Fordist literature emphasizes the importance of inducing more heterogeneity in production and adjusting more flexibility to the scale and sort of production needed (Ash 1994). Considering the above theoretical developments, the model of creative production discussed here describes a system where the boundaries between audience and producer blur, where production and consumption are entangled, and where production is more closely related to changes in contemporary society and culture. Here the established industry needs not only to react swiftly to cultural, social, and artistic changes in the market but also to find a way to extract creativity from the consumers themselves.

Put differently, marketplace interaction between professionals, amateurs, and audience constitutes a synergetic system where industrial interests and individual creativity reciprocate. This system constantly draws new recruits from the audience to become active participants in the commodification and coproduction of popular culture. At the same time, it nurtures cooperation between professionals and audiences in the development of new products. What distinguishes the production system described in this chapter from the post-Fordist literature is the extensive utilization of technology as part of the creative process. Allowing amateurs to take an active part in the work of the media industries means that anyone with a creative idea, a digital camera, and a good computer has a chance to become part of the industry that produces commodified cultural products. Audiences are thus constantly involved in production, making consumption an integral part of the production cycle, rather than merely its final destination.

Being so culturally and socially integrated in Japan, is this hybridized system of cultural production transferable and can it be duplicated in other cultural and social contexts? Can it work in the US, Switzerland, South Africa, or Israel? Some parts may be transferable, especially the notion of easing restrictions and realign the boundaries of media and cultural production, cultivating closer communication with fans, and extracting creativity from below. In some respects, Japan is not unique. America's rap culture scene, for instance, started from ground level before being commercialized by the USA's music production companies. But in manga and animation, the Japanese example of allowing the infringement of copyright laws and royalties for the sake of creativity might be too difficult for US and European companies to accept. There, the Walt Disney model of zero tolerance for big groups of amateurs infringing their copyright on a daily basis as part of the creative process still prevails.

References

Aksoy, A., & Kevin, R. (1992). Hollywood in the 21st century: Global competition for critical mass in image markets. *Cambridge Journal of Economics*, 16:1–22.

All Japan Magazine and Book Publishers (APJEA). (2017). *2016nen no Komikku Shijo wo Happyō Shimashita* [Talks about 2016 Comics Market]. Available at: http://www.ajpea.or.jp/information/20170224/index.html. Accessed May 1, 2018.

Allison, A. (2006). *Millennial monsters: Japanese toys and the global imagination*. Berkeley, CA: University of California Press.

Ash, A. (Ed.). (1994). *Post-fordism: A reader*. Bodmin: Blackwell.

Association of Japanese Animators (AJA). (2016). *Anime Industry Report 2016*. Available at: file:///C:/Users/nissim/Downloads/Anime_ind_rptsummary_en%20(1).pdf. Accessed May 1, 2018.

Association of Japanese Animators (AJA). (2017). *Anime Industry Report 2017*. Available at: file:///C:/Users/nissim/Downloads/Anime_ind_rptsummary_en%20(2).pdf. Accessed May 1, 2018.

Azuma, H. (2009). *Otaku: Japan's database animals* (J. E. Abel & S. Kōno, Trans.). Minneapolis, MN: University of Minnesota Press.

Brienza, C. (2016). *Manga in America: Transnational book publishing and the domestication of Japanese comics*. New York: Bloomsbury.

Caves, R. (2000). *Creative industries: Contracts between arts and commerce*. Harvard, MA: Harvard University Press.

Condry, I. (2013). *The soul of anime: Collaborative creativity and Japan's media success story*. Durham, NC: Duke University Press.

Daliot-Bul, M., & Otmazgin, N. (2017). *The rise of anime in the US: Lessons for global creative industries*. Harvard: Harvard University East Asia Press.

Dentsū Communication Institute. (2009). Jōhō Media Hakusho [White Paper on Information and Media]. Tokyo: Daiyamondosha.

Elsbach, K. D., & Kramer, R. M. (2003). Assessing creativity in hollywood pitch meetings: Evidence for a dual-process model of creativity judgments. *Academy of Management Journal, 46*(3), 283–301.

Hartley, J. (ed). (2005). *Creative Industries*. Cornwall: Blackwell Publishing.

Holroyd, C. and Coates, K. S. (2015). *The global digital economy: A comparative policy analysis*. Amherst, NY: Cambria Press.

Iwabuchi, K. (2002). *Recentering globalization: Popular culture and Japanese transnationalism*. Durham, NC: Duke University Press.

Japan External Trade Organization (JETRO). (2006). Jōhō Media Hakusho [White Paper on Information and Media]. Available at: http://www.jetro.go.jp/en/. Accessed August 31, 2018.

Kelts, R. (2007). *Japanamerica: How Japanese pop culture has invaded the U.S.* New York: Palgrave.

Kinsella, S. (2000). *Adult manga: Culture and power in contemporary japanese society*. Honolulu: University of Hawai'i Press.

LaMarre, T. (2009). *The anime machine: A media theory of animation*. Minneapolis, MN: University of Minnesota Press.

Leonard, S. (2004). *Progress against the law: Fan distribution, copyright, and the explosive growth of Japanese animation*. Cambridge, MA: Massachusetts Institute of Technology.

Media Innovation Lab. (2017). *Information media trends in Japan*. Information Media White Paper. Available at: http://www.dentsu.com/knowledgeanddata/publications/pdf/information_media_trends_in_japan_2017.pdf. Accessed May 1, 2018.

Morisawa, T. (2013). Producing animation: Work, creativity, and aspirations in the Japanese animation industry. Ph.D. Thesis, Oxford University.

Mulcahy & Kevin V. (2006). Cultural policy: Definitions and theoretical approaches. *The Journal of Management, Law, and Society, 35*(4), 319–330.

Nomura Sōgō Kenkyū Sho [Nomura Research Institute]. (2005). Arata na Konsyūmā-tachi no Pawā: Otaku Shijō wo Saguru [The New Power of Consumers: Visit the *Otaku* Market]. Tokyo: Nomura Sōgō Kenkyū Sho [Nomura Research Institute].

Norris, C. (2009). Manga, anime and visual art culture. In Y. Sugimoto (Ed.), *The Cambridge companion to modern Japanese Culture* (pp. 236–260). New York: Cambridge University Press.

Oh, Ingyu, & Koo, Bonwon. (2010). Japanese Webtoon: Digitalizing and Marketing Manga Online Using South Korean App Designs. In Park Gil-Sung, N. Otmazgin & K. Howard (Eds.), *Transcultural Fandom and the Globalization of Hallyu* (pp. 181–206). Seoul: Korea University Press.

Otmazgin, N. (2013). *Regionalizing culture: The political economy of Japanese popular culture in Asia*. Honolulu: University of Hawaiʻi Press.

Otmazgin, N., & Ben-Ari, E. (2013). Introduction: History and theory in the study of cultural collaboration. In O. Nissim & B.-A. Eyal (Eds.), *Popular culture co-productions and collaborations in East and Southeast Asia* (pp. 1–25). Singapore: NUS Press and Kyoto University Press.

Pellitteri, M. (2012). *The dragon and the Dazzle: Models, strategies, and identities of Japanese imagination—A European perspective*. Bloomington, IN: Indiana University Press.

Pink, D. H. (November, 2007). Japan ink: Inside the Manga Industrial Complex. *Wired*, no. 15.

Piore, J. Plore, & Sabel. J. Charles. (1984). *The second industrial divide: Possibilities for prosperity*. New York: Basic Books.

Richie, Donald. (2003). *The image factory: Fads and fashions in japan*. London: Reaktion.

Ryan, B. (1992). *Making capital from culture: The corporate form of capitalist cultural production*. De Gruyter Studies in Organization 35. Berlin: Walter de Gruyter.

Shimoku, K. (2008). *Genshiken Official Book*. New York: Del Rey.

Shiraishi, S. (2013). *Grōbarukashita Nihon no manga to anime [Globalized Japanese Manga and Anime]*. Tokyo: Gakujutsu shuppankai.

Steinberg, M. (2012). *Anime media mix: Franchising toys and characters in Japan*. Minneapolis, MN: University of Minnesota Press.

Stevens, Carolyn S., & Shūhei Hosokawa. (2001). So Close and yet So Far: Humanizing Celebrity in Japanese Music Variety Shows, 1960s–1990s. In Brian Moeran, (Ed.) *Asian Media Productions* (pp. 223–245). Honolulu: University of Hawaiʻi Press.

Storper, M. (1994). The transition to flexible specialization in the US film industry: External economies, the division of labour and the crossing of industrial divides. In A. Amin (Ed.), *Post-fordism: A reader* (pp. 195–226). Oxford: Blackwell.

Tomaney, J. (1994). A new paradigm of work organization and technology? In A. Amin (Ed.), *Post-fordism: A reader* (pp. 157–194). Bodmin: Blackwell.

Ueno, T. (2002). Japanimation and techno-orientalism. In B. Grenville (Ed.), *The uncanny: Experiments in cyborg culture*. Vancouver: Arsenal Pulp Press.

Schwak, J. (2016). Branding South Korea in a Competitive World Order: Discourses and Dispositives in Neoliberal Governmentality. *Asian Studies Review, 40*(3), 427–444.

Yano Research Institute. (2017). Otakushijō ni Kan suru chōsa [Survey of the Otaku Market]. Available at: file:///C:/Users/nissim/Downloads/1773.pdf. Accessed May 1, 2018.

Nissim Otmazgin is the Director of the Institute for Asian and African Studies, The Hebrew University of Jerusalem, and a member of the Israeli Young Academy of Science and Humanities. A political scientist in training, his research interests include cultural diplomacy in Asia, popular culture and regionalization in East and Southeast Asia, and cultural industry and cultural policy in Japan and South Korea. His Ph.D. dissertation (Kyoto University, 2007), which examines the export of Japan's popular culture to Asia, won the Iue Asia Pacific Research Prize for outstanding dissertation on society and culture in Asia. As a part of this research, he conducted extensive fieldwork in Hong Kong, Singapore, Shanghai, Bangkok, and Seoul. He is the author of Regionalizing Culture: the Political Economy of Japanese Popular Culture in Asia (University of Hawaii Press, 2013) and (together with Miki Daliot Bul) of The Anime Boom in the US: Lessons for Global Creative Industries (Harvard University Asia Center Press, 2017).

Chapter 6
Dilemma: Professional Identity Work Among Tokyo-Based Designers

Jakob Thestrup

Given the context of this volume, the chapter sets out to elucidate broader insights into the phenomenology of creative work—indeed the process of creativity—by applying a prism of professional identity work. Specifically, it empirically explores professional identity dilemmas from the vantage point of graphic and fashion designers based in Tokyo, Japan. Drawing on career- and work-narratives, it investigates the role of potentially competing work imperatives as well as market uncertainty. The two groups diverge in unexpected ways and support extant literature in others. Notably, both groups exhibit a distinctly commercial logic that informs ideas of success and failure as well as the professional identity construct itself. As such, the often academically discoursed tension of art vs commerce seems curiously absent, however, a different dilemmatic space, associated with structure and agency, emerges in a salient fashion. Narrated dilemmas are further compounded by significant market uncertainty, but coping strategies differ greatly. Fashion designers are shielded from market uncertainty by virtue of their socially embedded design praxis whereas graphic designers are more vulnerable. All in all, fashion designers share a highly coherent professional identity narrative with regards to success criteria, aspirations and boundaries. Graphic designers, on the other hand, exhibit a very fluid and fragmented field of professional identity narratives and generally struggle more with dilemmas.

This chapter will start by introducing the creative industries; it highlights inherent dynamics of said industries and elaborates on the contemporary organizational context of designers as creative professionals. It subsequently presents the theoretical prism of professional identity work and discuss it in the context of identity dilemmas. We then turn to the empirical findings where work imperatives and market uncertainty as central themes are explored and discussed while drawing on a broader set of salient findings. The professional identity dilemmas are ultimately presented and discussed with reference underlying determinants—in particular what Bamberg (2011)

J. Thestrup (✉)
The University of Tokyo, Tokyo, Japan
e-mail: jakob_thestrup@hotmail.com

© Springer Nature Singapore Pte Ltd. 2020
N. Otmazgin and E. Ben-Ari (eds.), *Creative Context*, Creative Economy,
https://doi.org/10.1007/978-981-15-3056-2_6

describes as *'the management of agency between the double-arrow of a person-to-world versus a world-to-person direction of fit'* or what is typically viewed as "who is in control".

6.1 Creative Industries and Designers

Creative industries are typically defined as the industries where a production function with artistic creativity as a key input in the production process, and with an art product or a creative product as the main output. It emerged as a defined sector some twenty years ago and has since gathered increasing attention from scholars, media and policy-makers alike. This is in part because there is increasing recognition of the economic significance, and partly because the creative industries are often thought to complement urban and regional renewal policy goals, are relatively low-polluting, and have intrinsic cultural cache for many stakeholders. As a sector it encompasses independent artists, performing arts, music, film, media, architecture and design, advertising, photography and crafts and it is imbued with a set of distinct characteristics, naturally varying depending on the specific creative field, but on the whole diverges significantly from other industries (Caves 2000; Hesmondhalgh 2007).

The creative industries have partly led, and are partly a product of, major economic changes over recent decades. Whereas products used to compete based on utility and objective specifications, the widespread dissemination of technologies of quality control in mass production, and faster capabilities for emulation of industrial products, has seen sustained falls in production costs and rising average quality. Together with the increase in off-shoring of remaining labour-intensive elements of mass production from the 1990s, the imperative to promote 'value adding' became more salient in both business and public policy discussions. Companies have subsequently come to compete more through the subjective differentiation of their standardized products—customer perceptions and experiences—rather than objective product attributes. Whilst this has had its influential critics, aggregate consumer welfare has been much enhanced, and seen consumer expenditure increasingly diverted to services, giving rise to the so-called 'experience economy' effect (Pine and Gilmore 1999), and also created new demand for products that are differentiated by distinctive material, form, concept and origins. This has ultimately led to a recognition of creativity as constituting 'the decisive source of competitive advantage' (Florida 2002: 4), and also entails an important epistemological shift in the understanding of value.

Specifically, the creative industries are characterised by deep ambiguity and uncertainty as opposed to more traditional industries where goods are utilitarian and may be compared based on measurable standards (Lampel et al. 2000). Although creative actors or enterprises might have access to substantial amount of past data, the extrapolation of such knowledge far from guarantees success. Rather, with regards to market success, predictability in these industries remains very low—a point that

Caves (2000) has famously named the 'nobody knows' property. Additionally, creative actors themselves are subject to tensions as they are catering to two seemingly paradoxical imperatives; economic viability and the need to constantly create new products, genres and formats (DeFillippi et al. 2007). The creative process is far from straight forward and the management of said process is therefore not viable on a command-and-control basis (Lampel et al. 2000).

This has profound implications for the organisation of work in the creative industries, and is frequent reason for failure by more traditional industry enterprises that venture, through expansion or acquisition, directly in the creative industries. Moreover, for all firms that need to 'add value' to their product line-up, they face challenges in adapting established managerial practices and organizational cultures to working with 'creatives', either within the boundaries of their own enterprises or across firm boundaries as procurers of design services or collaborators with creative enterprises. Caves' (2000) seminal account of the creative industries identified seven dimensions across which creative industries could generally be differentiated from other industries, of which the most salient for this study are the aforementioned 'nobody knows' effect, and what he referred to the 'art for art's sake' dynamic. By this Caves was referring to the high level of intrinsic motivation of many artists in the cultural industries, which meant that their primary motivation was not financial, with complex implications for business. Whilst high intrinsic motivation may imply less need for monitoring, as in the command-and-control hierarchical firm, financial incentives were also less likely to be effective, and professional identity much less aligned with the interests of employers and clients than their own cultural and creative reputations. Among other studies, Eikhof and Haunschild (2006) nicely elucidate the salience of said tension in a study of German theatre actors where adopting a 'bohemian entrepreneur' identity was found to enable bridging of the gap between self-management and artistic work. Caves' framework, however, was developed principally with a view to explain the distinctive contracting practices, and organisational features at the firm and industry level for what we might classify as the 'cultural industries': music, visual and performing arts, literature and cinema. He gave less direct consideration to 'design', which often involves creative workers working to a brief from a client outside the creative industries. The exception to this is fashion design, which functions rather like the music industry or publishing in that specialised enterprises develop new creatively differentiated products directly in consumer markets. As such, this chapter will explore the degree to which such relationships—directly client-centred, or mediated through the larger scale of retail markets and distribution systems, impacts on the extent to which designers' professional identities are reconciled to commercial compromise.

6.1.1 Creative Professionals

As for individual professionals (or workers), extant 'Creative industries' literature often cluster them together as 'Creatives' implying a categorical membership. This is particularly apparent when discoursed in reference to 'humdrum', professionals who are distinctly non-creative in their work function. Creatives are often understood as having a cluster of common traits that are distinct—a cluster nicely exemplified by the Richard Florida's (2002) 'Creative Class'. There can be very good reasons for such clustering though. In the context of policymaking, for example, it serves an obvious purpose of reducing complexity and thus strengthening the communicability of an argument. The 'humdrum' versus 'creatives' binary construct, however, entails a notion of a shared social identity among 'creatives' engaged in professional work (i.e. individual agents in the creative industries). One potentially risky consequence of such discourse, indeed ontology, is that research findings of specific types of creatives may be uncritically generalized and ascribed to an increasingly crude idea of a 'creative'. Emphasizing graphic and fashion designers, this chapter explores the extent to which they identify with a shared social identity (or meta-identity) as 'creatives' and/or 'designers' in addition to—or as a substitute for—their immediate professional label.

The idea of 'design' has radically expanded since the early 1990s with palpable ramifications to the design profession. Increased societal complexity, digitization and technological development have preceded a multitude of professional labels such as 'UI/UX designer' and 'motion graphics designer'. The advent of Design Thinking in the early 1990s and its subsequent popularization has also contributed to a more salient design ethos whereby a codified methodology as well as a notion that anybody can be a designer has emerged [particularly through influential publications such as Kelley and Kelley (2013) and Brown (2009)]. To what extent fashion designers and/or graphic designers draw on a shared design ethos, and indeed identify with each other, remains unclear, but the salience of design in public discourse warrants a closer look.

When exploring the construction, interplay and performance of professional identities, the majority of studies so far have empirically drawn on rigidly hierarchical fields and matured institutional settings. In healthcare, for instance, doctors and nurses are often subjects of research (Cruess et al. 2015; Pratt et al. 2006) and education (whether it be academia or other levels) also constitute a common used research site (Archer 2008; van Lankveld et al. 2017). In addition to the key industry tensions and dynamics introduced earlier in this chapter, designers (as subject of research) is a distinct departure in several ways. Firstly, designers do creative work—and in doing so there is an inherent tolerance for failure in their work relative to non-creative professions. A medical doctor (or another agent in the healthcare field) is by contrast, and for very obvious reasons, not tolerated to fail as it could have very fatal consequences. Secondly, designers are not defined by having obtained a specific certificate through an approved educational program allowing for the exclusion of non-certificate holders, but rather, they are able to work equally as designers with autodidact backgrounds. Other actors in the creative industries, such as architects populate a gated profession where the professional identity is inculcated through long training and significant licensure requirements (Ahuja et al. 2017). Thirdly, design work in practice, whether it be fashion design or graphic design, is not a linear process. It is profoundly iterative and draws on the expertise of many disparate agents before coming to fruition (often referred to as the 'motley crew' property).

The collaborative nature of design work, however, and as exemplified by the two groups of designers presented in this chapter, are embedded in very different institutional contexts serve different market domains and the subsequent implications for the respective professional identity work and the nature of associated dilemmas consequently differ.

The creative industries are at the forefront of changes in the nature and organisation of work, in what has come to be referred to as 'the unbundling of the firm', and the rise of 'free agent' or 'gig' economy. Taken together with the increasing importance of subjective, relative to objective, forms of knowledge in an era of 'selling sensibility' and providing experiences (Pine and Gilmore 1999), a study of the professional self-identities of fashion and graphic designers may elucidate broader insights into contemporary creative work.

6.2   Professional Identity Work

Anchored in a constructivist approach, identity in a broad sense is not viewed as innate traits of any given person, but rather, an identity (or identities) is performed and negotiated in accordance with social, cultural, economical and historical factors. As such, identities are both contextual—dependent on circumstances—and relational—created in relation to something/someone else, for instance, something that is not. The 'difference' is thus central in the construction of an identity (Woodward 2002). Analytically, this underlines the importance of narrated others as it may elucidate ideas of self and identity boundaries alike (Ybema et al. 2009). Sims (2005) sums up this point by stating: *'I am, to a significant extent, the the stories that I tell about myself, although quite a lot can be discerned about my identity from the stories I tell about others too.'* (Sims 2005: 89)

The concept of 'professional identity' as presented in this chapter, is defined as an individual's subjectively constructed image of who he/she is as a professional (Slay and Smith 2011). In the context of work-life, professional identity implies the particular type of work individuals do and typically denote a specific type of training or set of skills that one possess (Pratt et al. 2006; Stockhausen 2005). As such, there is an emphasis on the work praxis as a differentiating factor from other people and an underlying notion of being unique as a product of what you do. Moreover, professional identity also entails a social dimension and may be viewed as a social identity allowing for individuals to become part of a certain community based on a shared methodology or certain type of work (Van Maanen and Barley 1984). For Crossley and Vivekananda-Schmidt (2009: 603), a professional identity "...is a prerequisite for accepting the responsibilities and obligations of the professional role and it can be key to developing the confidence to work as a qualified professional." As such, it holds distinctly enabling properties and regardless of being viewed as a role identity or social identity, professional identity is of great importance in that it organises the subjective ontology and thus constitute behvioural guidance (see Caza and Creary 2016; Siebert and Siebert 2005; Ibarra 1999). Beyond behavioural effects, a strong identification with a profession also serves to reduce uncertainty and provide self-enhancement (Hogg and Terry 2000). Grey (1994: 482) notes that, for better or worse, occupation has become a major source of identity and may be 'a place where the self may become that which it truly is or desires to be' (Bauman and Raud 2015).

In conjunction with the concept of professional identity, this chapter also draws on the theoretical notion of what Sveningsson and Alvesson (2003) refer to as 'identity work'. Identity work, as opposed to a more essentialist conceptualisation, emphasises the dynamic nature and the 'on-going struggle' associated with answering the question: Who am I? (Brown 2015). As such, identity work is the work we engage in when we continuously maintain, strengthen or modify the constructions that are productive in terms of having a sense of **coherence** and **distinctiveness**. Sveningsson and Alvesson (2003) argue that in any given organisational context, individuals will strive for comfort, meaning and integration as well as seek to integrate or balance one's definition of self and a work situation. Organisational discourses, role expectations and narrative self-identities are all part of this what is here referred to as *professional identity work*.

Following DeFillippi (2009) who notes that 'a solid sense of self as a creative has long been seen as central to creative workers' identity', this chapter introduces **identity dilemmas** as when a 'solid sense of self', in this case as a professional designer, is being or at the risk of being undermined. Identity dilemmas have thus far been explored by elucidating tensions/paradoxes and have been approached from the perspective of organizations, managers and creative professionals alike (DeFillippi et al. 2007; Ahuja et al. 2017; Beech et al. 2012; Gotsi et al. 2010). As already described, the art vs commerce tension is the most salient in the context of creative professionals whereby different coping strategies are applied in search for an 'optimal balance' (Kreiner et al. 2006). However, there may be other sources of dilemmas—Hogg (2009), for instance, argues that self-categorization and social identification is fundamentally a way to reduce self-uncertainty. In the context of a professional self, a strong (and stable) institutional context imbued with a clear set of logics (Thornton et al. 2012), aspirational career paths and training/education that is aligned with post-graduation work practices (Alvesson and Willmott 2002) may attenuate self-uncertainty and thus positively affect professional identification. Severe self-uncertainty, on the other hand, may constitute an identity dilemma and would require identity work to restore a 'solid sense of self'.

The nature of experienced identity dilemmas, however, is arguably rooted in key structural positions and the schematic below constitutes a presupposition of professional identity positions with reference to level of identity fluidity and the art/commerce imperative. Based on Ahuja et al. (2017) the professional identity of architects have moved from an imperative anchored in art and aesthetics to a commercially driven construct with the advent of managerialism. The certifications required and long education required has informed the position of a less fluid and thus more socially structured and bounded professional identity.

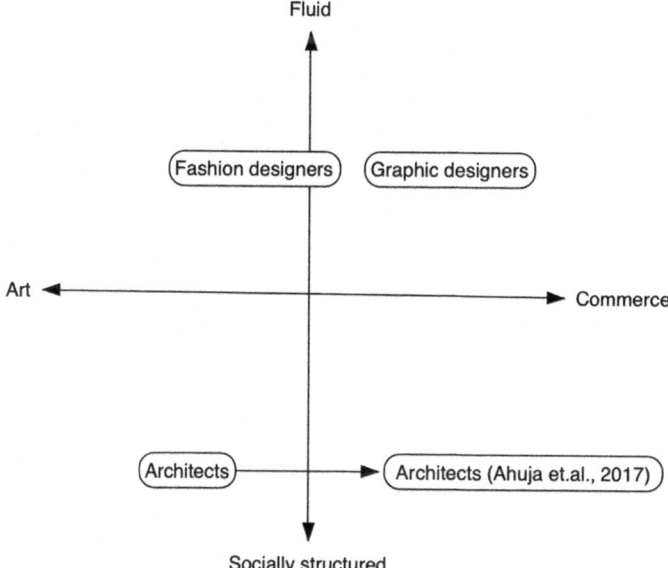

As for the two groups of designers, they are presupposed to be situated in the fluid end of the spectrum based on the non-certified/non-gated nature of their profession (vis-a-vis the already mentioned architects). However, given the brief-driven nature of graphic design work as well as their ongoing client-focused iterations, graphic designers are likely to inhabit a stronger commercial imperative.

6.2.1 Analytical Strategy and Methods

With the above schematic in mind this chapter makes use of three ways to explore the professional identity work and associated dilemmas. The first is through work practice narratives. For instance, stories of interesting work tasks, work situation where the interviewee felt successful or had a feeling of failure. The second way is by career narratives where the interviewee both makes sense of a him/herself in a broader temporal context and also elucidate 'turning points'. The third and last way is through reflexive meetings with others, i.e. stories of interactions with other professionals from similar industries and dissimilar industries alike. These narratives constitute the unit of analysis and are considered voices in what Hazen (1993) refers to as the polyphonic organisation. They continuously create meanings whereby professionals in and around organisations articulate and negotiate individual, group and organisational self-perceptions. In this particular context, the stories expressed in an interview situation are considered a performance and thus the narratives are identity work.

The empirical basis of this research consists of in-depth interviews with 30 different designers all based in Tokyo, Japan. The majority of the designers are clustered in

two groups—graphic designers and fashion designers—and the remaining interviewees are somehow crossing the boundaries of one of the two groups. For example, a
UI/UX designer who sees himself as a hybrid between a programmer, manager and
a graphic designer or a self-proclaimed fashion illustrator who applies her drawing
skills exclusively in the context of fashion. The interviewees are equally male and
female and span from 23 to 56 years of age. The interviews have provided a range
of qualitatively rich narratives that upon collection have been analyzed thematically
(Riessman 2006) while paying particular attention to plot, discursive strategies and
positioning (Czarniawska 1998; Davies and Harre 1990). An iterative approach was
adopted when moving from descriptive categories (first order) to more analytical
concepts and—in the context of this particular chapter—particular emphasis has
been placed on *market uncertainty* and *economic imperatives* that are forming the
basis of the analysis and findings.

6.3   Design for Design's Sake?

As already mentioned, the salience of the 'art for art's sake' effect, experienced as
the pain of artist aspirations foundering on the rocks of hard commercial reality, has
been well established across the creative industries. Interestingly and in contrast to
expectations, the interviews revealed little evidence in support of this. Most designers
narrated themselves as different from (and in some cases opposite to) artists. Fashion
designers, however, were particularly explicit about the importance of commanding a
positive market response and industry peers would actively perpetuate this perception
and even police it as a boundary condition.

> When I was young and designing a controller told me "we have to sell and you are a designer,
> not an artist!". I really agreed with that and I still do. Cause if you are an artist you just do
> whatever you want and try to find someone to buy your stuff. But in the fashion industry
> there is a market and there is shop and employees sell it. So we have to make it sell. (Fashion
> Designer)

The degree to which commercial success is important in being a fashion designer is
striking throughout the collected narratives. In conjunction with displaying resilience
toward failure, commercial success entails peer recognition and prestige: *"I made a
really casual and easy design and nobody expected it would sell really well and I
didn't think that way either. But it actually sold a lot more than we thought and for
many weeks it was the top selling piece in the shops. We had to re-order and re-order
and re-order many times. Because of this I became pretty famous inside the company
- a lot of people said 'oh you are the one who did that design, it was great!'"* (Fashion
designer)

Beyond prestige and peer recognition, positive career outcomes directly related
to commercial success was also saliently narrated: *'Later when I was interviewing
for another job (…) they asked me what I did that sold the most and I told them
about the piece and how much it sold and when I described the design they say "oh I*

remember that piece, that sold amazingly well". So they remembered the design and that was cool.' (Fashion Designer)

Graphic designers would—contrary to fashion designers—reflect on the different imperatives in the context of their own work. However, this is often narrated in a matter-of-fact way more so than a source of frustration or tension. There is a general a clear understanding that graphic design work is a way (and sometimes fun way) to make ends meet and pay the bills—and that naturally includes occasionally doing less interesting project for the sake of getting paid. Although not highly salient, a few accounts reveal tension-like dynamics as this graphic designer who implicitly characterized his aspirational self as not embodying a commercial imperative; *'I don't really wanna be the kind of person that just accepts jobs because it's money, but obviously sometimes you have to do it.'* This highlights a need to balance the different imperatives in the context a professional self and is thus a departure from fashion designers at large.

6.4   Market Uncertainty

As predicted and supporting Caves (2000), the empirical material of this research unequivocally shows that market uncertainty is highly salient for both groups of designers, however, as their work style and contexts differ greatly so does the impact of said uncertainty. One notable difference between the two groups of designers is the frequency of experienced failure. Although the idea of 'nobody knows' profoundly resonated with all designers, the frequency of actual experienced failure was very different; fashion designers would, through weekly meetings with merchandisers, receive quantitative data on sales and would thus come face to face with market failures on a very frequent basis compared to graphic designers, who in spite of this discrepancy, seemed less resistant to the prospect of perceived failure.

One fashion designer working for an upscale in-market brand narrated the failure of a particular design. She did a lot of research by consulting with several co-workers and sales staff in order to gain assurance that she was reading the market trends correctly and increase the chance of the garment selling well. Yet, it severely underperformed to the surprised of everybody involved.

> (…)everybody involved said "This will sell a lot!". So when everybody said that, I thought that was gonna happen and I felt relaxed and good about it being produced in large numbers. But when it actually got in the shops, it didn't sell at all. Nobody expected that. (Fashion designer)

Although she acknowledged her own responsibility, the sense of failure was mediated by the fact that she took all the necessary steps to ensure a successful outcome. Upon realizing the poor market performance of design, however, nobody criticized her as *'it happens to everyone'*.

Even though I was the person in charge of the design, I asked a lot of peoples opinion, I checked last year sales of the corresponding design, I talked to shop assistants and the controller so I did a lot of research in the company. (Fashion Designer)

This narrative of market failure resonates with many accounts and highlights several points; firstly, the acknowledgement of uncertainty and the prospect of market failure as an integral premise of the industry and subsequently the complete acceptance hereof. Insofar as the praxis norms have been followed when designing, managers will not penalize fashion designers for market failures. Secondly, the social dimension of the fashion designer is emphasized where working in close physical proximity to colleagues allow for crucial mutual assurance (even when a given design ends up under performing) and what can be described as hedging of responsibility. As such, the fashion designer emerges as a 'team player' where the sense of collective responsibility leads to remarkable resilience in the face of potential failure. Beyond shielding from market failures, the collective nature of the work praxis is also often narrated as a significant resource; '*I really prefer working where there are other designers so I can consult them whenever I am in doubt or want another opinion. When I am alone sometimes I think too much about problems and I become unable to solve them. It's easier with other designers around.*' (Fashion designer)

The socially embedded work-style of fashion designers, however, goes beyond solving problems and hedging responsibility—it also serves to reinforce ontologies of design work and bolster the perception of the role of a fashion designer. In contrast, graphic designers mostly engage in solitary work and, on occasion, nomadically located in/with different teams. They often narrate being left with limited to no feedback after a given project and although a repeat client can be viewed as a measure of success it is temporally disassociated from the project. In the context of failure, clients simply don't come back and there is nothing but the imagination of the given graphic designer to construct an explanation. The inability to share responsibility combined with the ambiguous or non-existent feedback of failures often creates strong emotional feedback.

Several graphic designers narrated that unambiguous client feedback as a luxury in the context of failure and success alike. The inability to know if a given product or pitch would be well received caused trepidation; '(…) *it is very hard to know if you are doing the right thing or not. It's like, sometimes people just don't like what you do. That can really hurt.*' (Graphic designer)

In the case of graphic designers, boundary conditions of the professional identity are rarely policed by peers and subjects alike and the apparent lack of a distinct and shared ontological narrative leads to graphic designers often struggling with 'imposter syndrome', self doubt and anxiety. Additionally, it may compound uncertainty when navigating a career. One graphic designer narrated a feeling of being a crossroads in his career and was unable see a natural progression. A big perceived problem in this regard, was his lack of expertise; '*I feel like I don't have any particular field of expertise. It's fine to be more of a generalist I think, but I can't call myself an expert in brand design or an expert in UI/UX design. I am just thinking a lot about that at the moment. I just don't feel that I have any deep level of knowledge in any of those areas.'* (Graphic designer)

Building and maintaining a particular skillset is an important part of a professional identity, however, the narrated ambiguity surrounding what a graphic designer does or is supposed to do to further her/his career speaks to a more fluid professional identity construction. Such fluidity may hold a positive or negative impact depending on context. Some graphic designers for instance feel enabled by this ambiguity and continuously re-invent themselves either by appropriating other designer identities such as 'interior designer' or related creative identities. This kind of expansive identity work is absent among fashion designers.

The importance of market performance in the narration of design success undoubtedly compounds the effects of market uncertainty and further exacerbate associated dilemmas. Had a designer only been preoccupied with the his or her own vision for a given product, whether or not it would manifest as a commercial success would—to a larger extent—become unimportant.

6.5   Other Factors

Beyond market uncertainty and work imperatives, however, a broader set of empirical factors where found to inform professional identity as well as associated dilemmas. **Firstly**, they operate in distinctly different technological domains, which, among others, result in different levels of outcome tangibility. Graphic designers are completely and solely dependent on a computer and internet connection allowing for them to complete all work functions. Fashion designers, on the other hand, have yet to integrate digital technologies to any meaningful degree and the materiality and intricate nuances of fabrics and sample designs are simply impossible to capture digitally. As such, the creative process of fashion design is almost exclusively based on analogue technologies whether it be drawing a design on paper or testing a garment sample by having a model wear it. **Secondly**, fashion designers ultimately cater to a consumer market whereas graphic designer are working with (and sometimes for) a client. Consequently, they are relatively removed from the end-user experience. The client relation also holds significance in terms of perceived design ownership (authorship)—when graphic designers work to a brief, it is often narrated that they assume the transactional role of a supplier to the client and, to a large extent, have to follow the clients wishes even when these pertain to aesthetic judgments. The sense of ownership is subsequently diminished and that is particularly apparent in the discursive strategies employed by the different designers. Specifically, fashion designers almost exclusively refer to their design as *'my design'* while remaining aware of the multitude of actors involved in the production function. Such explicit framing of ownership is curiously absent among graphic designers who instead refer to *'a project that I work(ed) on'*. **Thirdly**, the institutional field—defined in part by the prevailing understanding held by institutional actors concerning appropriate industry practice (Sydow 2006)—also differ greatly between graphic and fashion designers with potentially profound implications for professional identity construction and dilemmas. One example of institutionalized practice in the fashion industry is the temporality and fixed product 'rhythm'. All creative work is organized around the production of two collections (autumn/winter and spring/summer) and there is a very clear script for which phases need to be completed at which times in order to make the deadline for a given collection. Graphic designers have no such 'temporal script' and—as projects often vary in size and scope—it is organized on a case by case basis. Additionally, as graphic designers engage in various institutional fields according to client and project there is an inherent uncertainty around 'appropriate industry practice'. **Fourthly**, the praxis of design work itself, as narrated by the designers, differs in that fashion designers rely heavily on co-workers in their day to day tasks. This is supported by a close *physical proximity* and a profound culture of sharing. It enables fashion designers to be resilient in the face of market failures by 'hedging' perceived responsibility and ultimately shields from an experience of personal failure. Graphic designer narrate less stability in terms of daily interactions and often express the lack of trusted professional peers to spar with as a cause of dread. This is sometimes exacerbated when changing projects and a new client emerges with different expectations and communications styles. As such, anchored in the design praxis, fashion designers, contrary to their graphic counterparts, encounter a more pervasive and shared understanding of responsibilities, accepted behaviour and success criteria. Such understandings are continuously policed in various situations, whether it be in the office or at a job interview, and the professional identity is thus continuously reaffirmed.

6.6   Dilemmas

The immediate dilemmas exhibited by the two groups of designers differ significantly, however, they arguably inhabit the same dilemmatic space. Graphic designers oftentimes, explicitly and implicitly, exhibit imposter syndrome directly caused by ontological uncertainty. This can be narrated as anxiety and confidence issues associated with constantly 'faking it' or as a constant need to expand ones area of expertise (based on the idea of being insufficient). Other times when experiencing success, it is ascribed to factors divorced from the design praxis itself: '*Another way I justify to myself that I am faking it is - If I look at my past I can see that clients have been very happy, they've come back to me on numerous occasions so there is not reason to think I am doing a bad job, right? - but then I know for sure that people enjoy working with me, I think they kind of consider me to be a nice person and they get along with me and that's the reason they work with me, it's not for my design.*' (Graphic designer). In a similar vain, there is a distinct hesitation to embody the 'graphic designer' label. Such hesitance is also rooted in the uncertainty of what it means to be a good graphic designer and a lack of institutionalized benchmarks of success or quality: '*you see so much work, especially with social media, so much work in the industry that's amazing. Sometimes it is difficult to… put yourself in that line and say; well if they are a designer does that make me a designer too? yeah, there is this internal conflict of do I call myself a designer? Am I on that level? Do I need to be on that level to be a designer?'* (Graphic designer)

Among fashion designers, an immediately salient dilemma was found in the career narratives. Once a professional identity as a fashion designer has been established, it is perceived to be very difficult to re-invent oneself and change careers without having to start from scratch. One effectively becomes 'locked in' by the institutionalized label as narrated by this aspiring fashion designer who entered the labor market twelve years ago: *'I always wanted to be a fashion designer, but when i finished studying* [fashion design] *my teacher introduced me to a company that needed a pattern maker. I have been a pattern maker ever since and it is difficult to change that (…) I still want to do it some day, but now everybody knows me as a pattern maker so I feel I am stuck.'* (Aspiring fashion designer)

On a meta-level, however, these dilemmas rooted in ontological uncertainty or being transfixed, respectively, speak to different loci of control and levels of autonomy and ultimately to the debate of agency vs structure. Invoking the above displayed schematic, the professional identities diverge and empirically inhabit two distinct positions.

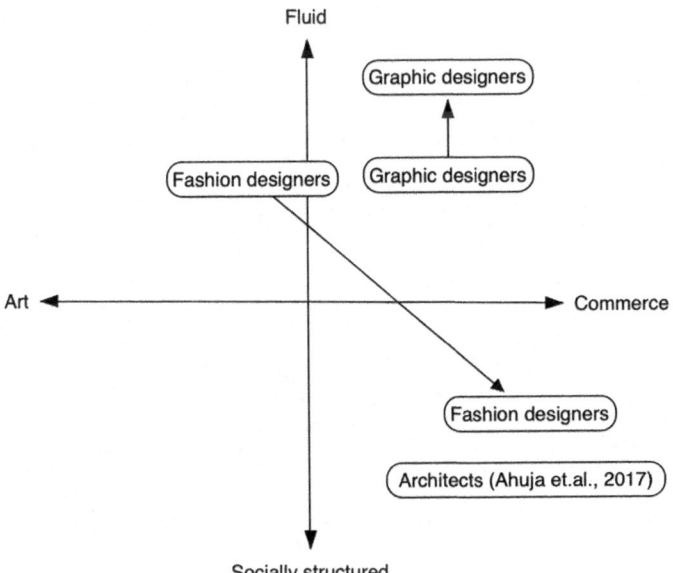

As such, it constitutes a significant departure from the presupposed positions described above where fashion and graphic designer identities were both argued to be fluid. The empirical material, however, revealed that, in the case of fashion designers, the structure is largely dictating the construction of a highly institutionalized professional identity with clear boundaries. Such a professional identity is arguably relatively easy to inhabit as the individual need not construct a career path or re-invent a professional self-image from scratch. Rather, what to do, how to act and, to a certain extent, how to succeed, are ultimately answered in shared professional identity narratives enabling fashion designers to navigate at the workplace and in their career at large. In the case of graphic designers, however, the empirical material suggests that agentic factors play a central role in shaping behaviour. The ambiguous and malleable boundaries of the graphic designer identity enables individuals to be orchestrate their own career trajectory and re-invent themselves, their work-styles or even migrate into related professional fields while retaining a value proposition in the labor market. The cost of all this autonomy, as evidenced in the dilemmas, comes in the absence of external guiding structures and can make everyday work life riddled with stress and anxiety. Further, it places a not unsubstantial amount of responsibility on the individual—both in the already evidenced context of (market) failure and when seeking to progress a career. Fashion designers, on the other hand, narrate dilemmas associated with excess external control and lack of autonomy whereby feeling unfulfilled is sometimes expressed, but the general level of anxiety remain low.

6.6.1 Meta-Identity as Possible Resource

Although graphic and fashion designers may have attitudinal and methodological approaches in common (Michlewski 2015), fashion designers make no reference to a meta-level identity in the shape of a 'designer' in the collected narratives. There is an institutionally set path to becoming a fashion designer which includes being an assistant after completing training and then get promoted to fashion designer. The few accounts of switching professional category involved staying in the fashion industry, but changing to a different work function such as 'buyer' or 'merchandiser' (with substantial difficulty). These accounts are rare and the majority remain fashion designers throughout their career (or restart a career in a different field). Some graphic designers successfully use the expansive nature of the 'designer' label as a resource—what Côté (1996) refers to as 'Identity capital'—when changing fields or as response to market opportunities. As such, the elastic meta-identity constitute a significant resource in the professional identity work of graphic designers—and quite possibly among closely related designers too (as "UI/UX designer" or "brand designer", for instance). 'Creative' was less explicit, however, salient as well. One graphic designer nicely illuminated the importance of being creative and having autonomy when at work while juxtaposing it with stereotypical humdrum work: '*I hate when I am just a factory worker. When a boss says "do this and do that" I just feel like a robot and I am not doing anything creative.*' (Graphic Designer). Thus, there is cause to believe that designers working in a digital space and in the same market domain may hold similarities with regards to professional identity fluidity and dilemmas alike, however, that is an empirical question for future research.

6.7 Conclusion

For Tokyo-based creative professionals, a fashion designer is a fashion designer, but a graphic designer is not a graphic designer. Or put differently, the professional identity of fashion designers is significantly more coherent and supported/policed through a matured institutional setup. It is shared across multiple organizations and stakeholders and permeates the industry. Graphic designers, on the other hand, narrate a significantly more fragmented 'field' of professional identities. Although there is a pervasive understanding of the importance of a commercial imperative, there is a very limited shared ontological narrative to assign meaning and ultimately help navigate work and career and this places a rather heavy burden on graphic designers to create themselves as professionals. There are a some who relish this ambiguity and change their self-category and 'area of expertise' according to circumstance, interest and opportunity (one example from photographer to graphic designer to product designer to business consultant drawing on 'design thinking'). For most this ambiguity led to struggles manifested as identity dilemmas.

As illuminated by the work practice and career narratives, the degree to which designers are different in terms of self-perception or professional identity construct—particularly in the face of salient industry traits—makes referring to 'a professional designer' in a singular and archetypical way implying a coherent designer group-identity close to non-sensical. There are no doubt methodological and attitudinal similarities between graphic designers and fashion designers, however, they operate in two distinctly different institutional fields whereby, among others, physical proximity, outcome tangibility and design praxis differ. In the case of graphic designers, and particular when navigating their career, a meta-identity of 'designer' proved a valuable resource. It enabled the utilization/integration of different designer labels, indeed identities, while still drawing on and valuing from past design-related work. The use of such meta-identity is arguably a function of the highly fluid nature of the graphic designer identity at large, but the more intricate dynamics of such expansive identity work constitute a topic for future research.

It may be possible to draw wider implications from this study, however, limitations should be carefully considered before doing so. Firstly, this study is limited to two distinct design-based professions. A broader array of professional practices in the creative industries may yield different findings. Secondly, it does not claim that the implications are universal within the two professional fields. For instance, there might be particularly cases of designers who do not adhere to a commercial logic in the same way as this study has found. Haute couture fashion designers come to mind has a quantitatively small, but highly visible, group who may operate with a different professional self-conception and perhaps face a different set of identity dilemmas associated with the constraints of a 'signature style'. Thirdly, as the institutional practices and structures change over time and place, a comparative study with designers based outside of Japan may prove valuable. These limitations certainly emphasize the need for a more nuanced view of professional identity in the context of the creative industries.

References

Ahuja, S., Nikolova, N., & Clegg, S. (2017). Paradoxical identity: The changing nature of architectural work and its relation to architects' identity. *Journal of Professions and Organization 4*(1).

Alvesson, M., & Willmott, H. (2002). Identity regulation as organizational control: Producing the appropriate individual. *Journal of Management Studies 39*(5).

Archer, L. (2008). Younger academics' constructions of "authenticity", "success" and professional identity. *Studies in Higher Education. Routledge, 33*(4), 385–403.

Bamberg, M. (2011). Who am I? Narration and its contribution to self and identity. *Theory & Psychology, 21*(1), 3–24.

Bauman, Z., & Raud, R. (2015). *Practices of selfhood*. Cambridge: Polity.

Beech, N., Gilmore, C., Cochrane, E., & Greig, G. (2012). Identity work as a response to tensions: A re-narration in opera rehearsals. *Scandinavian Journal of Management, 28*(1), 39–47.

Brown, A. D. (2015). Identities and identity work in organizations. *International Journal of Management Reviews, 17*(1), 20–40.

Brown, T. (2009). *Change by design: How design thinking transforms organizations and inspires innovation*. New York: Harper Collins.

Caves, R. E. (2000). *Creative industries—contracts between art and commerce*. Cambridge, Mass.: Harvard University Press.

Caza, B. B., & Creary, S. J. (2016). The construction of professional identity. Retrieved June 23, 2018 from Cornell University, SHA School. https://scholarship.sha.cornell.edu/articles/878/. In A. Wilkinson, D. Hislop & C. Coupland (Eds.), *Perspectives on contemporary professional work: Challenges and experiences* (pp. 259–285). Cheltenham, UK: Edward Elgar.

Côté, J. E. (1996). Sociological perspectives on identity formation: The culture-identity link and identity capital. *Journal of Adolescence, 19*(5), 417–428.

Crossley, J., & Vivekananda-Schmidt, P. (2009). The development and evaluation of a professional self identity questionnaire to measure evolving professional self-identity in health and social care students. *Medical Teacher, 31*(12), e603–e607.

Cruess, R. L., Cruess, S. R., Boudreau, J. D., Snell, L., & Steinert, Y. (2015). A schematic representation of the professional identity formation and socialization of medical students and residents. *Academic Medicine, 90*(6), 718–725.

Czarniawska, B. (1998). *A narrative approach to organization studies*. Thousand Oaks, Cal.: Sage Publications.

Davies, B., & Harre, R. (1990). Positioning: The discursive production of selves. *Journal for the Theory of Social Behaviour 20*(1), 43–63.

DeFillippi, R. (2009). Dilemmas of project-based media work: Contexts and choices. *Journal of Media Business Studies, 6*(4), 5–30.

DeFillippi, R., Grabher, G., & Jones, C. (2007). Introduction to paradoxes of creativity: Managerial and organizational challenges in the cultural economy. *Journal of Organizational Behavior, 28*(5), 511–521.

Eikhof, D. R., & Haunschild, A. (2006). Lifestyle meets market: Bohemian entrepreneurs in creative industries. *Creativity and Innovation Management, 13*(3), 234–241.

Eikhof, D. R., & Haunschild, A. (2007). For art's sake! Artistic and economic logics in creative production. *Journal of Organizational Behavior, 28*(5), 523–538.

Florida, R. (2002). *The rise of the creative class, and how it's transforming work, leisure, community and everyday life*. New York: Basic Books.

Gotsi, M., Andriopoulos, C., Lewis, M. W., & Ingram, A. E. (2010). Managing creatives: Paradoxical approaches to identity regulation. *Human Relations, 63*(6), 781–805.

Grey, C. (1994). Career as a project of the self and labour process discipline. *Sociology, 28*, 479.

Hazen, M. A. (1993). Towards polyphonic organization. *Journal of Organizational Change Management, 6*(5), 15–28.

Hesmondhalgh, D. (2007). *The cultural industries* (2nd ed.). Thousand Oaks, Cal.: Sage.

Hogg, M. A. (2009). Managing self-uncertainty through group identification. *Psychological Inquiry, 20*(4), 221–224.

Hogg, M. A., & Terry, D. J. (2000). Social identity and self-categorization processes in organizational contexts. *Academy of Management Review, 25,* 121–140.

Ibarra, H. (1999). Provisional selves: Experimenting with image and identity in professional adaptation. *Administrative Science Quarterly, 44*(4), 764–791.

Kelley, D., & Kelley, T. (2013). *Creative confidence: Unleashing the creative potential within us all.* New York: Crown Business.

Kreiner, G. E., Hollensbe, E. C., & Sheep, M. (2006). Where is the 'Me' among the 'We'? Identity work and the search for optimal balance. *Academy of Management Journal, 49*(5), 1031–1057.

Lampel, J., Land, T., & Shamsie, J. (2000). Balancing act: Learning from organizing practices in cultural industries. *Organization Science, 11,* 263–269.

van Lankveld, T., Schoonenboom, J., Kusurkar, R. A., Volman, M., Beishuizen, J., & Croiset, G. (2017). Integrating the teaching role into one's identity: A qualitative study of beginning undergraduate medical teachers. *Advances in Health Sciences Education, 22*(3), 601–622.

Michlewski, K. (2015). *Design attitude.* New York: Routledge.

Pine, B. J., & Gilmore, J. H. (1999). *The experience economy: Work is theatre & every business a stage.* Boston Mass: Harvard Business School Press.

Pratt, M. G., Rockmann, K. W., & Kaufmann, J. B. (2006). Constructing professional identity: The role of work and identity learning cycles in the customization of identity among medical residents. *Academy of Management Journal, 49*(2), 235–262.

Riessman, C. (2006). Narrative analysis. In V. Jupp (Ed.), *The SAGE dictionary of social research methods.* Thousand Oaks, Cal.: Sage.

Siebert, D. C., & Siebert, C. F. (2005). The caregiver role identity scale: A validation study. *Research on Social Work Practice, 15,* 204–212.

Sims, D. (2005). Living a story and storying a life—a narrative understanding of the distributed self. In A. Pullen & S. Linstead (Eds.), *Organization and identity* (pp. 86–104). New York: Routledge.

Slay, H., & Smith, D. A. (2011). Professional identity construction: Using narrative to understand the negotiation of professional and stigmatized cultural identities. *Human Relations, 64,* 85–107.

Stockhausen, L. J. (2005). Learning to become a nurse: Students reflections on their clinical experiences. *Australian Journal of Advanced Nursing, 22*(3), 8–14.

Sveningsson, S., & Alvesson, M. (2003). Managerial identities: Organizational fragmentation, discourse and identity struggle. *Human Relations, 56,* 1163–1193.

Sydow, J. (2006). Managing projects in network contexts: A structuration perspective. In D. Hodgson & S. Cicmik (Eds.), *Making projects critical* (pp. 252–264). Palgrave: Houndmills, Basingstoke.

Thornton, P. H., Ocasio, W., & Lounsbury, M. (2012). The institutional logics perspective. In *Emerging trends in the social and behavioral sciences* (pp. 1–22). Hoboken, NJ, USA: John Wiley & Sons, Inc.,

Van Maanen, J., & Barley, S. R. (1984). Occupational communities: Culture and control in organizations. *Research in Organizational Behavior, 6,* 287–365.

Woodward, K. (2002). *Understanding identity.* Arnold.

Ybema, S., Keenoy, T., Oswick, C., Beverungen, A., Ellis, N., & Sabelis, I. (2009). Articulating identities. *Human Relations, 62*(3), 299–322.

Chapter 7
Creativity at the Margins in the 'Golden Age' of Japanese Cinema (1945–1965)

Jennifer Coates

We often think of popular cinema as one of the more accessible creative arts. But where is this creativity located, and how is creativity fostered or suppressed within the cinema industry? For creativity to exist within the creative industries, an industry or workplace must allow that creativity to develop. While some forms of creativity are explicitly supported in financial, material, and motivational terms, others are inadvertently blocked, deliberately suppressed, or lack encouragement. In such instances, creativity in the creative industries can take on different forms, and constructing a career in such restricted circumstances becomes in itself an exercise in creativity. For example, finding a way to work in an unsupportive workplace, or with limited funds, is an exercise in creativity. This kind of creativity exists not only within the industry workplace, but also at its margins. In some cases, agents even convert cultural capital from outside the industry workplace into creative power within the workplace. Making space to produce creative work can include rhetorically invoking or physically inhabiting roles and spaces outside the creative industry in question, for example, in the domestic sphere. Taking the 'golden age' of the postwar Japanese cinema industry as a case study, this chapter explores how individuals pushed to the margins of the studio system took creative measures to increase their own creative capacities.

Strictly censored by the Allied Occupation forces, and with a constant eye on the financial bottom line, the postwar Japanese film industry was not a free creative space. Directors and actors were restricted by exclusive long-term contracts with the dominant studios, enforced by inter-studio cooperation that prevented anyone who broke contract with one studio being employed by another for a set period of time. Studio executives relied on the popular press to both promote and discipline actors and directors. This chapter explores the marginalization and subsequent creative triumphs of actor Kogure Michiyo (1918–1990) and director Ichikawa Kon (1915–2008) to demonstrate how creative strategies for overcoming bureaucratic studio obstacles developed in unusual places, including the gossip press, the advertising

J. Coates (✉)
The University of Sheffield, Sheffield, UK
e-mail: jennifer.coates@sheffield.ac.uk

© Springer Nature Singapore Pte Ltd. 2020
N. Otmazgin and E. Ben-Ari (eds.), *Creative Context*, Creative Economy,
https://doi.org/10.1007/978-981-15-3056-2_7

industry, and the domestic sphere. By understanding creativity in the 'golden age' of Japanese cinema as a response to industrial, economic, and bureaucratic restrictions, we can better understand what creativity entails.

This chapter does not focus solely on the kinds of creativity analyzed by much extant scholarship, such as, for example, an actor's creative portrayal or a director's creative aesthetic. Instead the case studies to follow highlight the forms and processes by which filmmakers demonstrate organizational creativity by finding innovative ways to pursue a career in spite of significant obstacles. In this respect, this chapter addresses not only scholarly blindness to the margins of creative endeavour, but also a persistent lack of acknowledgement of the forms through which careering is made within the creative industries. Informed by Pierre Bourdieu's "The Forms of Capital" (1986) the analysis which follows demonstrates how forms of capital can be converted to allow for greater creative opportunities within a restrictive industry.

7.1 Making Films in Postwar Japan

Based on the name, we might expect the second 'golden age' of Japanese cinema to be a peak point of creativity. The period 1945–1965 saw rapidly growing audience numbers, peaking in 1958. Audience attendance was calculated at 733 million (rounded to the nearest million) in 1946, increasing by 3.2% in 1947, 1.7% in 1948 and 3.7% in 1949, and surpassing one billion in 1957 (Izbicki 1997: 46). The number of cinema theatres increased steadily year on year before peaking at 7457 in 1960. The cinema industry was supported and funded by a dedicated mass audience without many competing attractions and enjoyed a diverse range of exhibition opportunities.

Audiences watched both domestic and imported film content in the new cinema theatres of the postwar era. During the Occupation of Japan (1945–1952), the offices of the Supreme Commander for the Allied Powers (hereafter SCAP) controlled the import of foreign films to Japan, with a heavy bias for American Hollywood productions (Terasawa 2010: 55). In the early years after defeat, as the domestic film industry recuperated, almost half the films screened in Japan were not created at home. In 1946, thirty-nine American films, five foreign films of non-American origin (all imported before the war) and sixty-seven Japanese films were screened. By 1950 foreign imports had risen to 185, 133 of which were American. A new quota system was introduced in the same year to cap foreign imports based on the number of films from a particular country shown over the previous ten years. After the control of foreign film importation was given over to the Japanese government in 1951, the percentage of foreign films released in Japan declined from 52.7 to 40.7% between 1951 and 1952 (Terasawa 2010: 56). In 1955, 514 Japanese films were released, accounting for 65.8% of all films screened in commercial cinemas, while by 1960 the percentage of domestic productions screened had risen to 78.3%. Occupation era import laws and the post-Occupation cap on foreign imports further supported the well-attended Japanese cinema by restricting competition from international film industries.

At the same time however, Occupation era cinema content was heavily censored. The offices of SCAP, headed by General Douglas MacArthur, explicitly positioned the cinema as a means to change the attitudes of the general public. Cinema content was developed under strict information dissemination and censorship guidelines. After beginning the Occupation of Japan on 2 September 1945, SCAP quickly circulated the Memorandum Concerning Elimination of Japanese Government Control of the Motion Picture Industry on 16 October 1945 (Hirano 1992: 39), indicating the importance to the Occupiers of placing the cinema industry under new controls (Kitamura 2010: 42). SCAP personnel instructed Japanese filmmakers in the kind of content understood by the Occupiers to be desirable, assessing synopses and screenplays, before final film prints were censored or suppressed.

In the first years of the Occupation, SCAP personnel were proactive in encouraging the production of films that reflected the Allied Occupation's democratic agenda. The Motion Picture division of the Civil Information and Education Section (hereafter CIE) checked synopses, screenplays, and filming plans, while the Civil Censorship Detachment (hereafter CCD) examined prints. Finished products were sent back to the studios for cuts. SCAP even attempted to formulate a hypothetical typical audience member known as Moe-san (Mayo 1984: 303). Moe-san was a composite of information gathered by Allied intelligence and researchers during and immediately after the war. Based on their understanding of wartime schooling and social indoctrination, Occupation personnel attempted to predict Moe-san's reaction to the media of the postwar period, with the intention of influencing the ideal audiences' 'democratization' through this same media (Mayo 1984: 303).

Removing Home Ministry controls after 1945, SCAP encouraged major studios Tōhō, Shōchiku, and Daiei to resume production as soon as possible (Kitamura 2010: 43). Smaller studios were merged to create industry giants, as the 1947 merger of Tōyoko Eiga, Ōizumi Eiga, and distribution company Tokyo Eiga Haikyū created Tōei studios. Formally established in 1951, Tōei was known as "the production factory of the popular" (*tsūzoku no seizō kōjō*) (Standish 2005: 272), indicating the large output and competitive over-production encouraged at the major studios. Yet the actual creative production inside the studio system was strictly controlled. SCAP was invested in turning the Japanese studios into productive powerhouses, but not necessarily creative ones.

Nonetheless, the studio system managed to produce not only popular entertainment films, but also the classics that won Japanese cinema's first international awards. Japanese films came to dominate the international film festival scene in the early postwar era, winning a significant number of awards at European film festivals during the 1950s, as well as at US award ceremonies. Path-breaker Kurosawa Akira received numerous awards for *Rashomon* (*Rashōmon*, 1950) including the Golden Lion at the Venice Film Festival in 1951 and the Academy Award for Best Foreign Language Film in 1952. Gosho Heinosuke's *Where Chimneys Are Seen* (*Entotsu no mieru basho*, 1953) won acclaim at the 3rd Berlin International Film Festival. Kurosawa's *Ikiru* (1952) and Ōzu Yasujirō's *Tokyo Story* (*Tokyo monogatari*, 1953) competed at the 4th Berlin International Film Festival in 1954, while Mizoguchi Kenji won the Silver Bear at the Venice Film Festival for *Tale of Ugetsu* (*Ugetsu monogatari*, 1953).

Gate of Hell (*Jigokumon*, Kinugasa Teinosuke, 1953), the first Japanese colour film to have an international release, received an Oscar in 1954 for Best Costume Design (Wada Sanzo) and an Honorary Award for Best Foreign Language Film and became the first Japanese film to win the Palme d'Or at the Cannes Film Festival in the same year. Inagaki Hiroshi won an Academy Award for Best Foreign Language Film for Part I of his *Samurai* trilogy (*Miyamoto Musashi*, 1954) in 1955, and Ichikawa Kon's *The Burmese Harp* (*Buruma no tategoto*, 1956) was nominated for Best Foreign Language Film at the Academy Awards. Inagaki also received the Golden Lion at the Venice Film Festival for *Rickshaw Man* (*Muhōmatsu no issho,* 1957) in 1958. Kobayashi Masaki's *Kwaidan* (*Kaidan*, 1965) was awarded the Special Jury Prize at Cannes and nominated for Best Foreign Language Film at the Academy Awards, and Teshigahara Hiroshi's *Woman in the Dunes* (*Suna no onna*, 1964) won the Special Jury Prize at the Cannes Film Festival and was nominated for Oscars for the Best Director and Best Foreign Language Film. In the first decades after World War II, Japanese cinema broadcast the creative triumphs of the defeated nation struggling back to international recognition.

Given this commercial and artistic success, we could reasonably assume the major studios to be hotbeds of creativity. This era of film production certainly conforms to a definition of creativity understood as the creation of new market opportunities, as Japanese cinema found new audiences and fans overseas through successful competition at international film festivals. Yet looking more closely at the social, political, legal, and structural constraints imposed on key groups of creatives such as actors, directors, and scenario writers, the picture becomes more complicated. Actors, directors, and scenario writers often appear to have achieved universally recognized creative excellence in spite of, rather than with the support of, the film industry and its bureaucratic personnel. In this respect, the era was also a period of career building innovation at the personal or micro-level, as well as market expansion at the structural or mezzo level, and the international or macro level.

7.2   Restrictions on Creativity Within the Studio System

The new postwar studios remained vertically integrated, developing film content in-house with teams of staff contracted to the studios, and exhibiting new films in studio-owned theatres before renting them out to the second- and third-run cinemas that charged lower entrance fees and showed older films. When a studio produced a popular film, the profits went straight back into the studio, but when a film lost money at the box office, the cost was borne by the studio. In the early postwar era of rationing when raw materials, including film stock, were in short supply, a studio could lose a lot of money very quickly due to the vertical integration model. For this reason, the box office performance of a film was of ultimate importance to the studio heads, and directors such as Ichikawa Kon were penalized for making films that failed to earn big box office receipts. Actors were rarely entrusted to lead big-budget films unless they could demonstrate a loyal audience following large enough to ensure a good turnout at the box office. Studio personnel monitored film content, style, and casting with an eye on the bottom line.

The Allied Occupation bureaucracy imposed further restrictions by censoring film content both before and after production. CIE officers would meet with studio personnel to review planned film projects, striking out any elements on a pre-circulated list of banned topics which included direct mention of the Occupation itself, as well as sympathetic depiction of Japan's war effort, defeat, or Imperial ideology. CIE personnel exhorted filmmakers to include preferred topics, themes, and characterizations at the planning stages of a new film. Policy documents such as the Political Information-Education Program prepared by the CIE in June 1948 called for all media branches to coordinate in an effort to make Japanese audiences aware of the rights and responsibilities of democratic citizens (Tsuchiya 2002: 196). The document advised liaising directly with Japanese film producers to persuade them to include material and themes related to the political education of the Japanese populace. In November, this document was developed into a 158-page book titled *Information Programs*, designed as reference material for all CIE officers (National Archives II at College Park, Maryland, RG 331, GHQ/SCAP, CIE, Box 5305, file 12 and 15). When a film had been shot and edited, the CCD then removed any material violating the censor's code.

Films were expected to educate their viewers as to how a modern, postwar, democratic life should be lived. Central to this agenda was gender equality, a goal SCAP identified with the destruction of perceived 'feudal' attitudes in Japan. To this end, the Allied bureaucracy instructed Beate Sirota Gordon and others to draft Article 24 for the 1947 Constitution, which outlawed discrimination on the basis of sex and granted new rights to women and girls. Filmmakers were commanded to create strong democratic female characterizations and stories, in an attempt to use the aspirational power of cinema to make the new gender ideals into reality. Cinephile David Conde, head of the Motion Picture and Theatrical branch of the CIE until July 1946, encouraged studios to present a positive image of women on film, and banned the production of films which "deal with or approve the subjugation or degradation of women" (Freiberg 1992: 101). Conde instructed filmmakers to avoid confining women to domestic familial roles "considering their newly upgraded social status" (Hirano 1992: 149). Studios and scriptwriters were encouraged to produce narratives and imagery that depicted emancipated Japanese women as aspirational and instances of female subservience were deleted from film scripts (Kitamura 2010: 60). SCAP influence over film content continued until June 1949, when the Motion Picture Code of Ethics Committee (*Eiga Rinri Kitei Kanri Iinkai*), a self-regulating organization modeled on the Motion Picture Producers and Distributors of America (later the MPAA) took over. By then, certain elements of studio infrastructure mandated by SCAP had become standard, such as the hiring of large numbers of female actors to meet SCAP's demand for female leading roles. In this way, SCAP ideological goals influenced the material structure and staffing of the Japanese studio system, and this influence outlasted the Occupation itself in several aspects.

7.3   The Actor as Creative: Working in the Postwar Studio System

The postwar studio system controlled not only the production and distribution of films in Japan (subject to SCAP approval), but also determined to an extent which actors could star in particular films. The heads of the major studios participated in a monopoly agreement that held each studio to a collective promise not to employ stars that had left other major studios within a set period of time. This agreement allowed the major studios to build big-budget productions around star personae, but the monopoly also served the interests of some stars, as a budding star persona could be based around the 'persona' of the studio. Young stars at Nikkatsu, for example, formed their public personae around the showy and nihilistic aura of the *taiyōzoku* 'sun tribe' film genre, while Ozu Yasujirō's gentle home dramas for Shōchiku cast a classic nostalgia over their stars.

Competitive overproduction created a demand for new stars, and at the same time, studios that had focused on male-centric war epics until 1945 were suddenly faced with a mass of new censor-mandated roles for women, and few actresses to take them on. In response, the studios developed recruitment drives such as the New Faces search, which became a public event in which young actors were chosen from open auditions and from the choruses of review shows and the popular Takarazuka Opera. Creating public star-searches that doubled as publicity stunts, the major studios hired a large number of actresses over the first four years of the Occupation. When censorship was handed over to the Film Ethics Regulation Control Committee in June 1949 (effectively becoming industry self-censorship), the predominance of female roles continued for a number of years due to the large number of actresses contracted to each studio, despite a decreasing political focus on gender equality.

Much like the Hollywood studio system, the Japanese studio system strictly forbade contracted staff to work with other studios, unless hired out by their home studio. Major stars were in such high demand that studios could refuse to lend them, while an unpopular or low-earning performer could be hired out or dropped from their contract. Studios controlled actors' means of self-publicization by managing journalists' access to stars, and used the industry and gossip press to promote or discipline actors. Though a major star could survive an attack from the gossip press, the public personae of less popular stars could be seriously damaged by bad publicity.

This added an element of risk for individual actors, potentially restricting the playfulness or 'play with form' that generally characterizes creativity. Standing out amongst the massed ranks of 'New Faces' that arrived at the studios each year could ensure access to greater opportunities for creativity in the form of bigger parts, more screen time, and the opportunity to play challenging characters. At the same time, standing out for the wrong reasons put an actor at risk of condemnation by the gossip and industry presses, which could lead to rejection from audiences, and becoming stigmatized as box office poison. This outcome would block off career opportunities that offered more creative acting practice. In this situation, actors had to balance opportunity against risk and craft their star persona carefully. While the creation of an everyday persona was a subtler art than the dramatic acting skills captured onscreen in this era, in many ways it required more creativity. To make matters more difficult, a convincing star persona required an element of playfulness to appear natural and warm, and so actors learned to simulate the playfulness of creativity under risky circumstances.

Personal creative power was largely dependent on audience following; while bankable stars had a degree of creative freedom, choosing and shaping acting roles and even taking on directorial projects, less popular stars were at the mercy of their studio. Popularity, power, and independence were closely connected. Sufficient popularity and artistic renown allowed actors to make bold career moves unavailable to those considered less valuable within the studio system. High profile actors could even test the studio's monopoly agreements to move between studios. In 1956, Hidari Sachiko moved from Shin-Tōhō to Nikkatsu, Minamida Yōko moved from Daiei to Nikkatsu, and Kitahara Mie from Shōchiku to Nikkatsu. All three converted their popularity and box office earning power into the freedom to choose their creative environment. Hidari even became Japan's third female director, directing an episode of the ensemble film *Hot Pants* (*L'Amour Au Féminin*, Jean-Gabriel Albicocco, Thomas Fantl, Hidari Sachiko) in 1971 before planning, producing, and directing *The Far Road* (*Toi ippon no michi*) in 1977. A carefully crafted yet seemingly spontaneous star persona could pay off quite significantly for the lucky or creative actor who managed to get it right.

Prizes such as leading parts and greater independence within the studio system were offset by horror stories about those who got it wrong—unlucky actors cast out from or abused by the studio system, published in the popular gossip press (Coates 2016: 40). In extreme cases magazines even reported on death from neglect and overwork at the lowest ends of the star spectrum (Anon 1947: 53), clearly connecting unsuccessful star personae with personal as well as professional risk. Stars were disciplined both through the vertical hierarchies of the studio system and by the popular press to understand greater popularity as greater earning power, and therefore greater success, resulting in increased freedom, compensation, and opportunity. On the other hand, failures lead to public shame and potential financial and physical ruin.

In this respect, we can think of star persona in the postwar studio system as a kind of capital. Oliver Driessens argues for extending Bourdieu's field theory to the study of contemporary celebrity, understanding celebrity as a kind of capital that can be converted into other resources such as economic or political capital (2013). This chapter is focused more narrowly on the conversion of the cultural and social capital held by famous actors and stars into economic capital that is used within the studio system itself to attain creative freedom. As Bourdieu argues, in certain circumstances, capital "amounts to the same thing" as power (1986: 243). Within the restrictive environment of the postwar Japanese film industry, actors had to get creative about self-presentation in order to convert their skills and popularity into the earning power that bought creative freedom. This off-screen creativity (in the service of greater on-screen opportunity) is the focus of the following case studies.

7.4   Creative Career Strategies: The Case of Kogure
Michiyo

In 1947, actress Kogure Michiyo became a target of the gossip press when *Eiga bunko* (*Film Library*) magazine's gossip column "Star Record" (*Sutā toroku*) took aim at the organization of her domestic and working lives (Anon 1947: 15). An anonymous columnist expressed snarky concern about how Kogure balanced her domestic roles with her career. "As a housewife and mother, how does she keep up home life and her life as an actress without failing in either?" (*Katei no shufu de ari, ko no haha de aru kanajo ga, katei seikatsu to joyū seikatsu to o ika ni hatan naku ikinukō ka*) (Anon. 1947: 15). Kogure was a moderately popular actress, a style icon for women and something of a sex symbol for male critics, who appreciated her "sex appeal" (*iroke*) (Matsubara 1948: 13). Within the studio system however, negative public perceptions of one's domestic arrangements and off-screen life could cost an actress valuable fans, and thereby box office bankability. With her creative future at stake, Kogure found a creative way to defend her public persona against this attack, and in the process stumbled on a winning formula for workplace success that guaranteed future opportunities for a wide variety of acting roles.

Kogure attempted to create a more coherent onscreen/off-screen persona by penning a small personal advice column in *Eiga Fan* (*Film Fan*) magazine titled "The Key to My Life as a Housewife" (Kogure 1949: 33). Her advice was carefully crafted to support key aspects of her onscreen star persona, shaped by warm comedic supporting roles such as Umetaro, the friendly local geisha of *Blue Mountains* (*Aoi sanmyaku*, Imai Tadashi, 1949).

> You should lovingly depend on your husband [*otto ni amaeru*] and make use of women's gentle nature [*yasashisa*] to make harmony in the home. Getting a little silly in the home is the secret to housewife life I think. When I'm alone in the house I like to do childish foolish things [*baka*], like play "Catch ball." You should take time apart from your husband sometimes [*tokidoki otto to hanareru*]. We are separated due to work, so thanks to this everyday is like a honeymoon [*shinkon*]! Housewife life keeps you in beautiful health [*shufu seikatsu wa utsukushiku kenkō*]. (Kogure 1949: 33)

Kogure's account of her home life mirrors her onscreen persona in the inclusion of anecdotes about playing childish physical games, repeating playful actions she was often seen performing on film. Her appeal to woman's "gentle nature" positions the reader, imagined as female, in the same category as Kogure, emphasizing their similarities to create feelings of sympathy and understanding. Positioning the reader in intimate relation to the star in this way was also highly seductive, as the glamour of Kogure's star persona was reflected onto the reader by way of her claim to a shared experience. Kogure fostered this intimate affect with phrases such as "when I'm alone" and "the key [or secret, *hiketsu*] to my life," which imply that the reader is a privileged observer to the private aspects of her off-screen 'real' life. This could encourage warm feeling towards the actress, and an enjoyable sense of inclusion. Bourdieu argues that the "non-monetary investments" of cultural and social capital are "affective" and can be converted to have significant yield in the marketplace

(1986: 255). Kogure's writing demonstrates clearly how affect can be created, converted, and then banked as social capital in her successful appeal for her readers' loyalty and affection.

Kogure's depiction of her life as a stay-at-home housewife was also highly aspirational. Though the popular press followed SCAP's lead in championing the stay-at-home wife and mother as the ideal modern, emancipated woman, few nuclear families could afford to leave half the workforce at home (Uno 1993: 303; Liddle and Nakajima 2000: 175). Kogure downplayed her non-household-related work in her writing (though the writing itself was an example of this kind of work), referencing outside employment only in positive relation to its impact on her home life; for example, being apart during working hours was credited (*sono okage de*) with improving her marital relationship. Kogure obfuscated the fact that *both* she and her husband worked outside the home, making it possible for the reader to interpret her advice in the context of the idealized housewife waiting for her husband to return home. The reader was implicitly encouraged to believe that Kogure's housework was her whole work experience, even though this was clearly not the case. In this rhetorical move, Kogure leveraged the cultural capital attained by implying that her household is wealthy enough to have a stay-at-home housewife to encourage admiration in her readership. This converted her cultural capital into social capital by increasing the number of readers in her fan group, "a durable network of more or less institutionalized relationships" as Bourdieu might put it (1986: 248). The potential resources of this fan group would become actual resources when the fans invested economically in Kogure, buying tickets to her movies and purchasing the goods she promoted. Kogure would in turn give back to the fan group with images of and narrative accounts about herself and her fictionalized private life.

Kogure's ultra-domestic, ultra-feminine re-creation of her star persona also aligned her with SCAP's socio-political agenda, while selling her 'just one of the girls' persona to audiences primed by censor-shaped popular press content to recognize her domestic life as the postwar female ideal. By blending Occupation-compliant imagery with relatable beliefs and humour, Kogure fashioned a star persona that proved convenient for a studio system caught between meeting censors' demands and attempting to increase fan loyalty and thereby box-office commerce. Shōchiku studio soon promoted Kogure to her first leading role in Ozu Yasujirō's groundbreaking divorce comedy, *The Flavour of Green Tea Over Rice* (*Ochazuke no aji*, 1952), while Sanyo Electric hired her for a long-running advertising campaign (Yoshimi 1999: 158). Kogure's reward for her creative response to the disciplining and gender-conservative gossip press was greater work opportunities, fame, and money, paradoxically achieved by posing in the gossip press as a devoted housewife.

In this way, creative stars could convert the cultural capital of an idealized home life into public popularity, which could then be converted into greater power and freedom within the studio system, leading often to increased earnings. This process can be analyzed by understanding each stage of exchange as a mode of capital as defined by Bourdieu.

Depending on the field in which it functions, and at the cost of the more or less expensive transformations which are the precondition for its efficacy in the field in question, capital can present itself in three fundamental guises: as economic capital, which is immediately and directly convertible into money and may be institutionalized in the form of property rights; as cultural capital, which is convertible, in certain conditions, into economic capital and may be institutionalized in the form of educational qualifications; and as social capital, made up of social obligations ("connections"), which is convertible, in certain conditions, into economic capital and may be institutionalized in the form of a title of nobility. (Bourdieu 1986: 243)

Cultural capital takes three distinct forms: the embodied state ("long-lasting dispositions of the mind and body"); the objectified state (cultural goods); and the institutionalized state (for example, educational qualifications). Furthermore, "ability or talent is itself the product of an investment of time and cultural capital" (Bourdieu 1986: 244). Not only the actor's carefully crafted personal representations, but also their acting talent, can be understood as cultural capital in the sense of requiring an investment of time and training.

Kogure's personal advice column can be read as an exercise in converting cultural capital into social capital. By demonstrating her familiarity with the objects and forms that constituted an agreed-upon 'good life' in early postwar Japan, Kogure inferred a degree of elite status, education, and training in the field of homemaking, with the cultural capital such qualifications are "presumed to guarantee" (Bourdieu 1986: 243). The column is littered with references to objects and household goods than suggest a wealthy lifestyle, supported by Kogure's insistence on the physical nature of housework. Her home was clearly to be imagined as spacious and full of tasteful objects. In this way, she leveraged an objectified form of cultural capital to encourage an aspirational response from readers. Her claim that "everyday is like a honeymoon!" not only depicted her everyday life as enviously joyful, but also referenced a new and expensive way of marking wedding celebrations that reminded the reader of her wealth, modernity, and good taste.

Kogure also channelled the embodied form of cultural capital in a number of ways. Her reference to "women's gentle nature" suggested an elite upbringing learning the manners that indicate social capital in the form of membership of an elite group. In fact, actors at the major studios were often subjected to a kind of hot-house equivalent of elite etiquette training, as women in particular were required to learn certain dance and movement forms associated with the upper classes in their first years at the studio. Nonetheless, the "long-lasting dispositions of the mind and body" resulting from this training could be passed off as embodied social capital. Kogure also boasted of her "beautiful health", supported by an author portrait showing the star in full make up with her hair stylishly arranged, looking out at the viewer with her head resting on one hand, as though listening attentively. While describing her elite and aspirational home life, Kogure nonetheless represented herself as paying careful attention to the everyday women to whom her column was directed, modelling the consideration for others expected of well-brought up women.

In painting Kogure as an aspirational yet relatable member of an elite class in order to increase her fan base, the advice column converted her demonstration of cultural capital into social capital. Within the studio system, stars with greater fan bases and media exposure were considered more bankable, and offered bigger roles, better projects, and opportunities outside the studio, such as advertising contracts. In this way social capital could be converted to economic capital in the form of increased wages for the star and bigger box office takings for the studio. Popular stars could "mobilize by proxy the capital of a group" (Bourdieu 1986: 256) in order to buy themselves a stronger position within the studio system.

Yet the process of generating and converting cultural capital into social capital and eventually into economic capital never ends. Kogure's appearances for Sanyo Electric continued the process into the 1950s as she played the role of Mrs. Sanyo, marked as a qualified homemaker by her marital status and display of physical skill. The object markers of her status as elite homemaker surrounded her in each advertisement – electric household goods such as washing machines complemented bright white aprons and flawless styling, demonstrating cultural capital in its objectified form. This was converted into social capital as Kogure became a ubiquitous face familiar even to those who did not follow cinema culture, and successfully convinced a number of households to invest in Sanyo goods, the sale of which boosted her own and the company's economic capital. This conversion cycle continued throughout her career and is evident in the career histories of a number of creatives working in the golden age of studio production. As Bourdieu observes, "reproduction of social capital presupposes an unceasing effort of sociability, a continuous series of exchanges in which recognition is endlessly affirmed and re-affirmed" (1986: 250). Stars continuously demonstrated their recognition of their fan base by sharing intimate details through the gossip press, in order to keep producing the social capital that could command mass turnouts at the box office.

7.5 Locating Creativity: Work Versus Family

We could say that Kogure leveraged the cultural capital of her family life to achieve greater freedom and power in her workplace. To increase her creative power at work, she built a public persona around her role in the home. For female-focused home dramas of the type in which Kogure appeared, box office sales were made on the strength of star appeal as much as on the reputation of the director. The word choice and positioning suggest that Kogure created her advice column to directly appeal to female readers, building her fan base and increasing her box office appeal for the demographic most likely to have been the readership of the gossip magazines which had previously criticized her. This approach certainly convinced Shōchiku and Sanyo, who hired her on a more prominent basis thereafter. In this example, the home is no longer a space of leisure but becomes a secondary workplace, an arena where valuable cultural capital is generated, to be exchanged for social and then economic capital within the primary or officially recognized workplace. While the home has long been the workplace for women, whether primary or secondary, Kogure's career move demonstrates how the home and the professional workplace are inextricably linked in the conversion of capital. We must therefore broaden our understanding of the kinds of workplaces in which creative work takes place.

The home as workplace reappears in the creative narratives of directors as well as actors. Like Kogure, director Ichikawa Kon's frequent battles with the studios were mediated through public representations of his married life. Studios were reluctant to waste the in-house training received by directors in the era before film schools, and often signed young men graduating from assistant director to director roles to long-term exclusive contracts. For this reason, the studios would penalize rather than fire unsuccessful directors, assigning them salvage operations on pre-purchased text adaptations, or vehicles for contracted actors. Thanks to his wife, respected scenarist Wada Natto, Ichikawa was able to turn such impossible projects into creative successes; Audie Bock characterizes their professional relationship as the "reliance" of the director on the scenario writer (Bock 2001: 40). When Ichikawa was assigned to direct *An Actor's Revenge* (*Yukinojo henge*) as punishment for a series of box office failures by Daiei studio, Wada stepped into help, and public discourse on their romantic partnership became part of the legend of this creative success.

7.6   A Screenwriter's Revenge: Besting the Studio System

After disappointing box office returns on a string of literary adaptations including *Conflagration* (*Enjō*, 1958) and *Odd Obsession* (*Kagi*, 1959), Daiei Studios instructed Ichikawa to re-make Kinugasa Teinosuke's *Revenge of a Kabuki Actor*, a 30-year-old silent film that had lain in storage for years (McDonald 1994: 145). The film had been the biggest box office hit in the history of Japanese cinema in 1935, and starred Hasegawa Kazuo, then preparing to make his 300th film with Daiei. Studio personnel decreed that *An Actor's Revenge* would be that film, and that Ichikawa would direct it. To add insult to injury, the director was required to use the studio's new DaieiScope format, which he resisted to no avail (Ichikawa 2001: 303). *An Actor's Revenge* was clearly not an economic priority for the studio in terms of expense but was nonetheless expected to earn some return at the box office. Ichikawa's restricted budget was evident in the outdated scenery and use of aging matinee idol Hasegawa Kazuo in not one but two roles, playing both a loveable thief and an *onnagata*, or female role actor. Through stylized camerawork, clever casting, and ironic use of the tacky set however, Ichikawa created a stylishly camp story of mis-read lesbian romance wrapped up in a crime caper. This new reading of an old film depended largely on a dramatically re-written script.

Wada amped up the dialogue, making the comedic most of Hasegawa's hopelessly deep voice, now quite unsuited to the performance of female roles due to his advanced age. Ichikawa built on this core absurdity at the heart of the film by adding a visual counterpart to the requirement for theatrical suspension of disbelief on the part of the audience and other cast members. He treated the widescreen DaieiScope format as a very modern stage, sending actors on and off the edges. The backgrounds of key scenes were often simply blacked out, lending a Brechtian simplicity to monologues while covering for sparse or missing settings, props, and extras. Ichikawa and Wada updated the second-hand narrative for the 1960s by turning weak dialogue into surreal farce, an aging star into a camp event, and minimal scenery, props, and lighting into an avant-garde style statement. The innovations of Ichikawa's film, as well as its sheer audacity and unique visual style have earned it a place in the golden age canon, perhaps even more popular overseas than at home.

The story of Wada and Ichikawa's collaboration is as long lasting as the legacy of the bizarre success of *An Actor's Revenge*. Unlike Kogure, who introduced a stylized account of her family life into her professional persona to convert her cultural capital into social and later economic capital, Wada and Ichikawa were creative collaborators before they were family members, marrying in 1948 after meeting at Tōhō studio, where she was working as an interpreter. Under the pen name Wada Natto, Mogi Yumiko (later Ichikawa Yumiko), wrote a great number of film scripts including 30 for Ichikawa Kon. Ichikawa regularly made a point of noting her imprint on finished films. For example, continuity assistant Nogami Teruyo recalls Ichikawa vocally insisting that Wada had "such an ear for dialogue" while on set (Nogami 2006: 102). In a documentary film made two years before his death, Ichikawa even credits Wada for his debut, recalling that she chose the novel from which his first feature film was adapted, *Machiko* (Nogami Yaeko, 1928), which became *A Flower Blooms (Hana Hiraku*, 1948). In this way Ichikawa verbally constructed an image of Wada as supremely skilled and qualified, with exceptional taste, building cultural capital that could be exchanged for social and ultimately economic capital.

In *The Kon Ichikawa Story (Ichikawa Kon monogatari*, 2006), Iwai Shunji's documentary celebrating the director's life, we learn that the pen name Wada Natto was originally a shared pseudonym used between the two on collaborative writing projects, before Mogi Yumiko took it on alone to become the famous screenwriter of the 1950s and 1960s. Their creative partnership was not always harmonious—Ichikawa recalls a home life featuring creative differences and arguments so intense that they would eat dinner together in silence. Eventually, he remembers, he would concede that her ideas were the better ones. Stories of the two arguing long into the night at home tie their authorship/auteurship to a collaborative domestic space, and Ichikawa explicitly connects Wada's creativity with the domestic sphere and feminine-ascribed qualities like tidiness and domestic order. Arguing for an imagined and idealized feminine mode of creativity based on domestic skills, Ichikawa converts one kind of cultural capital into another, as Wada's homemaking skills become applicable to the professional area of scenario writing. "'Women..., well, my wife is very meticulous,' he sighs, 'So she always did a complete and very beautifully detailed scenario'" (Ichikawa quoted in Bock 2001: 40). Like Kogure, Wada's domestic cultural capital is converted into professional institutional cultural capital in the collapsing of home-as-workspace and professional workplace.

Wada herself also insisted on her domestic identity alongside her professional one in her own written discourse. In an article on her writing process, for example, she answered a question about decisions related to her adaptation of Ishihara Shintarō's novel *Punishment Room (Shokei no heya*, 1956), with reference to her identity as a mother. "Like mothers everywhere, I was shocked by the novel" (Wada 2001:

192). Wada's reference to her son follows a passage devoted to the technicalities of adapting literary works for the screen, marked literally as such with the opening phrase "To get slightly technical" (Wada 2001: 191). Like Kogure, Wada highlighted her domestic roles, but unlike the actress she did not avoid directly addressing her professional creative capabilities. Here the cultural capital of an educated middle-class domesticity blends more seamlessly into institutional cultural capital, before being converted into social capital in the professional sphere.

While Wada is often positioned as the woman behind the scenes, or the silent partner in Ichikawa's creative life, we see everywhere Ichikawa's insistence on her presence, her input, and her own creativity, all of which are subtly gendered. In this aspect, Ichikawa's public performance also recalls Kogure Michiyo's, in that both insist on their domestic attachments in order to further their creative possibilities. In Kogure's case, focusing public attention on her domestic role through creating an advice column in a popular magazine allowed her to leverage her home life to increase her fan base, popularity, and power at work, leading to greater opportunities for creativity and financial compensation. In Ichikawa's insistence on foregrounding his marital relationship as the creative force in his career, we can see a similar strategy.

Ichikawa's positioning of Wada as the generative force in his creative output at first appears to be a simple case of muse-creator inspiration. Yet the significant detail of the two sharing a pen name in their early years brings us back to *An Actor's Revenge*, in which the titular actor is an *onnagata* (female role impersonator) in the Kabuki theatre. The Japanese title of the film is in fact 'Yukinojo's revenge' (*Yukinojo henge*), and the main character sets out to avenge a wrong done not to Yukinojo the *onnagata*, but to the young boy he was before becoming a female impersonator. As a child, the main character witnessed a wealthy businessman ruin his parents, leading to their deaths. As Yukinojo, he gains access to the businessman's home and daughter, planning to ruin him slowly in revenge. For a creative partnership so skilled in converting the cultural capital of their domestic life into cultural, social, and then economic capital in the workplace, it is striking that their most enduring text identifies the domestic familial sphere as the most vulnerable capital in the villain's holdings. The narrative of *An Actor's Revenge* underlines the trend we can see in Kogure, Wada, and Ichikawa's life narratives, where the home is the starting point of a cycle of building cultural capital to convert into social and then economic capital, only to feed back into the domestic sphere in the form of consumer goods, education, and physical cultivation. Yukinojo understands that destroying the villain's home and family destroys the space and raw materials which generate this profitable cycle.

The narrative also mirrors Wada and Ichikawa's career in gendered terms, in that the story follows a male actor leveraging a feminized creative identity to achieve his personal goals. Yukinojo is one public persona containing two persons of different genders—the female role actor and the man behind, with the memories of the orphaned male child. Conversely, Ichikawa and Wada/Mogi began their careers as two individuals operating under one name, Wada Natto. Years later, when Ichikawa was victimized by Daiei studios and forced to create under commercial and bureaucratic constraints, Wada's script saved his doomed film, returning Ichikawa to a position of creative power in the prestige and box office reliant studio system. *An Actor's*

Revenge is also Wada Natto's revenge, and Wada and Ichikawa are both one person, and at the same time two different people.[1] Ichikawa and Wada/Mogi's written and recorded discourse reveals this powerful creative agent as forged in the domestic sphere, where male and female creative identities struggle for creative control, and yet ultimately merge in the conversion of domestic cultural capital into professional cultural capital, social capital and fame, and economic reward.

7.7 "Living with the Material": Creativity and the Domestic Sphere

Using family and the domestic sphere, Kogure, Ichikawa, and Wada/Mogi's strategic innovations opened up roads for more, and more creative, work in their restrictive studio environments. In these cases, creativity is physically located at the margins of the studio system rather than within the system itself, in the home-as-workspace rather than the professional workplace. Kogure, Wada, and Ichikawa carved out space and resources for future creativity through the public performance of domestic roles and relations, in many ways embodying SCAP's ideal of the nuclear family as a base unit of democratic capitalist productivity. The cultural capital generated within the domestic sphere was converted through public discourse into social and economic capital, which returns to the domestic sphere in a cycle of increasing power that creates increased opportunity for creativity with reduced personal risk.

While leveraging family and the domestic to increase their power in the workplace, thereby opening up the possibility for greater creativity and independence in their careers, both Kogure and Ichikawa also used the domestic sphere as a space from which to create. Kogure's writing is a creative practice that draws from the space of the home, describing housework, furnishings, and the feeling of being domestic. Ichikawa more explicitly described his and Wada/Mogi's creative practice as "living with the material" (Bock 2001: 40), taking scripts and plans home, fighting about them while making and eating dinner, and collaboratively developing a creative approach for a particular project. In thinking about creativity and the creative industries then, we must not allow our focus on industry to blind us to the margins, including the very non-industrial space of the domestic sphere, as a place where creativity also takes place. In some cases, the possibility for creativity in the workplace might even depend on creative use of the domestic as a place (both material and ideological) from which to build a power base (of popular acclaim as well as financial reward) that can persuade an industry to make space for different kinds of creative agency. When we recognize the creative practices performed in the domestic sphere, we can better understand the process by which domestic cultural capital is converted into workplace cultural capital, becoming social capital and ultimately economic

---

[1]Ichikawa Kon also used thriller writer Agatha Christie's name as a pen name for his writing (Bock 2001: 41). Given the cross-gender nature of Yukinojo's character in *An Actor's Revenge*, it is interesting to note that Ichikawa often takes on the names or personae of female creative.

capital. By analyzing how one set of resources is converted into another, we can also see the crafting and maintenance of a career as a creative process in itself. In fact, we can even see the creation of a career that can generate social and economic capital as the first creative act of an actor, director, or scenario writer.

References

Anon. (1947). Ai wa uruwashi: sutâ to kekkon [Love is beautiful: Stars and marriage]. *Eiga bunko*, *2*, 51–56.

Anon. (1947). Sutā tōroku [Star record]. *Eiga bunko*, *1*, 34–36.

Anon. (1947). Sutā tōroku [Star record], *Eiga bunko*, *3*, 14–15.

Bock, A. (2001). Kon Ichikawa. In J. Quant (Ed.), *Kon Ichikawa* (pp. 37–52). Toronto: Toronto International Film Festival Group.

Bourdieu, P. (1986). The forms of capital. In J. Richardson (Ed.), *Handbook of theory and research for the sociology of education* (pp. 241–258). Westport, CT: Greenwood.

Coates, J. (2016). How to be a domestic goddess: Female film stars and the housewife role in postwar Japan. *US-Japan Women's Journal, 50*, 29–53.

Dreissens, O. (2013). Celebrity capital: Redefining celebrity using field theory. *Theory and Society, 42*(5), 543–560.

Freiberg, F. (1992). Tales of Kagayama. *East-West Film Journal, 6*(1), 94–110.

Hirano, K. (1992). *Mr. Smith goes to Tokyo: Japanese cinema under the american occupation 1945–1952*. Washington: Smithsonian Institution Press.

Izbicki, J. (1997). *Scorched cityscapes and silver screens: Negotiating defeat and democracy through cinema in occupied Japan*. PhD diss. (unpublished). Cornell University.

Kitamura, H. (2010). *Screening enlightenment: Hollywood and the cultural reconstruction of defeated Japan*. Ithaca: Cornell University Press.

Kogure, M. (1949). Watashi no shufu seikatsu no hiketsu [The key to my life as a housewife]. *Eiga fan, 9*(2), 33.

Liddle, J., & Nakajima, S. (2000). *Rising suns, rising daughters: Gender, class and power in Japan*. London and New York: Zed Books.

Matsubara, I. (1948). Iroke to joyū [Actresses and sex appeal]. *Eiga goraku, 2*(2), 13.

Mayo, M. (1984). Civil censorship and media control in early occupied Japan: From minimum to stringent surveillance. In R. Wolfe (Ed.), *Americans as proconsuls: United State military government 1944–1952* (pp. 263–320). Carbondale: Southern Illinois University Press.

McDonald, K. I. (1994). *Japanese classical theater in films*. Fairleigh Dickinson University Press.

Nogami, T. (2006). *Waiting on the weather: Making movies with Akira Kurosawa*. New York: Stone Bridge Press Inc.

SCAP (Supreme Commander of the Allied Powers) General HQ. (1946). Statistics and reports section. In *Summation of the non-military activities of the occupation of Japan 7*.

SCAP (Supreme Commander of the Allied Powers) General HQ. (1948). Political Information-Education Programme. National Archives II at College Park, Maryland, RG 331, GHQ/SCAP, CI&E, Box 5305, file 12 and 15.

Standish, I. (2005). *A new history of Japanese cinema*. London, New York: Continuum.

Terasawa, K. (2010). *Enduring encounter: Hollywood cinema and Japanese women's memory of the postwar experience*. PhD diss. (unpublished). Birkbeck, University of London.

Tsuchiya, Y. (2002). Imagined America in occupied Japan: (re-)educational films shown by the U.S. occupation forces to the Japanese, 1948–1952. *The Japanese Journal of American Studies, 13*, 193–213.

Uno, K. S. (1993). The death of 'good wife, wise mother'. In A. Gordon (Ed.), *Postwar Japan as history* (pp. 293–322). Berkeley, Los Angeles, Oxford: University of California Press.

Wada, Natto. (2001). The 'sun tribe' and their parents. In J. Quant (Ed.), *Kon Ichikawa* (pp. 191–196). Toronto: Toronto International Film Festival Group.

Yoshimi, S. (1999). 'Made in Japan': The cultural politics of 'home electrification' in postwar Japan. *Media, Culture and Society, 21*, 149–171.

Jennifer Coates is Senior Lecturer in Japanese Studies at the School of East Asian Studies at the University of Sheffield. She is the author of Making Icons: Repetition and the Female Image in Japanese Cinema, 1945–1964 (Hong Kong University Press, 2016). Jennifer's research and teaching is situated at the intersection of Japanese Studies, Film Studies, History, History of Art, and Anthropology, and can best be characterized as Japanese Cultural Studies. Her wider research interests include Japanese and East Asian cinema, photography, gender studies, filmmaking, and ethnographic methods.

Part IV
Social Conditions of Creativity

Chapter 8
Several Things that We Know About Creativity: History, Biography and Affordances in Entrepreneurship

Heung Wah Wong and Karin Ling-Fung Chau

Creativity is a fuzzy concept—there are many ways to define creativity and different approaches to the study of creativity. We are not going to present here a comprehensive review of the literature relevant to either the definition of creativity or the approaches to the understanding of creativity. We instead would like to say several things that we know about creativity. Notwithstanding the contentious debates around the definition of creativity, Sternberg and Kaufman (2010: 467) succinctly point out there are two key dimensions of creativity: novelty and quality, or, usefulness. The dimension of novelty must imply a change from one state or form to another, which is also to say that novelty is difference-making practices. To say a difference is useful, evaluation must be involved whereby the difference is assessed as valuable to a person or a community, for not every difference is valuable. The value of a difference here is like Sahlins's (1976: 169) idea of 'utility' that it 'is not a quality of the object but a significance of the objective qualities'. The significance of differences here is to be understood in double senses: meaningfulness and importance, which are acquired from the cultural context in which differences are created. Putting all of this together, creativity as significant differences necessarily involves two processes. The first is a process of difference-making, the other an evaluative process that determines whether the differences made are meaningful and important. The former is a forward-looking process, while the latter a retrospective assessment.

If we understand creativity as making meaningful and significant differences, creativity is, we contend, not unlike the anthropological concept of historical agency. It follows that the theoretical framework anthropologists adopt to analyse historical agency can also be used to examine creativity in a *particular* historical context because anthropological discussions of historical agency are always context-specific.

H. W. Wong (✉)
The University of Hong Kong, Pok Fu Lam Road, Hong Kong
e-mail: hwwongc@hku.hk

K. L.-F. Chau
King's College London, London, UK

© Springer Nature Singapore Pte Ltd. 2020
N. Otmazgin and E. Ben-Ari (eds.), *Creative Context*, Creative Economy,
https://doi.org/10.1007/978-981-15-3056-2_8

In this chapter, we are going to examine the entrepreneurial process of Fong Bou Lung,[1] a Hong Kong entrepreneur who has developed his company, Fong Bou Lung Jewellery International Limited (FBL), from a small jewellery workshop to a well-known retail brand in Southeast Asia, by the anthropological framework of historical agency. The reason that we choose Fong's entrepreneurship to examine creativity is that entrepreneurship likewise is akin to the concept of historical agency. As we shall show in a moment, entrepreneurship is also about making meaningful and significant differences. Analysing entrepreneurship as historical agency can therefore enable us to discuss the several things that we know about creativity. More importantly, understanding Fong's entrepreneurship as a creative process, as readers can see by themselves, can help clarify the nature, the process and the evaluation of creativity.

8.1 Who Is Fong Bou Lung?[2]

Fong Bou Lung was born in Hong Kong in 1936. His father was a hawker who sold snake meat and soup in a local market. His mother was a housewife. He has an elder brother and a younger sister. The Fong family had to share a 600-ft^2 flat with six other households and squeeze themselves into a 100-ft^2 room on the veranda. It was very common in Hong Kong, at least before the 1970s, for several households to share a single flat as the lower-class people were simply too poor to afford individual housing.

The poor life of the Fong family had become even more miserable since the Japanese army conquered Hong Kong in 1941. Fong was five years old at that time. His father could not resume his trade in the market during wartime. Fong's parents had to sell off all their belongings for food. Later, they even had to sell their eldest son to another family as they were too poor to raise him. To survive, Fong's father became a rag-and-bone man and Fong became his assistant. They had to walk from block to block every day to collect second hand items. Fong recalled that he was almost killed by an air raid when he was doing his business on the street.

Following the Japanese surrender, Fong, who was around ten years old then, got the chance to go to school. Just two years later, however, he was forced to drop out. The Fong family was haunted by poverty again. Fong's father fell ill so he could no longer get to work. Not only did Fong have to cease his study since his parents could not afford it, he also had to help support the family. At the age of thirteen, Fong was sent to a goldsmith to take up an apprenticeship in goldsmithing. All of this happened so suddenly that Fong simply had to accept the arrangement.

---

[1]To protect the identity of our informants, the names of the entrepreneur and the company are pseudonymised. In the Chinese language, the surname precedes the first name. We follow the convention in the chapter.

[2]The following discussion on Fong and his entrepreneurial process is based on our research on FBL conducted from 2003 to 2008.

Fong was sent to a traditional Chinese goldsmith in Kowloon. His apprenticeship was to last for five years. During the period, the boss provided Fong meals and accommodation. In return, Fong was required to live in the goldsmith to help guard the store. He was not entitled to any salary or holiday. Fong could at best get one dollar[3] each month from the cashier to get a haircut.[4]

Altogether there was ten staff in the goldsmith. Fong was the only apprentice, meaning that he was at the bottom of the hierarchical ladder. Fong's major duties were to satisfy every need of the seniors and do the cleaning, grocery and cooking for everyone. No one taught Fong anything on goldsmithing. He learnt the craft through self-learning. Fong was frustrated by the system as he thought that it was a complete waste of time.

Despite the hardship, the apprenticeship did guarantee Fong's own survival. Although he did not have any salary, he still managed to save some money from the grocery allowance and give it to his parents because he had to support his family as his father could no longer work.

Five years later, Fong completed his apprenticeship. He could have become a goldsmith 'master', but he chose to work in a cotton mill as an intern. Money was the reason for the twist. The money did not come easily, however. The cotton mill adopted a rotating shift system. Fong took up the night shift for two weeks followed by a week of day shift. For each shift, Fong had to work for 12 h either from 7:00 am to 7:00 pm or vice versa without air-conditioning. Fong described the work experience in the cotton mill as one of the toughest moments in his life.

The cotton mill, however, was shut down without any prior notice one year after Fong had started to work there. Fong was at a complete loss when he suddenly became unemployed. "I was very anxious," Fong recalled. "I needed to feed myself and my family. I needed a job desperately." Through the recommendation of his masters at the previous goldsmith, Fong took up another apprenticeship in a workshop attached to a jewellery store in Tsim Sha Tsui[5] to learn the craft of gemstone-setting. In early post-war Hong Kong, 'goldsmith' and 'jewellery stores' were two distinct categories of business establishments. Traditional goldsmiths mainly sold pure 24 K gold products to general local customers, while jewellery stores predominantly sold karat gold accessories set with gems or diamonds to tourists and upper class local customers. The masters of the latter generally earned much more than those of the former. That's why Fong chose to take up an apprenticeship in the jewellery workshop.

Fong's second apprenticeship lasted for two years. This time, he received $30 a month as 'salary'. After completing the apprenticeship, Fong continued to work in the workshop for a while, but his master did not mention anything about the salary increase. Fong then left the workshop and found a job in a large jewellery company in Tsim Sha Tsui. Fong's income increased to $600 a month. The work was very

---

[3]Unless specified, the currency in the chapter refers to Hong Kong Dollar (HKD).

[4]In the 1950s, a fish ball noodle cost around twenty cents in Hong Kong.

[5]Tsim Sha Tsui is located in southern Kowloon. It was and still is a major tourist area in Hong Kong. It was also the hub of jewellery stores on the Kowloon side.

tough, but Fong did not complain because he was simply preoccupied with making more money.

Fong's biographical background helped nurture the trademark of his personality that can be summed up in a colloquial Cantonese term: *'faat cin hon'* (發錢寒, extreme craze for money). Fong not only suffered from extreme poverty during his childhood, but also had to assume the role and responsibility of the breadwinner in his family when he was very young as his elder brother was sold and his father could not work due to illness. The pressure on him was enormous. This explained why Fong would work in a cotton mill after completing his apprenticeship in the goldsmith, and why he would take up another apprenticeship in gemstone-setting later. Money maximization was the connecting logic behind Fong's seemingly unconnected moves. We have to emphasize that Fong *did not* choose to become a cotton mill intern, an apprentice in gemstone-setting nor a master in a jewellery store because he aspired to develop a career; he did so simply because he wanted to get more money for his family.

The series of unexpected events that took place during his formative years— the outbreak of the war, the sudden termination of his study, the undertaking of an apprenticeship in a goldsmith and the closure of the cotton mill—also reinforced Fong's *'faat cin hon'* mentality as he learned from these events that he could survive in the storm of uncertainty and change the fate of himself and his family *only* through earning more and more money. Fong's *'faat cin hon'*, however, is not simply about advancing his own material condition or enhancing his family's financial wellbeing; it has become an overriding value and a guiding principle of Fong's life. We shall see how Fong's mentality of *'faat cin hon'* motivated him to set up and develop his own jewellery business.

8.2 Fong's Entrepreneurial Adventure

Around 1960, a visit of the owner of the jewellery retail shop where Fong took up his apprenticeship, changed Fong's whole life. The owner asked Fong if he would like to take over the workshop of his former master. Fong did not hesitate and said yes, and this was the beginning of Fong's entrepreneurial adventure. Fong explained that he just thought that it was a good chance for him to earn money:

> I had never thought about setting up my own business. I mean I didn't have time to dream about that…I didn't think much [regarding the owner's proposal]. I just thought that being a boss could earn a lot more than being a worker. I only have two hands; but if I employ people, I can multiply what I earn.

In the early stage, the jewellery retail shop was the only client of Fong's workshop. Since the retail shop was just a small business, it could not provide enough orders to support Fong's workshop. Fortunately, the owner of the jewellery retail shop not only allowed Fong to take orders from other clients but also recommended him to other jewellery stores.

8.2.1 To Produce or to Die

In the next several years, Fong devoted his energy to the expansion of his workshop, which was primarily driven by his distinctive business logic: to maximize production at all costs. Fong's business logic was very different from that of most of the owners of jewellery workshops in Hong Kong, who were usually very cautious about their investment in equipment and labour. Their caution was a result of the business model of the jewellery manufacturing industry in Hong Kong between the 1960s and 1970s.

The jewellery manufacturing industry was characterized by the dominance of small workshops and the reliance on labour-intensive production. Most of the workshops provided OEM (original equipment manufacturer) services to the local jewellery retailers and trading houses that engaged in the export business of jewellery. The profit margin of jewellery manufacturing, however, was very small. Since the manufacturers could only earn very little per order, they, in order to survive, had to win by quantity through obtaining as many orders as possible, which required them to recruit a sufficient number of skilful workers to work for them as jewellery products were largely hand-made before the widespread of the casting technique in the late 1970s. Once skilful workers were recruited, jewellery manufacturers also needed to continue to provide them enough work to do otherwise they would simply move to other workshops. If jewellery manufacturers failed to get sufficient orders after they expanded their labor force, they would lose money because the profit they generated would not be enough to pay for their skilful workers. Given the fact that jewellery manufacturers in Hong Kong had low bargaining power vis-à-vis foreign buyers, the owners of the local jewellery workshops tended to neither overproduce their products nor expand their labour force vigorously. Their production was basically demand-determined.

Fong's business logic, however, was completely supply-driven. He was not concerned about the demand side or the risks associated with overproduction and overexpansion. Fong was only guided by his desire to maximize profit. To maximize profit, as Fong's previous experience as a master taught him, was to maximize outputs. Fong thought that there was nothing mysterious about his strategy:

> My logic is very simple. I just thought that, one worker, say, could help you earn $100 for an order, if you got 100 workers then you got $10,000. If you got 1,000 workers, wow, the sum would be very large!

Fong thus had to actively recruit new blood to strengthen his team. In the early stage, Fong recruited a lot of apprentices. He reformed the system so that the apprentices did not have to do the irrelevant work as he once did. From day one, Fong taught the apprentices to master the craft so that he could turn the apprentice into skilful labour force as soon as possible and at a very low cost. Fong also focused on recruiting junior masters who had just completed their apprenticeship at the renowned workshops.

8.2.2   The 1967 Riots

While Fong was busy expanding his business, the Hong Kong society was experiencing tremendous changes. In 1967, for the first time, the British colonial rule in Hong Kong was under a serious threat. The Cultural Revolution in China evoked a series of protests and boycott of the local workers supported by the left-wing groups. The protests soon turned into a large-scale opposition movement against imperialism and colonialism in Hong Kong. The opposition movement became more and more violent. Bombs were set up randomly on the street causing widespread anxiety and panic among the people. It was a time of chaos. Many people lost confidence in the future of the city and attempted to emigrate. A number of workshops stopped operating or were simply shut down.

Fong, however, was unaffected by the turmoil. His workshop continued to operate as usual as if nothing had happened. Since some of his competitors suspended or even abandoned their business, Fong grasped the chance to absorb their orders as well as workers. Fong emphasized that he had never for a second thought about shutting down the business or emigrating during the riots.

After the riots, the number of Fong's workers doubled. Fong had already established his name in the local jewellery manufacturing sector. In 1971, Fong incorporated his company and named it after himself, which became a milestone of his entrepreneurial adventure.

8.2.3   The Export Business

Fong's strategy in maximizing production through expanding the labour force soon put him under immense pressure to secure more orders for his workers. To retain the workers, Fong had to create new demand for his products. He first started to engage in the wholesale trade, asking some of the workers to become middlemen to help sell the products. Fong, however, still needed to obtain more big orders. A golden chance came in 1971.

In that year Fong was invited by the Hong Kong Trade Development Council (HKTDC) to participate in an international jewellery fair held in the United States. The HKTDC was a semi-official organization established by the Hong Kong government in 1966 to promote local products to, and link the local traders and manufacturers with, the international market. Fong gladly accepted the HKTDC's invitation. It was in fact a very bold decision, given that Fong doesn't speak English and had no prior experience in export. However, Fong believed that going overseas would be a good chance for him to promote his products and, more importantly, to get new and big orders as the volume of transaction in the export business was much bigger than OEM orders, which could help Fong to solve the overproduction problem. He recruited staff with high educational background and experience in export business to help him.

With the help of the HKTDC, Fong, unlike many other owners of the local jewellery workshops, engaged in the export business zealously and connected his business directly with the world market.

8.2.4 The Showroom Business

When Fong started to embark on his export business, he faced a very big problem at home. He received an official 'notice to quit' from the government which ordered him to evict his workshop because the building where Fong's workshop was located was a residential premise and it was illegal to undertake any industrial activities in a residential building in Hong Kong.

Given the ever-expanding scale of his workshop, Fong understood that it would be very difficult to find another suitable place in Tsim Sha Tsui. He thus decided to relocate the workshop to Hung Hom, an industrial area adjacent to Tsim Sha Tsui. Eventually, he rented several units on the eighth floor of an industrial building. With a 10,000-ft^2 space, the workshop was much bigger than before. The immediate problem was solved, but new problems emerged, as Fong told us:

> The new workshop was really large and I got several hundreds of workers at that time. I had to think of some ways to make full use of the space and get enough jobs for the workers. Another problem was that it took some time to travel back and forth between Tsim Sha Tsui and Hung Hom. The jewellery stores were all located in Tsim Sha Tsui, it was inconvenient for us to deliver the products.

The ongoing expansion of the workshop also propelled Fong to explore new business opportunities since Fong had to find new channels to sell the stock of his workshop. As Fong recalled:

> After we moved to the new place, some friends of mine working at local tour operators visited my new workshop. They suggested that they could take some tourists to the workshop to buy the jewellery. I thought it was a promising idea. I then recruited people to help start and run a showroom to sell our products to the tourists.

This is how Fong began his showroom business. Once established, Fong's showroom business grew rapidly as a result of the boom of the tourism industry. The showroom business was a special form of retail business designated especially for group tourists. All the customers were brought in by the travel agents or tourist guides; no individual tourist or local shoppers would be expected. The establishment of a showroom marked the monumental shift of Fong's company from the manufacturing sector to the retail sector.

8.2.5   The Retail Empire

In 1977, Fong opened his first jewellery retail branch in one of the most high-end shopping malls in Hong Kong. The business, however, did not turn out to be as good as Fong had expected. Fong was very frustrated until he came across an idea, as he explained to us:

> My store just got very few customers. I kept thinking what I could do to attract the customers. Then I suddenly got an idea. At that time, it was popular for people in Hong Kong to buy gold coins. I remember the bank sold a coin at the price of $328. I bought some coins from the bank and sold them at $320 each in the branch. People rushed to my store to buy the coins because they were cheaper! You may think that I did attract people, but I also lost money, right? It's not true. Some of the customers preferred to wear the coins, so they bought necklaces in my store. At the end, I was able to attract customers and earn money at the same time.

The success prompted Fong to come up with an unusual strategy in the industry at that time: to use mega sales to attract the consumers. Fong's strategy proved to be very successful. The sales and promotion events did attract a lot of customers to visit Fong's store. The success of Fong's campaigns ironically led to the closure of his store in the shopping mall. As Fong explained:

> The owner of the shopping mall refused to renew the lease. They didn't tell me the reason directly, but I knew that's because I held those sales events and attracted a bunch of people. They thought that my store was too 'low', damaging their high-end image. When the lease expired, they immediately kicked me out. Even until today, we still don't have any stores there.

In addition to the store in the shopping mall, Fong had also set up branches in areas such as Central and Causeway Bay[6] on Hong Kong Island. In 1986, after the shopping mall refused to renew the lease, Fong returned to the goldsmith industry. He established a goldsmith and jewellery store in Yau Ma Tei.[7] With the distinctive marketing emphasis on the low pricing of the products, Fong expanded the retail network of his company rapidly.

Fong listed his company on the Hong Kong Exchange in 1987. He became the chairman and the executive director of the listed company. According to the prospectus, the turnover of his company was estimated to be $448 million.[8] By that time, Fong had already extended the retail network to cover the New Territories, Kowloon and Hong Kong Island. In 1989, according to the annual report of the company, it became 'the largest chain of jewellery stores in Hong Kong in terms of number of retail outlets' employing over one thousand employees.[9] An ordinary goldsmith had

---

[6]Central and Causeway are the major commercial areas in Hong Kong.

[7]Many traditional goldsmiths were located in Yau Ma Tei including the one at which Fong started his apprenticeship when he was 13 years old.

[8]In order to protect the identity of the company and Fong, we omitted the reference information. If you need the information, please feel free to contact the two authors.

[9]In order to protect the identity of the company and Fong, we omitted the reference information. If you need the information, please feel free to contact the two authors.

become a chairman of a listed company. Fong of course could not have foreseen this and would never have dreamed about this.

8.3 An Analysis of Fong's Entrepreneurship

In light of Fong's entrepreneurial process described above, several observations can be made. The first is his extreme pragmatism. Fong did not care much about the means adopted or the details of the process through which the goal was achieved. He was open to every option available as long as they could enable him to maximize profit. For example, Fong did not care what he made or sold as long as the products brought him profits. For a brief period, Fong converted some of his jewellery retail branches into optical stores when the business was not good. But why optical stores? The reason, as Fong told us, was simply because the layout of an optical store is like that of a jewellery store so that it did not cost him much when he converted a jewellery store into an optical store.

Secondly, Fong's decision-making was not completely arbitrary. We have shown that the entrepreneurial process was underpinned by Fong's production maximization logic, which was driven by his distinctive '*faat cin hon*' mentality that was developed from his unique biographical background and experiences during his formative years. This logic guided the way Fong made decisions during his entrepreneurial process. Fong had to constantly deal with the consequences, if not problems, of his business logic of production maximization. For example, Fong had to engage in the export, showroom and retail business because he had to keep creating sufficient demand for his production and clearing the stock arising from overproduction at the same time rather than because he had sensed some new opportunities in those markets and chose to diversify his business accordingly. In short, Fong's entrepreneurial adventure was guided by his business logic of production maximization and set in motion by his ongoing attempts to deal with the problems and contingencies arisen from this very logic.

Fong's entrepreneurial process, we therefore contend, should be understood as a forward-looking process driven by his idiosyncratic business logic of production maximization, which was in turn informed by his distinctive '*faat cin hon*' mentality. It is Fong's '*faat cin hon*' mentality and the resulting production maximization logic that shaped the specific way he interpreted and responded to the changing circumstances and made the major decisions that shaped the course of his entrepreneurial process.

We have to add hastily that Fong's '*faat cin hon*' mentality should not be seen as the only motivation, especially at the later stage of his entrepreneurial adventure. As we have argued elsewhere (Wong and Chau 2020), Fong's company was organized and governed in a way more like a '*bong paai*' (幫派, referring to a small, close group formed to pursue private interests) set up in pursuit of business than a modern corporation.[10] The *bong paai* metaphor is used here to highlight one important feature that characterizes Fong's company: FBL is organized around personal relationships maintained by loyalty and dependence. As the founder and chief of a *bong paai*-company, Fong was the unchallengeable centre in the sense that the *bong paai*-company was an embodiment of his will—he was basically the sole decision-maker and the supreme arbitrator. His employees were expected to demonstrate their absolute loyalty to Fong in a sense that they always put Fong's interest above those of others including themselves, especially when there were conflicts of interest. Loyalty in the *bong paai*-company therefore is the sacrifice of oneself for the sake of the founder-chief. Fong, in return, was obligated to compensate his followers not just with immediate and practical monetary reward but, more fundamentally, a sense of security. In fact, we have observed many occasions during our fieldwork inside the company that Fong repeatedly emphasized that his major concern was to guarantee the livelihood of the employees. We therefore suggest that the obligation to take care of the livelihood of his employees by continuously expanding the company was another major motivation for Fong's persistent entrepreneurial effort.

Thirdly, Fong had never had any strategic plan in his mind to transform his jewellery workshop into a retail brand. Fong just responded to contingencies. Fong's workshop experienced an explosive growth after the 1967 riots not because Fong foresaw the situation would turn better very shortly but because he had to keep up the production of the workshop for survival; he engaged in the export business because he had to settle the problem of overstock of the workshop and to generate enough orders to feed the employees; he engaged in the showroom business because he was forced to relocate his workshop to an inconvenient location; and he established his retail store because he still had to create demand for the production of his workshop. Fong's decisions were more an outcome of his reacting to contingencies than of any strategic planning, which is also to say that the transformation of Fong's company from a manufacturer to a retailer in the local jewellery industry is an *unintended* and *unexpected* consequence.

We argue that all the unintended or unexpected consequences of Fong's entrepreneurship emerge from what Sahlins calls 'conjunctural situations' in which Fong's decisions and actions mediated with the socio-economic context of Hong Kong to produce the specific development path of Fong's company and its historical effects on the jewellery industry, which were not what Fong intended or planned to do (Smith 2002: 288). The socio-economic context of Hong Kong is therefore also relevant to Fong's entrepreneurial process.

---

[10]Due to the limited space we are not able to elaborate the '*bong paai*' metaphor here. For the detailed discussion on the concept, please refer to Wong and Chau (2020).

8.3.1 Hong Kong's Post-war Economic Development

Hong Kong, as a British crown colony between 1842 and 1997, was occupied by Japan during the Second World War. After the War, Britain regained control over Hong Kong. The political situation during the early post-war period was very unstable due to the Cold War power structure. The outbreak of the Korean War in 1950, for example, had an enormous impact on Hong Kong. In December 1950, the United States decided to impose an embargo on the export of goods to China, Hong Kong and Macao. The General Assembly of the United Nations also passed the resolution to impose an embargo on the shipment of strategic goods to China in 1951. As China was the principal trading partner of Hong Kong, the embargos became a serious blow to the economy of Hong Kong. The government stated bluntly that 'it is no exaggeration to say that the Korean [W]ar and the world events following it have put Hong Kong in an economically impossible position' (Hong Kong Government 1952: 9). In order to survive, local entrepreneurs had been forced to turned to the manufacturing sector since the 1950s. The industrialization of Hong Kong was largely facilitated by what Hamilton and Kao (2018: 98) describe as 'the retail revolution' in the United States. The revolution in the U.S. brought about a high demand for cheap consumer goods from overseas manufacturers that in turn produced a market opportunity for the entrepreneurs in Hong Kong. The industrialization of Hong Kong was also made possible by the supply of an almost inexhaustible labour force due to the emigration of people from China after the establishment of the Communist China in 1949, the supply of fresh capital from businessmen from China, especially those from Shanghai (Wong 1988), and the transfer of the entrepreneurial and management skills of these immigrants. All of this enabled the local manufacturers to produce at a lower cost and with higher efficiency, which helped attract the multinational companies to outsource their production to Hong Kong. By the 1970s, Hong Kong had transformed from an entrepôt into an export-oriented industrial centre which gave rise to the famous 'Hong Kong model' (Riedel 1973).

The 'Hong Kong model', however, was very vulnerable to the increase in production cost, especially the labour cost. In the 1980s, the production cost of the manufacturing sector rose very rapidly because of the booming property market and the rising wage rate. More importantly, the manufacturers could no longer use the new immigrants as low-wage workers after the government cancelled the 'touch base' policy[11] in 1980. The Hong Kong government, following the famous laissez-faire doctrine, did not offer special help to the local manufacturers. Without the support of the government, the local manufacturers had no alternatives but to relocate their production bases to South China to exploit the abundant supply of low-wage workers there. Such relocation strategy contributed to the transformation of the manufacturing-oriented Hong Kong economy to a service-based economy (Chiu et al. 1997: 71–7).

Retail and tourism have replaced manufacturing to become one of the major pillars of the newly developed service economy of Hong Kong. Back in the 1960s,

---

[11]This policy stated that any illegal immigrant from mainland China would be granted right of abode by the Hong Kong government if they could successfully reach the urban area of Hong Kong.

for most Hong Kong people, shopping was done primarily for practical rather than entertainment purposes. In the 1990s, shopping has become a major form of entertainment activities among Hong Kong people. The change was facilitated by several factors including the launch of the public housing programme providing cheap but good housing facilities for lower-class families, which alleviated considerably their financial burden, the development of a comprehensive public transportation system which largely reduced the travel time between the major shopping areas of Hong Kong and the residential areas, the improvement of shopping facilities resulting in the rapid growth of shopping centres in both public and private housing estates, and of course, the increase of wealth of the people.

The retail sector also benefited significantly from the development of the tourism industry in Hong Kong. The industry developed steadily after the Second World War. Since the 1960s, the growth of the tourism industry had been remarkable. The number of tourists visiting Hong Kong increased from around 50,000 in 1957 to more than ten million in the mid-1990s (Hong Kong Tourism Board 2008: 5, 10). One of the major reasons for the rapid growth of tourism is that Hong Kong was able to attract diverse groups of tourists at different stages. Throughout the post-war period, the source of foreign tourists in Hong Kong gradually shifted from the West to the East. Before the 1960s, most of the tourists visiting Hong Kong were from the U.S. and the British Commonwealth. In the 1970s, the U.S., Japan and Australia were the most important countries of origin of foreign tourists in Hong Kong. Japan became the top one in 1971 and remained to be so for the following twenty years (Hong Kong Tourist Association 2001: 2–8). During the same period, the number of tourists from Southeast Asia also increased rapidly. Taiwan and South Korea emerged as important sources of foreign tourists between the end of the 1980s and early 1990s. Taiwan even surpassed Japan to become the top country of origin in the tourist market in Hong Kong in 1990 (Hong Kong Tourist Association 1991: 4).

To summarize, Hong Kong had undergone rapid industrialization between the 1950s and 1960s. Until the end of the 1970s, the economy of Hong Kong was predominately driven by the export-oriented industrialization. The manufacturing sector had gradually declined in the 1980s as many manufacturers had to relocate their production bases to mainland China. The structure of Hong Kong's economy experienced a sectoral shift from manufacturing to financing, trading and services. The retail and tourism sectors have become the major pillars supporting the emergent service-economy.

8.3.2 The Mediations

The course of development of Fong's jewellery business followed closely the trajectory of the broader economic transformation taken place in Hong Kong. We argue that the manufacturing-to-retailing development of Fong's company would not have taken place without the broader production-to-service transformation of Hong Kong's economy. The growth of Fong's manufacturing business, for instance, was a result of the mediation between Fong's logic of production maximization and the broader growth of the jewellery industry driven by the increasing overseas demand for jewellery products manufactured in Hong Kong. Mediation here is similar to what Sahlins (2000: 301; italic original) calls 'a work of cultural signification' that 'can be similarly described as the appropriation of local phenomena that have their own reason *in* and *as* an existing cultural historical scheme', through which Fong's creative difference-makings acquired their significance as meaningful and important entrepreneurial activities. In other words, the broader production-to-service transformation of Hong Kong's economy helps amplify the historical effect of Fong's ongoing attempts to deal with the problems and contingencies arisen from his logic of production maximization. It is true that Fong's manufacturing regime developed very swiftly; but if there were no substantial increase of demand for the locally manufactured goods from the West, especially the American retail market, Fong's manufacturing business would not have grown so rapidly. It is also true that the large scale of Fong's workshop enabled him to secure orders directly from foreign importers; but if the Hong Kong economy were not characterized by the expansion of export in the 1970s, Fong could not have secured more orders by going overseas. Again, it is true that the competitiveness of Fong's workshop lay in his ability in expanding the labour force. However, his strategy was effective only because there was a vast pool of cheap labour made available by the influx of immigrants from China.

In a similar vein, the success of FBL's showroom business is the result of the mediation between Fong's entrepreneurial move into the showroom business and the growth of the tourism industry in Hong Kong. It is true that what made Fong successful in his showroom business is his capacity to move his business beyond manufacturing; it is also true that the success of Fong's showroom business is related to the fact that Fong is a go-getter as he did not really do any serious calculation or formulate detailed strategies before involving himself in the new fields. Fong simply acted. All of this, however, could not have happened without the growth of the tourism industry in Hong Kong.

The success of Fong's retail business likewise was enabled and facilitated by the advent of a new shopping culture in Hong Kong. We have shown that FBL's retail business was able to stand out because Fong successfully promoted the new idea of jewellery for ordinary people. However, Fong's idea of jewellery for ordinary people *alone* cannot be held responsible for the success of Fong's retail business because it cannot explain why ordinary people in Hong Kong were willing to spend money on luxury goods. All of this testifies that Fong's actions and profit-making intentions did not have a direct one-to-one relationship with their historical effect.

Parenthetically, the broader production-to-service transformation of Hong Kong economy, however, cannot dictate Fong's entrepreneurial activities, either. In this regard, Sahlins's argument about how individuals can live the universal in a particular way through Sartre's analysis of Flaubert is very illustrative and thus deserves a long quotation:

> Flaubert was a child of a mother with noble aspirations, memories of a sort of petite noblesse, and a father who was a doctor, a bourgeois scientist from the countryside. Flaubert's father was a scientist participating in the new rational, objective world view—what Peter Galison

calls 'the romantic objectivity of the nineteenth century'. And Flaubert and his family—
including an order brother who followed in his father's footsteps and with whom Flaubert
could not compete—were living during the Restoration, after the Church and the monarchy
came back to power. Flaubert lived this conflict between the feudal order, which his mother
in some ways represented, and the rational, scientific, modernized order, which his father
represented—although here again in very ambiguous, contradictory ways. Flaubert's father
had a kind of theocratic hold on his children by which he used to try to instil in them scientific
rationality and a disbelief in God. So it was those kinds of contradictions that he grew up
with. But what if Flaubert's father had been the noble and his mother the bourgeoise? What
if he lived his Oedipus relation with a bourgeois mother and a pious father? The history
of French literature would have been entirely different! So you could transpose to Flaubert
what Sartre also said of Valery: Flaubert was a bourgeois idealist, that is true, but not every
bourgeois idealist is a Flaubert. There's an individuality in the mediation of the totality to
the person. The process does not consist in inscribing the categories without residue and in
universal form on the person. Unlike the 'subjectivity' fiction, people do not simply embody
the larger categories; they live them in particular ways and likewise particularly express
them. (cited in Smith 2002: 289–290)

Fong's profit-maximization motives likewise cannot be reduced to the wider
socio-economic factors because they were also informed by Fong's own biographical background and the experiences he had during the formative years. End of
parenthesis.

What we attempt to argue here is that there is always a gap between Fong's action
and profit-making intentions and their historical effects. The gap is created by the
intervention of the broader socio-economic context. Our argument therefore involves
three terms: Fong's actions and intentions, the broader socio-economic context, and
the historical effect, in which the historical effect of Fong's actions and intentions
is the relationship between the other two; it is the result of the appropriation of
Fong's actions and intentions by the broader socio-economic context in which these
activities takes place. It follows that the same actions and intentions in different socio-
economic contexts will have different historical effects. The historical significance
of Fong's actions and intentions in terms of its determinations as entrepreneurial
activities and its historical effects as entrepreneurship is dependent on the broader
socio-economic context.

It follows that the effect of Fong's entrepreneurship can only be assessed *retrospectively* because it is always historical and thus cannot be known a priori. We
can only examine the historical effects of Fong's forward-looking entrepreneurial
process in retrospect. If Fong's business had failed, for instance, during the 1967
riots, we would not have spent a whole paper here discussing the entrepreneurship of
someone called Fong Bou Lung. It is only when Fong's entrepreneurial process has
been assessed retrospectively as having made significant historical effects, is he qualified as an entrepreneur. While the entrepreneur could only *look forward* by making
decisions without knowing the exact effects, we can only *look back* to evaluate the
historical effect of the entrepreneur's decision-makings and determine whether the
effect can qualify Fong's actions and intentions as 'entrepreneurial'.

8.3.3   Historical Effects In-the-Context

The historical effects of Fong's entrepreneurship are also relative to the level in which Fong's entrepreneurship takes place. In the context of the local jewellery industry in Hong Kong, the historical effects of Fong's entrepreneurial process can be described as what Sahlins calls 'revolutionary change' that changes or 'reverses course' (cited in Smith 2002: 287). Fong's forward integration of production and circulation was indeed very rare, if not unique, in the jewellery industry in Hong Kong. Most of the jewellery workshops tended to remain in the manufacturing sector. On the other hand, all major players in the jewellery retail market, except Fong's company, started out as a retail outlet. They would attempt to achieve backward integration after they had accumulated sufficient capital to claim control over the suppliers. The major reason Fong is considered a legendary figure in the industry is that he broke down the barrier between the manufacturing and retail sectors. Fong was among the few entrepreneurs who first operated a showroom in Hung Hom. After Fong's success in his showroom business, other entrepreneurs followed suit to establish jewellery showrooms in the area where has become a major cluster of jewellery showrooms in Hong Kong catering tourist groups specifically.

Fong also revolutionized the local jewellery industry by fostering the massification of the jewellery industry. He was the first major jeweller to popularize the use of sales campaigns in the industry. Instead of marketing the glamour and grandeur of the jewellery products like other jewellery retailers, Fong focused instead on underscoring the price worthiness of his products. Fong played an important role in transforming the public perception on jewellery from an untouchable luxury to an everyday necessity.

However, when we situate Fong's case in the broader Hong Kong context, the development of his company can only at best be described as following a 'developmental change'. A 'developmental change', according to Sahlins, refers to the change that 'continues a given course of development' (cited in Smith 2002: 287). In contrast to the revolutionary change, it is evolutionary by nature. The development of FBL simply followed the broader economic transformation of Hong Kong, capitalizing the opportunities created by the rise of the manufacturing sector, the tourism industry and the retail market. While Fong made significant differences to the local jewellery industry, he did not have the equal impact on the whole Hong Kong economy.

The above different modes of historical changes caused also determine the types of the historical subject of Fong's entrepreneurial process identified at the industrial and societal levels. At the industrial level, Fong is identified as the historical subject of the entrepreneurial process, while FBL, his company, is made the historical subject at the societal level. The difference in historical subject in these two levels can be attributed to the nature of historical changes. As mentioned above, what Fong did in the industrial level was revolutionary, while in the societal level, Fong's entrepreneurship only caused evolutionary changes. As Sahlins (2004: 127) effectively argues, historical subject is defined by the mode of historical changes the subject caused. Revolutionary changes are usually attributed to one single individual, while evolutionary changes to collectives. In other words, the historical subject causing revolutionary changes always refers to some individuals, while in the case of evolutionary changes, some collectives are often held responsible.

8.3.4 Systemic Agency Versus Conjunctural Agency

The different historical effects of Fong's entrepreneurship at different levels can also tell the different types of agency Fong possessed. Fong had the absolute power to determine the course of the development of FBL by virtue of his position as the founder and the controlling shareholder when his company was listed on the Hong Kong Stock Exchange. In other words, what Fong did must be agentive; although the effects, as we have shown above, were not always his intention. This is what Sahlins calls 'systemic agency' as it is the institutional position within the structure that enables the position holder to make significant differences (cited in Smith 2002: 288)

In the broader industrial context, Fong, however, was only able to make history because he was what Sahlins calls 'conjunctural agency' in the sense that he was put at a particular historical conjuncture (cited in Smith 2002: 288). It was not because of his position as an owner of a jewellery workshop that empowered him to bring changes to the industry as a whole, but because of the mediations we identified that enabled him to bring about significant changes to the local jewellery industry. The historical effects of Fong's entrepreneurship on the industry would be ephemeral. What we want to illustrate here is that the historical effects of Fong's entrepreneurship and the conditions for his history-making are related to the types of agency Fong possessed.

8.4 Several Implications for the Study of Creativity

The above long story of Fong and our brief analysis of the story are intended to shed some light on the understanding of creativity as we argue that entrepreneurship, as we have shown above, is also about making meaningful and significant differences.

We have explained how Fong had made significant differences to the local jewellery industry in Hong Kong. While Fong's business logic of production maximization was distinctive from other manufacturers, we cannot say that it was something completely new. What made Fong special is not the level of 'newness' of his way of doing business but the fact that he has made differences not just to his own company but also to the whole jewellery industry. Creativity therefore does not necessarily refer to the creation of new things; it is more about bringing about changes and making different-ness, however slight it is (Nixon 2006: 91).

The difference, however, must be evaluated and recognized by others. Not all differences are considered as creativity except those that are perceived as being significant in a certain context and in the double senses of being meaningful and important. Creativity, we contend, should be understood as a process of making differences that are evaluated as being both meaningful and important. In other words, creativity as a process of making meaningful and important differences is not necessarily used to describe any process of creating new products or devising new design; it can also be used to refer to novel ways of doing things. Fong's creativity likewise did not refer to new design of the jewellery of his company but his innovative attempts to deal with the problems and contingencies arisen from his idiosyncratic production maximization logic and the constraints imposed and the opportunities presented by the ever-changing environment.

8.4.1 Creativity as a Forward-Looking Process or a Retrospective Evaluation

This conceptualization of creativity immediately leads us to another central debate around the notion of creativity: whether creativity is innovation or improvisation. As Brian Moeran and Bo Christensen observe, some scholars understand creativity as innovation, which 'can be gauged only by looking backwards at past products' (Moeran and Christensen 2013: 3), while some others conceptualize creativity as improvisation, which can solely be evaluated in '*processes* of "in-the-making", rather than on the *products* made' (Moeran and Christensen 2013: 3). It follows that creativity as innovation is retrospectively determined, while creativity as improvisation is identified in forward-looking processes (Moeran and Christensen 2013: 3). Reflecting on Fong's case, we contend that the opposition between creativity as innovation and as improvisation is unnecessary. We have illustrated how Fong's entrepreneurial process should be understood as a forward-looking process and how his entrepreneurship must be examined as a retrospective historical effect. In a similar vein, creativity is prospective-cum-retrospective by nature. Creativity is constituted by both the looking-forward process and the post-event/product evaluation. The former enables the difference making while the latter determines if the differences are meaningful and important.

Recall that Fong simply focused on increasing the production of his workshop with the hope of generating more profit and on solving the problems and dealing with contingencies arisen from his own attempt to maximize production. Also recall the four critical decision-making moments of Fong's entrepreneurial adventure, which can be understood as what Howard Becker calls 'editorial moments' (Becker 1982: 198 cited in Moeran and Christensen 2013: 8). Moeran and Christensen (2013: 8) explain that these editorial moments are the 'actual choices made by different people at different stages during the performance of a creative work'. Throughout the process, Fong made use of whatever option available to him to achieve his goal without attempting to calculate the possible risks and possible consequences. Fong simply kept looking and going forward amidst the uncertainties. In this process, Fong was the principal actor who made the entrepreneurial choices during these evaluative practices. As we demonstrated, Fong had relatively few constraints when making the decisions during the editorial moments. It is because Fong possessed systemic agency in his company so that his structural position enabled him to make critical differences to the development of his company. Creativity is a forward-looking concept because the creator(s) just do/make whatever they can to solve the existing problems during the process without being able to predict the exact outcome.

Fong's agency, however, is conjunctural at the industrial level. His history-making was enabled less by his entrepreneurship than by a historical conjuncture which empowered Fong to make significant differences to the jewellery industry. In other words, Fong could not know a priori this historical impact of his entrepreneurship on the industry, which can only be evaluated retrospectively. In other words, creativity must be retrospective because it is necessarily historical for the effect of the creative process/product must be evaluated and recognized afterwards. We are only able to say that Fong is an entrepreneur because his entrepreneurship has already made meaningful differences to the jewellery industry in Hong Kong. As Moeran points out that creative products are characterized by what Howard Becker calls a 'fundamental indeterminacy' (Becker 2006: 24 cited in Moeran 2014: 23).

8.4.2 Affordances

Fong's case also gives us some new insights on the conditions of creativity. Moeran (2014) uses the concept of the circuits of affordances—techno-material, temporal, spatial, representational, social and economic—to examine the conditions enabling and restraining creativity. We propose to add at least two types of affordances to the list. The first is biographical affordance. In our analysis, we have illustrated how Fong's distinctive way of conceptualizing and interpreting the circumstances were shaped by his unique biographical background and experiences during the formative years. The same can also be applied to creators. We should examine the way how the biographical history of a creator shapes his or her specific creative process.

Second, we should add a 'self-imposed' affordance to the list. This refers to the self-imposed limitations inflicted on the creative process. Fong's extreme pragmatism enabled him to embrace every option available relative openly and minimize the effects of the self-imposed affordance. As we demonstrated, Fong was not constrained by his identity as a jeweller during the decision-making process. He would simply subscribe to the solutions that enabled him to achieve his goals of profit maximization. It did not matter if he had to sacrifice the brand image or to sell completely different things as Fong used to converted some of his jewellery retail branches into optical stores when the business was not good. He could always adjust the means to satisfy the end. Not many people, however, are like Fong. Very often, the creative processes of the creator are shaped, if not restrained, by their self-imposed identity constraints—such as the desire to maintain a distinctive artistic identity or to fit their works into a particular genre to get recognition.

The important implication to the understanding of creativity is that the opposition between art and commerce—and by extension, between creativity and commerce—as widely pointed out by scholars of cultural production (Caves 2001; Skov 2002; Taylor 2005) is not necessary as we can see from Fong's case that he has shown his significant creativity in his ongoing attempts to deal with uncertainties and problems while having made himself one of the most successful businessmen in post-war Hong Kong at the same time.

8.4.3 Creativity Is Relative

Creativity as a retrospective historical effect is relative to the contexts and levels in which it is situated. As we have demonstrated, the historical effects of Fong's entrepreneurial process varied in different levels. To the local jewellery industry in Hong Kong, Fong brought revolutionary changes in the sense that his company became a disrupter of the existing structure. However, Fong did not exert much historical effects on the Hong Kong society because the development of his company simply followed the trajectory of post-war economic transformation.

The relativity of creativity also speaks to the way historical subject is identified. As mentioned above, we usually refer to the individual as the historical subject if we refer to 'revolutionary changes'. In Fong's case, we say *Fong* established a showroom business or *Fong* broke down the barrier between the manufacturing and retail sectors when we describe the revolutionary changes *he* brought about to the local jewellery company. However, we say *FBL* followed the path of the post-war economic development in Hong Kong to describe the 'developmental change'. It is because the revolutionary change is brought about by the intervention of a particular actor, while the development change is brought about by the structural change in an enduring institutional order. This may explain why sometimes we emphasize the individual creator (such as Steve Jobs) while at other times we emphasize the brand/company when we talk about innovations and creative processes.

8.5 Concluding Remarks

In this chapter, we have indirectly said something about creativity by directly saying something about the entrepreneurship of a legendary jeweller, Fong Bou Lung, in Hong Kong through the concept of historical agency. We argue that creativity and entrepreneurship alike are concerned with making meaningful and significant differences and therefore the analysis of Fong's entrepreneurship through the concept of historical agency enables us to clarify the definition, the process and the evaluation of creativity. We contend that creativity should be primarily defined as the process of making differences that are evaluated as meaningful and important. Creativity therefore involves dual processes: a forward-looking process of difference-making and a retrospective evaluative process. We have explained how creativity is relative to the contexts and levels in which it is situated. The same activity can be evaluated differently because it can cause different historical changes in different contexts and levels. We have also shown that the mode of historical changes determines the type of the historical subject causing the changes. In other words, the mode of historical changes decides whether individuals or collectives should be designated as the creator(s) in a creative process.

One final point is that creativity and entrepreneurship are likewise about making meaningful and significance changes, which is also to say that they are concerned with historical agency. In fact, we can substitute 'historical agency' for 'entrepreneurship' as well as for 'creativity' in the above discussion of Fong's entrepreneurial process without much offence to any of these ideas. We are then tempted to ask: what can the study of creativity or entrepreneurship per se offer us? What makes the study of creativity *creative* and what makes the entrepreneurship study *entrepreneurial*? To answer these questions, however, would require another long paper. In this chapter, we just want to say and have already said several things that we know about creativity. If we say many things about creativity, to paraphrase Sahlins (1999: 415), several of them may be correct.

References

Caves, R. (2001). Contracts between art and commerce. *Journal of Economic Perspectives, 17*(2), 73–83.

Chiu, S. W. K., Ho, K. C., & Lui, T. (1997). *City-states in the global economy: Industrial restructuring in Hong Kong and Singapore*. Boulder, CO: Westview Press.

Hamilton, G. G., & Kao, C. (2018). *Making money: How Taiwanese industrialists embraced the global economy*. Stanford, CA: Stanford University Press.

Hong Kong Government. (1952). *Annual Report*. Hong Kong.

Hong Kong Tourist Association. (1991). *Annual Report 1990/91*. Hong Kong.

Hong Kong Tourist Association. (2001). *Annual Report 2000–2001*. Hong Kong.

Hong Kong Tourism Board. (2008). *Annual Report 2007/2008*. Available at: http://www.discoverhongkong.com/eng/about-hktb/annual-report/annual-report-20072008.jsp. Accessed April 27, 2018.

Moeran, B. (2014). *The business of creativity: Toward an anthropology of worth*. Walnut Creek, CA: Left Coast Press.

Moeran, B., & Christensen, B. T. (2013). Introduction. In B. Moeran & B. T. Christensen (Eds.), *Exploring creativity: Evaluative practices in innovation, design, and the arts* (pp. 1–42). Cambridge: Cambridge University Press.

Nixon, S. (2006). The pursuit of newness: Advertising, creativity and the 'narcissism of minor differences'. *Cultural Studies, 20*(1), 89–106.

Riedel, J. (1973). *The Hong Kong model of industrialization*. Kiel: Institu fuer Weltwirtschaft.

Sahlins, M. (1976). *Culture and practical reason*. Chicago, IL: Chicago Press.

Sahlins, M. (1999). Two or three things that I know about culture. *The Journal of the Royal Anthropological Institute, 5*(3), 399–421.

Sahlins, M. (2000). The return of the event, again. In *Culture in practice: Selected essays* (pp. 293-352). New York, NY: Zone Books.

Sahlins, M. (2004). *Apologies to Thucydides: Understanding history as culture and vice versa.* Chicago, IL: University of Chicago Press.

Skov, L. (2002). Hong Kong fashion designers as cultural intermediaries: Out of global garment production. *Cultural Studies, 16*(4), 553–569.

Smith, A. T. (2002). Endangered specificities: An interview with Marshall Sahlins, 16 October 2001. *Journal of Social Archaeology, 2*(3), 283–297.

Sternberg, R. J., & Kaufman, J. C. (2010). Constraints on creativity obvious and not so obvious. In J. C. Kaufman & R. J. Sternberg (Eds.), *The Cambridge handbook of creativity* (pp. 467–482). New York, NY: Cambridge University Press.

Taylor, M. (2005). Culture transition: Fashion's cultural dialogue between art and commerce. *Fashion Theory, 9*(4), 445–460.

Wong, H. W., & Chau, K. L. (2020). *Tradition and transformation in a Chinese family business.* London, New York: Routledge.

Wong, S. (1988). *Emigrant entrepreneurs: Shanghai industrialists in Hong Kong.* Hong Kong: Oxford University Press.

Heung Wah Wong is the Acting Head of School of Modern Languages and Cultures, The University of Hong Kong, and associate professor in Global Creative Industries. He receives his Ph.D. (social anthropology) from The University of Oxford. His research interest lies in the globalization of Japanese popular culture, anthropology of business, and cultural policies in East Asia. He is the author of *Japanese Bosses, Chinese Workers: Power and Control in a Hong Kong Megastore* (University of Hawaii Press and Curzon 1999) and co-author (together with Hoi-yan Yau) of *Japanese Adult Videos in Taiwan* (Routledge 2014), *Japanese Adult Video Industry* (Routlege 2018), and *Tradition and Transformation in a Chinese Family Business* (with Karin Ling-Fung Chau, Routledge 2020).

Karin Ling-Fung Chau is conducting her doctoral research on cultural policy and the animation industry in China in the Department of Culture, Media and Creative Industries, King's College London. Before starting her Ph.D., she was a part-time lecturer in the Global Creative Industries Programme, the University of Hong Kong. She is the co-author (together with Heung Wah Wong) of *Tradition and Transformation in a Chinese Family Business* (Routledge 2020).

Chapter 9
Rethinking Copyrights: The Impact of Copying on Cultural Creativity and Diversity

Jimmyn Parc

Abstract There have been a number of voices calling for the implementation of a tighter copyrights regime in this era of digitization that will help deter the copying of established works. Such an approach though is counterproductive. Although imitation is often considered as a negative practice in our time, throughout history it has been perceived very differently. This chapter focuses on the true role of imitation and reveals the real nature of the relationship between copying, creativity, and diversity. It argues that contrary to prevailing beliefs, imitation and copying do not restrict cultural creativity or diversity but in fact support them further. The findings of this chapter suggest that imitation within the copyrights regime should be carefully reconsidered and that maybe the core issue is about earnings, rather than cultural creativity or diversity.

The *Gran Madre di Dio* or Great Mother of God in Turin, Italy is a neoclassic-style church that was inaugurated in 1834 to commemorate the return of King Victor Emmanuel I of Sardinia to the throne after the defeat of Napoleon. One of the main features of this church is its dome, which on the inside has many rosettes engraved in the stone (see Fig. 9.1). Notable is the fact that the shape of each rosette is different from one another (see the right image in Fig. 9.1). In fact, most tour guides as well as local Turinians will claim that each one was crafted differently for ornamental reasons. This though raises an interesting but curious question on what would have been easier at the time: mass producing the same shape or crafting different shapes one by one? Given the challenges at the time in carving the same shape on stone, it would be more rational to assume that the dissimilarity of each rosette was more than likely due to a lack of technology for mass production, rather than a process of ornamentalization.

In fact, this way of ornament decoration where each item is unique and different can be found in other places across Europe as well as in Asia. For example, often thousands of small Buddha statues carved in stone or wood are found in small rooms

J. Parc (✉)
Sciences Po Paris, France
e-mail: jimmynparc@gmail.com

Seoul National University, South Korea

© Springer Nature Singapore Pte Ltd. 2020
N. Otmazgin and E. Ben-Ari (eds.), *Creative Context*, Creative Economy,
https://doi.org/10.1007/978-981-15-3056-2_9

143

Fig. 9.1 Rosettes under the dome (*Gran Madre di Dio*, Turin, Italy). *Notes* Exterior of *Gran Madre di Dio* (left top); cross section diagram (left down); dome (right). *Sources* Tripadvisor (left top); Museo Torino (left down); Vanupied, Photo by Gianni Caeddu (right)

of Buddhist temples across Asia. In order to emphasize the process of dissimilarity, people there too explain that the statues were carefully crafted to be different for ornamental and/or religious reasons. However, such an explanation should be carefully considered. It is not that long ago that we were able to produce identical products *en mass*; a good example is the Model T produced by Ford Motor company in 1908. The mass production of identical products was only possible due to the advancements of measurement and technology. It is noteworthy that the current metric system widely used around the world was only introduced in the eighteenth century and diffused widely in nineteenth century. With this accurate measurement of objects, technology was able to advance further. In this context, it can be easily assumed that copying or producing replicas would have been more difficult and thus appreciated more in the past.

It has only been in recent times that we have begun to highlight the importance of innovation which is often advocated as a contrary concept to copying and imitation. A good example is the lawsuits between Apple Inc. (hereafter Apple) and Samsung Electronics Co., Ltd. (hereafter Samsung) in 2012 because Samsung allegedly copied the design of smartphones and tablet PCs from Apple. Addressing this dispute, Peter Bressler, a former president of the *Industrial Designers Society* and the founder and board chair of product design firm Bresslergroup, explained that "my opinion (is) that there are a number of Samsung phones and two Samsung tablets that are substantially the same as the design in those (Apple) patents." In addition, he suggested that consumers could confuse one of Samsung's devices with Apple's (Lowensohn 2012). Following the legal proceedings, Apple was ranked as one of the World's Most Innovative Companies by the Boston Consulting Group in 2018—in fact it regularly has been since 2005—while Samsung was labeled as a copycat.

Despite these perceptions, the appreciation of copying or imitation in the present age is very much different from the precedent time. According to Godin (2017), in the fifteenth and sixteenth centuries, innovation was regarded as imitation of great (successful) men's deeds and imitation of (return to) ancient institutions (p. 19). The meaning of innovation as imitation changed in the early seventeenth century and meant introducing ideas and practices that are opposite to the established order, whether political or religious. In this respect, later innovation as imitation changed to innovation as subversive of the established order. In the nineteenth century, when innovation was theorized, imitation was replaced by original, difference, and creativity which all signify the introduction of something new, to be the first to have an idea, or to do something in a new way (p. 21). Afterwards, this connotation of innovation as opposed to imitation or copying has been implicitly or explicitly anchored in our society and world.

This connotation has further influenced the conceptualization on what innovation and imitation (or copying) are today. Legally speaking, copying, imitation, or plagiarism are all broadly defined as taking the creative ideas of another and selling and/or publishing them as one's own. However, this legal definition and even juridical approach are subject to considerable room for interpretation which is undoubtedly affected by the prevailing concepts of innovation and imitation. This sensitive issue effects even the attitude of artists concerning various activities which are not related much to selling or publishing someone else's idea. The case of when the Korean music group BTS or Bangtan Boys appeared on a music show explicitly reveals this typical attitude among "artists" regarding even a copying-like practice.[1] The following is the transcript of the most interesting part of the conversation that took place between RM or Rap Monster, a member of BTS and a Korean hip-hop MC known as B-free during a Korean show entitled "Bong-hyun Kim's Hip-hop live show" in 2013.[2]

B-Free	*You know the Kanye West song? It's called Black Skinhead. A friend of mine told me that someone made a song exactly like it. I looked it up. It was the same beat and you were rapping the same way. How did that happen? I was so mad at that time. So I swore.*
	[…]
RM	*The video was supposed to be a concept trailer. So, we weren't really trying to show our rap. […] So, with the purpose of using it for our concept. We just wanted to show our dance. If we cleared the copyrights, I know it would have been less problematic and you wouldn't need to tell us this. I know that, but we couldn't use it.*
B-Free	*Do you like Kanye West?*
RM	*Yes, I like him.*

[1] BTS debuted in June 2013 in Korea. This Korean boy band won the 2017, 2018, and 2019 Billboard Awards for Top Social Artist beating Justin Bieber, Selena Gomez, and other well-known American pop artists. They were invited to the American Music Awards and other well-known American TV programs such as *Ellen DeGeneres Show, Jimmy Kimmel Live!*, and *The Late Late Show With James Corden*. In addition, BTS even performed on *Dick Clark's New Year's Rockin' Eve 2018* and *2019*, which is a famous annual television event in the United States.

[2] MC: Master of Ceremonies; this term is often used as a term of distinction, referring to a hip hop musician with good performance skills such as lyrical ability and rapping technique; the episode can be found from YouTube, see Abi Abroad (2013).

B-Free   *If he's an artist you respect so much, then why use the same MR [music recorded],*
           acting like it's your own song? Uploading it to YouTube, rapping in that music
           video thing, and making the same kind of stage that Kanye West did. If you copy
           exactly like that, that's disrespectful to the artist you like in my opinion.

RM   *If you feel that way, I believe you can feel that way. But I don't understand what*
           you mean when you say the stage or performance is the same or alike. We only
           dance in that performance.

B-Free   *Then who is the one that raps?*

RM   *That was me, as exactly how Kanye West did it.*

Moderator *Let's end this talk right here.*

This conversation clearly demonstrates how the practice of copying or seemingly similar activities are perceived by artists these days, that it is a bad practice and immoral. Furthermore, it is regarded as not respecting other artists. In fact, the current attitudes toward the notion of copying is very much related to copyrights in modern society as RM hinted above.

9.1 Current Perspectives on Copying

In order to understand better how copying is perceived in our time, it is important to consider the fundamental purpose of copyrights as reflected in the mandates of key international institutions. The World Intellectual Property Organization (WIPO) focuses on protecting (i) the economic rights which allow the owners to derive financial rewards from the use of his/her works by others and (ii) the moral rights which protect the non-economic interests of the author (WIPO 2017). At the same time, the United Nations Educational, Scientific and Cultural Organization (UNESCO) is more interested in enhancing cultural creativity and diversity for society (UNESCO 2017). In other words, copying is considered immoral because it takes away the economic benefits from authors while hindering cultural creativity and diversity. This is in line with the prevalence of current concepts on innovation and copying.

In the real-world, since economic factors are more influential than cultural aspects, the current copyrights regime is more orientated toward economic interests and has evolved further toward a judicial approach which encompasses the current interpretations on innovation and copying. Meanwhile, alongside the economic interests, the overall goal of copyrights is to safeguard cultural diversity and creativity. These two have very distinguishable characteristics and need to be rigorously analyzed separately before understanding both of them in a comprehensive manner, theoretically and practically.

Despite the growing interest in cultural diversity and creativity, there are still a number of thinkers and scholars who often fail to distinguish between these two aspects. Furthermore, their work tends to be narrowly focused on a short period and/or limited examples instead of being based upon rigorous theories or practice. For example, Hatch (1998) highlights the fact that copyrighted work is like personal property and thus needs to be protected. From this, it is believed that the earnings generated from a protected work can help to enhance creativity among authors. Moreno et al. (2005) argue that copying weakens the development of creativity and many copied products have on average a low-minimum level of quality. They also highlight the fact that Italy has produced many highly creative products that are linked with local culture and traditional knowledge. Hence, they concluded that copying should be avoided in order to ensure cultural diversity which will then be further protected and promoted. Liebowitz (2007) insists that ownership provides values which can be reinvested in other works; therefore, unauthorized copying reduces appropriate revenues that are incentives to generate cultural creativity and diversity. In this regard, it can be concluded that most of these studies focus on economic rights and their consequences on cultural diversity and creativity, rather than "cultural diversity and creativity" per se.

In contrast, this chapter focuses on the non-economic issue of copyrights which is important but has been too often overlooked in other studies. More precisely, it explores whether copying hinders cultural diversity and/or creativity. For this kind of examination, it would be more credible and persuasive to adopt an historical approach by outlining a factual account of events. In this regard, this chapter presents several historical cases in order to seek answers to the question above. This can also be useful for further studies that integrate economic and non-economic issues on copying and cultural diversity and creativity. Contrary to prevailing conventional wisdom, the answer to this question is that copying does not limit cultural diversity and creativity.

9.2 Copying Cult Objects: Ancient Christian Art

In contrast to today, copying an object or a work in the past was not an easy task. With limited technology, it was particularly difficult to copy large-sized works on walls such as murals or frescos in massive cathedrals. Given this fact it is important to use a different standard to identify copying and approach it from a perspective that takes into account the technological limitations of the time. With such a refreshed view, we can then highlight several interesting points from the following religious works, in particular those that portray the crucifixion of Jesus Christ. In Fig. 9.2, these works portraying Jesus Christ were produced before or during the medieval period in Europe. The style of each work may be different from one another following the trends of the time. However, there is one similarity; the direction of Jesus' head, which is pointing down and to the right.

Many modern works that depict the crucifixion vary in which direction Jesus' head faces; right, left, middle, and sometimes even pointing up to the sky. However, a large number of works undertaken before and during the medieval period portrayed Jesus' head as pointing in the same direction, facing down and to right. In contrast to the direction of his head, the background of each piece is different. One might assume that these artists who all depicted Jesus' head as facing to the right did so for some important religious meaning (Boespflug 2008). However, there is no single part in the Bible that mentions about the direction of Jesus's head during the crucifixion.

Fig. 9.2 Depictions of the crucifixion and the direction of Jesus' head *Source* Wallraf das Museum

Although it is beyond the scope of this chapter, there is a strong argument that the choice of pointing the head to the right was chosen to reflect "right" as in the idea of right and wrong, which can be commonly found in other older civilizations (Roth 2009; McManus 2013).

This connotation of direction can also be found in the works that describe the way that Mary is holding Baby Jesus (see Fig. 9.3). Like the direction of Jesus' head, the relatively modern works vary in the depiction of Mary and Baby Jesus; Jesus can be in the middle or even on the left side. However, most works that appeared before and during the medieval period put Mary on the right side while Baby Jesus is on the left side of Mary. Again, the Bible does not mention anything specifically about the positioning. It can simply be human nature to hold a baby close to the heart, but many scholars have argued that this was influenced by ancient Egypt and the statues of Isis holding Horus (Werner 1972). Regardless of the origin, it can be easily assumed that these two positions have a ritual or religious meaning. Hence, artists copied the composition of the two figures.

Some would argue that the level of copying among the works examined before are not the same as in the modern age such as when Samsung copies the design of a

Fig. 9.3 The positions of Mary and Baby Jesus. *Notes* Enthroned Madonna with the Christ Child (left); Mary with the Child (middle); Our Mother of Perpetual Help (right). *Sources* Wallraf das Museum (left and middle); Church of St. Alphonsus Liguori, Rome, Italy (right)

smartphone from Apple. The similarity among the works shown previously is only the position of a certain figure rather than the entire composition. This is true, but under most current copyright laws, this type of copying would be considered as a violation of intellectual property rights. Regardless of the similarity of the works at the time, it did not hinder cultural diversity and creativity of religious works before and during the medieval period. It is also noteworthy to point out that these works were considered as cult objects and were not really conceived of as art. Later, the religious and spiritual values were replaced by artistic ones in the modern sense when they became associated with people and space in a lifelike way (Sonntag and Blühm 2016: 22–23). In brief, the notion of culture and art with these works only appeared very recently.

9.3 Copying in Emulation: Genre Art in the Netherlands

Art exists to satisfy its consumers. During the medieval period, the Catholic Church predominantly supported (or even hired) artists; in fact, it acted more like a consumer who provided investment (or remuneration) for artists to produce "cultural" goods. Therefore, countless works produced during this period contained themes related to the Bible or religious stories in order to meet the demands of their consumers. This trend changed significantly as royal families or aristocrats began to extend support (patronage) to artists, in other words they acted as consumers; the themes therefore shifted from biblical images to portraits of family members of royalty and aristocrats. This trend has changed further as the range of consumers has expanded to the bourgeoisie and middle class (Sonntag and Blühm 2016; Waibor 2017).

In order to meet this expansion (and/or change) of consumer markets, more works were needed thus more artists emerged. For example, in the seventeenth century the number of artists in work was more than the number of bankers to the extent that some paid their bills with their art works (Sonntag and Blühm 2016: 172–173). One interesting point is that Dutch artists never considered themselves as "artists," but rather as "craftsmen" during this period. Within this context, genre art emerged. The pictorial representation of genre art depicts interiors, parties, street scenes, and still life (Armenini 1977). And in order to meet the demands of the time, these depicted images were more realistic than the religious works of the precedent period. Figure 9.4 shows several typical works of genre art. Two different series of works are shown; one is about a woman writing a letter and the other is about a couple.

When the three works from each series are compared, a striking similarity can be found despite the fact that they were painted by different artists from around the same period. Regardless of the details of each piece, the posture of the figure(s)

Gerard Ter Borch (1655-1656)   Gabriel Metsu (1662-1664)   Johannes Vermeer (1665-1667)

Gerard Ter Borch (1658-1659)   Frans van Mieris (1661)   Jacob Ochtervelt (1664-1665)

Fig. 9.4 Selected paintings of Genre Art. *Source* Somogy and Louvre (2017)

is very similar. Furthermore, some pieces were painted with similar colors, either yellowish or ruddy. Under the current copyright law, this case would be considered as a violation and would therefore face criticism from various parties and the public. In this respect, why then did they paint in a similar style? There are two main reasons; by doing so (1) they can highlight their identification with the same school and (2) artists in the same school are usually in competition which brings about learning and improvement (Sluijter 2017; Waibor 2017). Artists learned from their peers and tried to show that they can paint the same object better than their peers at the same time through "dissimilar similarity" (Sluijter 2017). As a result, genre art flourished during the seventeenth and early eighteenth centuries and influenced future art forms such as realism and post-impressionism (Fuchs 1978). In short, copying in this case again did not hurt cultural diversity and creativity, but actually helped to promote it one step further.

9.4 Copying for Learning and Inspiration: Vincent Van Gogh versus Jean-François Millet

Some would argue that this copying practice only happened among a few schools or groups of artists who are not that well-known. In this section, two of the most famous painters are compared, Vincent Van Gogh and Jean-François Millet. Van Gogh is regarded as one of the greatest artists and his paintings are some of the world's most expensive works of art. This is in contrast to when he was alive and was unknown artist who only sold one piece. Figure 9.5 presents ten works by Van Gogh and ten works by Millet. One can easily see how similar these ten pieces by Van Gogh are to Millet's works when compared together; although several pieces such as *The Gleaners*, located on the left of the last row, show a difference in terms of the number of people and the presentation. Some even portray different images but still use similar titles, such as *Starry Night over the Rhone* by Van Gogh and *Starry Night* by Millet which are located on the right side of the last row.

After his death, Vincent Van Gogh left behind around 870 pieces of work. Among them around 520 pieces, almost 60%, are in fact copies of other painters such as Delacroix, Rembrant, Doré, and Millet, for which he copied from the most (Schwartz 1996: 248). Interestingly, Van Gogh and Millet were not in the same school nor did they even meet during their lives. Obviously Van Gogh never asked for permission from Millet nor did Millet give his consent. In the bundle of letters exchanged with his brother Theo, Vincent confessed many times that by copying Millet's works he was able to learn painting techniques, perception of light, usage of colors, and other artistic skills. For Vincent, copying Millet's works allowed him to enhance his artistry which indeed helped contribute toward cultural creativity and diversity, as other artists have done (Nagahiro and Singleton 2014).

Fig. 9.5 Vincent Van Gogh versus Jean-François Millet. *Sources* Various (please refer to references)

There is a prevailing view among cultural industries today that a copied work would hurt the original, resulting in a negative effect on cultural diversity and creativity. However, Millet's fame quickly declined because (1) as Napoleon III pushed for industrialization, Millet's works were regarded as old fashion by society and (2) he painted poor farmers and miserable rural life when people during that period preferred to see paintings with a more romantic vision (Sensier et al. 2007). As a result, most artists did not pay much attention to him. In other words, Millet's works devalued not because Van Gogh produced copies of them, but rather because other artists did not copy his works nor did they reference his works. The only exception was Vincent Van Gogh. This may also explain why Van Gogh had a hard time to be recognized as a good painter and sold only one piece during his lifetime.[3]

Under the current copyright regime, works are protected for 70 years after the death of the author or the copyright holder (*post mortem auctoris* or pma). In other words, copying a work that is over 70 years pma is not considered as a violation. Obviously, as shown in Fig. 9.5, the difference in the production year is much less than 70 years. Therefore, most of Van Gogh's pieces would be a violation under the current copyright law and he would have had a difficult time to avoid public criticism. Still, some may argue that these pieces by Van Gogh were intended to be only studies; in a way, it is very similar to the aforementioned case, BTS copying Kanye West. While that might be true of the time they were produced, today the works of both Van Gogh and Millet are exhibited in museums and auctioned for large sums of money. In the end, this is very similar to "taking the creative ideas of another and selling and/or publishing them as one's own." However, this fact does not hurt Millet's work nor his reputation.

Interestingly, Van Gogh's copied pieces are now usually more valuable than the originals. In order to understand this value gap, an in-depth analysis is needed. Why are Van Gogh's works more valuable in the market than that of Millet's? Who was the better painter, Van Gogh or Millet? Whose works are more original? Have Van Gogh's copied pieces devalued Millet's works? Furthermore, did Van Gogh's copying bring disgrace to him and hinder cultural diversity and creativity? All of these questions should be further studied carefully.

It is noteworthy to mention what Theo wrote to Vincent; "The copies after Millet are perhaps the best things you have done yet, and induce me to believe that on the day you turn to painting compositions of figures, we may look forward to great surprises" (Van Gogh 2000 [1896]: 569).

---

[3] While he was alive he only sold one piece, *The Red Vineyard near Arles*, for 400 Belgian francs in 1890 (roughly equivalent to six to eight month wages of a domestic servant) or about 1200 U.S. dollars at the current exchange rate. Today it is valued at more than 722 million U.S. dollars (Parc 2015).

9.5   Copying the Copied: Pablo Picasso and Others

Copying practices in culture can be found among the works of even recent painters. Another famous painter Pablo Picasso is at the core of such practice. In this section, four pieces by Picasso are shown next to the originals that he copied from (Figs. 9.6 and 9.7, right side). Compared to what Van Gogh did, Picasso's works can be viewed as a different interpretation of or inspired versions of existing works. In any case, the originals that Picasso copied or benchmarked were in the public domain when he produced his works.[4] Therefore, the two works by Picasso presented in Fig. 9.6 are free from the copyright violation.

However, the two pieces by Picasso presented in Fig. 9.7 leads to an interesting debate on the issue. The first piece by Picasso seems to copy a work by Manet in terms of composition. Interestingly though, according to the current copyright law, Picasso's 1951 work can be considered to have violated the law. This is because Manet's work is less than 70 years pma; Édouard Manet passed away in 1883 and

Pablo Picasso (1957)   Diego Vélasquez (1656)

Pablo Picasso (1962)   Jacques-Louis David (1796-1799)

Fig. 9.6 Pablo Picasso versus others. *Sources* Various (please refer to references)

---

[4]Public domain is the period beginning after the expiration of the copyright where any firm or individual can disseminate formerly copyrighted works without paying copyright-based earnings to the authors.

| Pablo Picasso (1951) | Édouard Manet (1868-1869) | Francisco Jose de Goya (1814) |

| Pablo Picasso (1960a) | Claude Monet (1865-1866) | Édouard Manet (1862-1863) |

Fig. 9.7 Copying and copied: Pablo Picasso and others. *Sources* Various (please refer to references)

his work would only be in the public domain after 1953. Yet, even Manet's painting is a copy of Goya's work which was produced in 1814. When Manet's and Goya's works are compared, Manet's work would not have been a violation of the law. If these three artists faced a court case, Picasso could argue that he did not copy Manet's work, but Goya's work. Hence, the court would reach a verdict that Picasso is not guilty because his work is produced 70 years pma after Goya's work.

A similar situation can be found with another work by Picasso, *The Luncheon on the Grass* (last row in Fig. 9.7). Here if Picasso were to argue that he copied Manet's work which was produced in 1863 not Monet's work of 1866, he would be free from copyright violation. In fact, the widely-known official title of Picasso's work is *The Luncheon on the Grass (after Manet)*. The more interesting point is that the production year of Monet and Manet's works differs by only two years, but important in regards to copyright law is that Manet died in 1883 whereas Monet died in 1926. This means that if Manet had lived as long as Monet did, Picasso's work would be considered a violation. This example shows that, the violation depends on the date when the artist passed away. If we recall the fact that copyrights insist artists do not copy each other's work in order to respect cultural creativity and diversity, then this argument does not make any sense with the Picasso-Monet-Manet-Goya case. How can it be argued that copying past works which are more than 70 years pma (due to the early production year or the author's early death) does not harm cultural diversity and creativity, but doing so with works that are less than 70 years pma does harm cultural diversity and creativity?

Another interesting point can be found in Fig. 9.8. *Judgement of Paris* was produced in the early sixteenth century. Initially, this piece was very different from the works of Picasso, Monet, and Manet entitled *The Luncheon on the Grass*. However, if we pay more attention to each corner of this work, we can see that Manet's work

Marcantonio Raimondi (1510-1520)

Fig. 9.8 The original: *Judgement of Paris. Sources* Metro Politian Museum of Art

copies a scene from the bottom right corner of the original piece. Thus, all three artists, Picasso, Monet, and Manet can be considered to have copied from the same work and "interpreted" it in their own way. Based on all of these facts, it is hard to argue that copying hinders cultural diversity and creativity.

9.6 Discussion

In the past, why did so many artists copy existing works? What was the purpose behind this trend? The reality is that this kind of practice can often be found throughout the history of "art". In fact, some artists have even collected images from existing works to make a "bank of images" which can be used as their own work (Sluijter 2017), although this tends to be viewed negatively in our time given the context of copyrights. There are several reasons why artists have copied other work. First, people copied as a form of admiration. Sometimes it has a meaning of veneration or worship, like the cult objects in the Catholic Church. Therefore, the same style should be maintained, such as the direction of Jesus' head on the crucifixion or the position of Mary and the Baby Jesus.

Second, as these works became more popularized, artists then sought to produce the same object but with more desire or even ambition, reaching the same style or technique used in the original work by examining their own ability. Third, they seek to show that they are doing better than their peers by copying an original work or learning from one another through imitation as shown with artists in the seventeenth century. Through this process many artists learn new techniques and enhance them; sometimes using it as even inspiration for further development as Vincent Van Gogh confessed many times in his letters. In brief, it is only in recent years that this practice of copying has come to be viewed negatively. Furthermore, given that we are in the age of mass production since the twentieth century, people have come to associate reproductions as commercial items rather than work, therefore different or unique works are more favored.

One interesting point that we should not miss is the fact that Van Gogh's copied works are more accurate and precise than other copies by genre artists, particularly when compared with the originals. Intriguingly, this is more related to technological advancements, like the rosette in the *Gran Madre di Dio*. Van Gogh could do it better because he had Millet's works in his hand and was able to copy as much as he could. In contrast to Van Gogh, genre artists had to visit galleries during the day to view originals to copy or benchmark and then paint them at home during the night.

Before the Van Gogh period, paper was expensive and only a limited number of people could afford it. It was only around the 1840s that Friedrich Gottlob Keller and Charles Fenerty invented the wood pull process for papermaking (Burger 2007). This reduced the price of paper significantly and after this technological advancement many people were able to use it more readily. With the popularization of paper and the advancement of etching techniques, many existing paintings were copied and printed out on paper. In some of the letters he exchanged with Theo who was working for a gallery in Montmartre, Paris, Vincent Van Gough asked him to send copies of specific works by Millet. Once he was in possession of the works, Van Gogh was able to freely copy Millet as much as he wanted to.

Furthermore, in the 1830s, Winsor & Newton, Ltd. began to produce paints, both industrialized oil and water color, and standardized brushes (Barnett et al. 2006). Compared to precedent times where each artist had to make their own color and colorant, the newly produced standardized paints and brushes helped artists to produce works that are more original-like than before in terms of color.

It is evident that as society entered the age of mass-production, people tended to appreciate items that are different and unique. This is why Picasso produced many "inspired" works that can be considered as different interpretations of existing works. In fact, Picasso produced many different versions of *The Luncheon on the Grass* after Manet's one. The initial version is relatively similar to Manet's original, but as he produces many contrasting versions he begins to develop his own style which is different from his earlier version (see Fig. 9.9). The last one would be considered as more of an inspired work. The evolution of Picasso's work shows explicitly that copying does not hinder cultural diversity and creativity, but rather helps it.

1960a   1960b

1961   1962

Fig. 9.9 The evolution of *the luncheon on the grass* (by Picasso)

9.7 Conclusion

In this era of digitization, the sharing of cultural contents through online intermediaries such as YouTube has increased steadily. In response, there have been a number of concerned voices pushing for copyrights to be tightened further in order to protect cultural creativity and diversity. In particular, international organizations such as the WIPO and UNESCO as well as some countries like the United States, have emphasized the need to respect copyright laws in relation to economic and non-economic rights. Economic rights allow the rights-owner to derive financial rewards from the use of his or her works by others, while non-economic rights are related to cultural diversity and creativity. Broadly, these copyright laws seek to establish two objectives. Firstly, by imposing restrictions on copying, authors must differentiate their work from others which helps to secure greater diversity. Secondly, having done this, authors will achieve a more stable financial backing and thus work toward exercising more creativity.

In reality though, this has not always been the case. Although copying is often considered as a negative practice in our time, throughout history it has often been perceived more positively. This chapter focuses on the true role of copying to reveal the relationship between copying and cultural creativity and diversity. Throughout history the perception of imitation has drastically changed from admiration, ambition, inspiration to immorality. By looking at the early Christian art work, genre art from the Netherlands in seventeenth century, and famous painters such as Vincent Van Gogh and Pablo Picasso, a new perspective on copying is presented in this chapter. It argues that contrary to current prevailing beliefs, imitation does not restrict cultural creativity or diversity. Furthermore, by comparing the aforementioned artists and their works, it is argued that the notion of copyright duration is too arbitrary which requires a different scope for further studies.

The findings of this chapter together with the historical evidence demonstrates that the current view on copying and copyright laws may be too limited, overwhelmed too much by the concept of innovation, and are narrowly focused on our time, rather than approaching cultural diversity and creativity as a whole from a historical perspective. When a cultural trend is prosperous, it can have a significant impact on culture and be recognized as part of history. Instead, the current concept of cultural diversity and creativity and its "supporting" copyrights law tend to view culture myopically rather than hypermetropically and protects only first-movers—but are they really the first?—while eliminating challenges from late-movers. This approach would promote various different styles for a short time, but cannot help a trend to become prosperous through copying and imitating over a longer period.

In order to foster the dynamics of cultural diversity and creativity, copying and its practice within the copyrights (or more likely intellectual property rights) regime should be carefully reconsidered. More importantly, the current copyrights regime may be more about earnings, rather than cultural creativity or diversity. One might argue that all of these clichés are invented to keep the economic hegemony derived from cultural goods which has been established through the wrong interpretation of neo-capitalism. This is a point that should be carefully assessed. If the world really wants to achieve cultural diversity and creativity, we should not miss what Isaac Newton once said, "if I can see further it is by standing on the shoulders of giants." He was insightful enough to use "standing" not "trampling" and this aspect should be kept in the back of our mind.

Acknowledgements This work was supported by the Laboratory Program for Korean Studies through the Ministry of Education of the Republic of Korea and the Korean Studies Promotion Service of the Academy of Korean Studies (AKS-2015-LAB-2250003).

References

Abi Abroad. (2013). B-Free disrespecting BTS Rap Monster & Suga? https://www.youtube.com/watch?v=A60nxqU_uIE, originally from Kim Bong-Hyun's hip-hop chodaeseok [Bong-hyun Kim's hip-hop live show], Nov. 21. Accessed February 7, 2018.

Armenini, G. B. (1977). *On the true precepts of the art of painting*, ed. and trans. E. J. Olszewski, B. Franklin, New York, NY.

Barnett, J. R., Miller, S., & Pearce, E. (2006). Colour and art: A brief history of pigments. *Optics & Laser Technology, 38*(4–6), 445–453.

Boespflug, F. (2008). *Dieu et ses images. Une histoire de l'Eternel dans l'art*. Paris, France: Bayard Editions.

Boston Consulting Group. (2018). *The most innovative companies 2018*. https://www.bcg.com/publications/collections/most-innovative-companies-2018.aspx. Accessed June 21, 2018.

Burger, P. (2007). *Charles Fenerty and his paper invention*. Gatineau, Québec, Canada: Peter Burger.

Fuchs, R. H. (1978). *Dutch painting: World of art*. London, UK: Thames and Hudson.

Godin, B. (2017). Why is imitation not innovation? In Benoît Godin & Dominique Vinck (Eds.), *Critical studies of innovation: Alternative approaches to the pro-innovation bias* (pp. 17–32). Cheltenham, UK and Northampton, MA, USA: Edward Elgar Publishing.

Hatch, O. (1998). Toward a principled approach to copyright legislation at the turn of the millennium. *University of Pittsburgh Law Review, 719,* 719–757.

Liebowitz, S. (2007). What are the consequences of the European Union extending copyright length for sound recordings? Document prepared for IFPI (International Federation of the Phonographic Industry).

Lowensohn, J. (2012). Apple design expert calls Samsung a copycat. *CNET* (6 August). https://www.cnet.com/news/apple-design-expert-calls-samsung-a-copycat/. Accessed June 21, 2018.

McManus, C. (2013). *Right hand, left hand: The origins of asymmetry in brains, bodies, atoms and cultures*. Hachette, UK: Phoenix.

Moreno, J. Y., Santagata, W., & Tabassum, A. (2005). *Material cultural heritage, cultural diversity, and sustainable development*. Working Papers, Ebla Center, University of Turin.

Nagahiro, K., & Singleton, K. (2014). From Van Gogh as intellectual history: The reception of reproductions and imagination. *Review of Japanese Culture and Society, 26,* 242–265.

Parc, J. (2015). Wrestling with or embracing digitization? http://ecipe.org/blog/wrestling-with-or-embracing-digitization/. Accessed March 1, 2018.

Roth, M. (2009). *The left stuff: How the left-handed have survived and thrived in a right-handed world*. Plymouth, UK: M. Evans & Company.

Schwartz, H. (1996). *The culture of the copy*. New York, NY, USA: Zone Books.

Sensier, A., Mantz, P., Lacambre, G., Deschamps, G., & Deschamps, R. (2007). *La vie et l'œuvre de Jean-François Millet*. Paris, France: Éditions des Champs.

Sluijter, E. J. (2017). Imitation: Chez les peinnre de genre. In Somogy and Louvre (Eds.), *Vermeer et les Maîtres de la peinture de genre* (pp. 69–89). Paris, France: Somogy Editions d'Art and Louvre editions.

Somogy and Louvre (Eds.). (2017). *Vermeer et les Maîtres de la peinture de genre*. Paris, France: Somogy Editions d'Art and Louvre editions.

Sonntag, S., & Blühm, A. (Eds.). (2016). *Wallraf das museum*. Cologne, Germany: Dumont.

The United Nations Educational, Scientific and Cultural Organization (UNESCO). (2017). Copyright. Accessed April 17, http://www.unesco.org/new/en/culture/themes/creativity/creative-industries/copyright/. Accessed December 2, 2017.

Van Gogh, V. 2000 (1896). *The complete letters of Vincent Van Gogh* (Vol. 3, p. 569). Bulfinch Press.

Waibor, A. E. (2017). Vermeer et les Maîtres de la peinture de genre. In Somogy and Louvre (Eds.), *Vermeer et les Maîtres de la peinture de genre* (pp. 15–43). Paris, France: Somogy Editions d'Art and Louvre editions.

Werner, M. (1972). The Madonna and child miniature in the Book of Kells Part I. *The Art Bulletin, 54*(1), 1–23.

World Intellectual Property Organization (WIPO). (2017). Copyright. Accessed April 17. http://www.wipo.int/copyright/en. Accessed December 2, 2017.

List of Works (Painting and Photos) Used

David, J.-L. (1796–1799). *The intervention of the Sabine women.* Paris, France: Musée du Louvre.

De Goya, F. J. (1814). *The third of May 1808.* Spain: Museo Nacional Del Prado.

Manet, E. (1862–1863). *The luncheon on the grass.* Paris, France: Musée d'Orsay.

Manet, E. (1868–1869). *The execution of the Emperor Maximilian of Mexico.* Mannheim, Germany: Staedtische Kunsthalle.

Martini, S. (1284–1344). *Mary with the child.* Cologne, Germany: Wallraf das Museum.

Metsu, G. (1662–1664). *Elegant lady writing at her desk.* Private Collection.

Millet, J.-F. (1850). *The sower.* Boston, MA: Museum of fine Arts.

Millet, J.-F. (1852–1853). *The sheep-shearers.* Boston, MA, USA: Museum of fine Arts.

Millet, J.-F. (1854). *Peasant woman with a rake.* New York, NY, USA: The Metropolitan Museum of Art.

Millet, J.-F. (1855). *The woodcutter.* Paris, France: Musée du Louvre.

Millet, J.-F. (1858). *The first steps.* Laurel, MS: Lauren Rogers Museum of Art.

Millet, J.-F. (1866a). *Noon–rest from work.* Boston, MA: Museum of Fine Arts.

Millet, J.-F. (1866b). *Two peasants digging.* Boston, MA, USA: Museum of Fine Arts.

Millet, J.-F. (1873). *Morning: Going to work.* Jerusalem, Israel: Matsart Auctioneers & Appraisers.

Millet, J.-F. (1875a). *The gleaners.* Paris, France: Musée d'Orsay.

Millet, J.-F. (1875b). *Starry night.* New Haven, CT, USA: Yale University Art Gallery.

Monet, C. (1865–1866). *The luncheon on the grass.* Paris, France: Musée d'Orsay.

Museo Torino. (2018). *Cross section diagram of Gran Madre di Dio,* http://www.museotorino.it/view/s/11e36cd6c6a04425ba9a8445e0c518d9. Accessed February 15, 2018.

Ochtervelt, J. (1664–1665). *The oyster meal.* London, UK: Guildhall Art Gallery.

Picasso, P. (1951). *Massacre in Korea.* Paris, France: Musée Picasso.

Picasso, P. (1957). *Las meninas (after Vélasquez).* Paris, France: Musée Picasso.

Picasso, P. (1960a). *The luncheon on the grass (after Manet).* Private Collection.

Picasso, P. (1960b). *The luncheon on the grass (after Manet).* Paris, France: Musée Picasso.

Picasso, P. (1961). *The luncheon on the grass (after Manet).* Lucerne, Switzerland: Galerie Rosengart.

Picasso, P. (1962a). *The luncheon on the grass (after Manet).* New York, NY: Collection of Catherine Woodard and Nelson Blitz, Jr. © 2017 Estate of Pablo Picasso/Artists Rights Society (ARS).

Picasso, P. (1962b). *The rape of the Sabine women.* Paris, France: Centre Pompidou.

Raimondi, M. (1510–1520). *Judgement of Paris.* Collection of Earls Spencer (British); Vendor: P. & D. Colnaghi & Co, https://www.metmuseum.org/toah/works-of-art/19.74.1/. Accessed March 1, 2018.

Ter Borch, G. (1655–1656). *A gentleman pressing a lady to drink.* London, UK: Royal Collection Trust.

Ter Borch, G. (1658–1659). *Woman writing a letter.* The Mauritshuis, The Hague, The Netherlands.

Tripadvisor. Photo of Gran Madre di Dio, https://www.tripadvisor.ch. Accessed February 15, 2018.

Unknown. (Various years). Various works on Jesus crucifixion. Wallraf das Museum, Cologne, Germany.

Unknown. (1250–1260). *Enthroned Madonna with the Christ child.* Cologne, Germany: Wallraf das Museum.

Unknown. (before 1499). *Our mother of perpetual help.* Rome, Italy: Church of St. Alphonsus Liguori.

Van Gogh, V. (1888). *Starry night over the Rhone.* Paris, France: Musée d'Orsay.

Van Gogh, V. (1889a). *Peasant woman with a rake (after Millet).* Private collection.

Van Gogh, V. (1889b). *The sower (after Millet).* Otterlo, The Netherlands: Kroller-Muller Museum.

Van Gogh, V. (1889c). *Two peasants digging (after Millet).* Amsterdam, The Netherlands: Stedelijk Museum.

Van Gogh, V. (1889d). *The woodcutter (after Millet).* Amsterdam, The Netherlands: Van Gogh Museum.

Van Gogh, V. (1889e). *The sheep-shearers (after Millet)*. Amsterdam, The Netherlands: Van Gogh Museum.

Van Gogh, V. (1890a). *The first steps (after Millet)*. New York, USA: The Metropolitan Museum of Art.

Van Gogh, V. (1890b). *The gleaners (after Millet)*. Bührle, Zürich, Switzerland: Sammlung E. G.

Van Gogh, V. (1890c). *Morning: Going to work (after Millet)*. Saint Petersburg, Russia: Hermitage Museum.

Van Gogh, V. (1890d). *Noon–rest from work (after Millet)*. Paris, France: Musée d'Orsay.

Van Mieris, F. (1661). *The oyster meal*. The Hague, The Netherlands: The Mauritshuis.

Vanupied. (2018). *Dome of Gran Madre di Dio* (photo by Gianni Caeddu), https://www.vanupied. com/turin/monuments-turin/eglise-circulaire-gran-madre-di-dio-a-turin.html. Accessed February 15, 2018.

Vélasquez, D. (1656). *Las meninas*. Spain: Museo Nacional Del Prado.

Vermeer, J. (1665–1667). *A lady writing*. Washington DC, USA: National Gallery of Art.

Jimmyn Parc is a visiting lecturer at Sciences Po Paris, France and a researcher at Institute of Communication Research, Seoul National University in Korea. He received a Ph.D. in international studies (with focus on international business and strategy) from the Graduate School of International Studies (GSIS), Seoul National University and another Ph.D. in economic history from University of Paris-Sorbonne (Paris IV). He has published numerous academic articles and conducted a number of research projects related to the competitiveness of organizations, industries, and countries. His current research focuses on cultural industries in Asia and Europe, which includes films and music. Currently, they are at critical juncture as they face a changing business and trade environment as well as new challenges from digitization.

Chapter 10
Tradition or Innovation? Creativity and Internationalisation in Kyoto's Craft Industries

Adam Johns

Traditional crafts may seem an unorthodox choice for an examination of creativity and innovation. When presented as a dichotomy of two contending forces, the continuity of existing practice, which tradition entails, seems the antithesis of proactive experimentation leading to change in the status quo. The current state of these industries in Japan, however, offers the opportunity to explore innovation in locally-embedded industries through the process of internationalisation.

Predominantly operating under a moniker of Japanese traditional industries (*dentō sangyo*) or tradition craft (*dento kogei*), these crafts—including a disparate variety of woven and dyed textiles, pottery, lacquerware, and specialised forms of woodwork and metalwork—have continued to decline year on year and are today a mere fraction of their size at the height of their production. Changes in consumer preferences, lifestyle, and taste has led to large-scale decline of traditional markets for these products. This has subsequently led to a collapse in the number of both artisans and merchants, the latter of whom have long fulfilled the role of market-making intermediary for many of these industries.

One of the major challenges—and opportunities—facing tradition craft industries is internationalization and its potential to reinvigorate production with new materials, processes, applications, and markets, while attracting new talent. But do they have the diverse skillset and flexibility required to achieve this?

Indeed, this "traditional" label seems to axiomatically suggest limitations to the amount of innovation that might be permitted within the sector, particularly where it relates to the modernizing of the craft to meet the needs of contemporary and indeed international markets. For this reason, some call for this label to be discarded—Murayama (2019) urges both industry and policymakers to consider the chronologically agnostic "cultural business".

Amid this backdrop, both private and public-sector initiatives have been increasing in an effort to both preserve and promote these industries. Artisans and merchants

A. Johns (✉)
Sophia University, Tokyo, Japan
e-mail: ajohns@sophia.ac.jp

© Springer Nature Singapore Pte Ltd. 2020
N. Otmazgin and E. Ben-Ari (eds.), *Creative Context*, Creative Economy,
https://doi.org/10.1007/978-981-15-3056-2_10

have increasingly been working with international designers and advisors, and often facilitated by newly emerged "producers" to develop new contemporary products for global niche markets. These efforts are often supported (and subsidised) by local, regional, and national government programs. But is such global innovation possible within such a domestic-focused tradition?

Having been the capital for over 1000 years, Kyoto was the site of widespread creativity and innovation that attracted artists and artisans from around the country to push their craft to the pinnacle of technical refinement and artistic endeavour. With an enduring concentration of traditional crafts, Kyoto makes for a unique case study to examine the nature of creativity and innovation in these attempts to modernize and internationalise.

This chapter examines "traditional" heritage crafts providers in Kyoto that have—through a mix of private and public initiatives—sought to dramatically alter their production process in order to ensure the survival of their craft. First, it examines the definition of traditional craft, discussing the relationship between tradition and innovation and the contending distinction between artisan and artist and the division of labour in the creative process before proposing theoretical challenges to innovation under a codified definition of tradition. Through a series of short case studies, it then assesses the effect that interventions to internationalise the sector has had on the level of innovation within the industry, and examines the extent to which the codification of tradition is compatible with the long-term sustainability and innovative flexibility of the industry.

Evidence from the craft industries in Kyoto indicates that the choice between tradition and innovation suggested in the title is very much a false dichotomy. While compromises in the creative process may disappoint purists, it indicates that innovation vis-à-vis internationalisation as a survival mechanism has begun to take hold in the industry. As a result, many artisans and merchants have begun to adapt new roles and professional identities in a realisation that not only products and processes but organisational structure need to change in order to survive.

10.1 Defining Traditional Craft

Defining craft—and traditional craft—is a complex endeavour. In the broadest possible sense, Adamson defines craft as a process and 'not a classification of objects, institutions, or people' (Adamson 2007: 4), while Gore considers craft as 'any human transformation of raw material into another object' (Gore 2004: 39). Murata similarly describes the definition of *kogei* as 'a representation of the process of creation itself where human and material/nature—subjects and objects—are fused together' (Murata 2015: 11–12).

In this vein, there is a significant volume of existing research in the art history and cultural studies disciplines that thoroughly examines the historical and philosophical distinctions between fine art, craft, and industrial manufacturing. Here, the definition of tradition craft will use the Japanese legal classification as a starting point, and distinctions between art, craft, and industry will specifically focus on the legal, organisational, and marketing ramifications, and the perspective of industry participants themselves.

A critical question is whether the classification sets stringent guidelines or limitations on new product innovation, the use of alternative materials, processes, or new products that currently have no history of traditional daily use or may be designed with global—not Japanese—markets in mind.

10.1.1 Designated Traditional Crafts in Japan

The Law for the Promotion of Traditional Craft Industries ("Densan Act") was enacted in 1974 to preserve and protect "officially designated traditional craft" in the belief that they not only supported regional economic development but to sustain the cultural fabric and legacy of Japanese society (METI 2011).

As of November 2018, there were 232 officially designated craft. This includes 38 different woven textiles, 12 dyed textiles, 32 ceramics, 23 lacquerware, 32 wood and bamboo craft, 16 metalwork, and 17 regionally-distinct Buddhist altar objects.

In contrast to the growing number of designated crafts, the industry declines year on year. After peaking at 540 billion yen (US$4.7 billion) in 1983, total production value of traditional craft fell steeply after the burst of the bubble economy in 1991, from over 500 billion yen (US$4.3 billion) in 1990 to 96 billion yen (US$835 million) in 2016.[1] Correspondingly, employment in the sector dropped from its approximately 288,000 peaking in 1979 to around 200,000 in 1990 then to 62,690 in 2016 (METI 2011; Densan Association 2018). Some insiders predict that without intervention many crafts will disappear within this generation of artisans (Kyoto Journal 2014).

According to The Act, craft must meet five criteria in order to receive designation by the Ministry of Economy Trade and Investment (METI):

1. The craft articles must be used mainly in everyday life.
2. The part of the craft that greatly influence its features should be made mainly by hand in the manufacturing process.
3. The craft articles must have a manufacturing history of at least 100 years, and must be made using traditional skills and techniques that continue to be used until the present.
4. As a general rule, the main raw materials of the craft articles must be those used continuously for more than 100 years.
5. Regional enterprises that produce the said craft should maintain a certain scale [at least 10 companies or over 30 people] and should be established as a local industry.

(Association for the Promotion of Traditional Craft Industries 2017)

---

[1] For consistency, Japanese yen to US dollar conversion is for reference only and takes a December 2016 average spot rate of 115 Japanese yen to 1 US dollar.

Yet in a modern post-industrialised world, some of these criteria come with inherent tension. To satisfy all of these criteria, a craft must be both historical and contemporary, yet neither art nor artefact. Likewise, to be predominantly handmade and yet created in a regional industrial agglomeration, a craft must have overcome pressures toward mass production and the shifting of production to low-cost centres throughout the world.

Pragmatically, the Densan Act defers specific criteria of each designation to the individual guilds responsible for registering and (self)regulating the traditional craft. This includes definitional decisions regarding raw materials, production processes, and provenance.

For example, the joint nomenclature of *kyo-yaki/kiyomizu-yaki* (often translated into English as "Kyoto ware") received its designation in 1977. Registered by the local guild (Kyoto Tojiki Kyodo Kumiai Rengokai), the notification specifies eight types of porcelain or clay, eight production techniques, sixteen ornamentation techniques, seven techniques for undercoat painting, six glazing techniques, and fourteen overcoat decorative painting techniques that can be used, as well as the five different cities in Kyoto Prefecture where production can be undertaken (Densan Association, n.d. a).

Likewise, for *Nishijin-ori* (also designated in 1976), registered by the local guild (Nishijin-ori Kogyo Kumiai), the designation specifies the allowed production techniques for the eleven different textiles classified as Nishijin-ori, allowing for different machines or handlooms that may make them, and specifies the permitted thread—silk, cotton, hemp/linen, gold and silver thread. *Tsuzure*, for example, specifies that it must be *sakizome* (yarn dyed prior to weaving) requiring extraordinary precision in both dying and weaving, and that the weft should be woven with a hand-operated shuttle with thread alignment by the weaver using their fingernails (Densan Association, n.d. b).

10.2 Challenging Traditional Craft

Yet as artisans and merchants develop new products, will these innovations may counter to the five qualifying criteria of traditional craft? Below, potential shifts away from the requirements of everyday, handmade, process, material, and provenance are considered as providers consider the imperative to internationalise.

10.2.1 Neither Art Nor Artefact

What if product innovation or market innovation resulted in a shift away from the "everyday life" criteria? For example, shifting the production to fine art, or for upmarket or foreign audiences (this could go to 'international section').

By specifying the relevance of craft to everyday life, the Act draws a clear line between craft (*kogei*) and fine art (*bijutsu*). Yet Sato (2011) indicates this distinction arising only in mid-Meiji Period, and Guth (2010) describes the distinction that has developed in Japan between arts and craft (and hence artist and artisan) as a false dichotomy exacerbated by a loss of respect for replication and copying (*utsushi*). A parallel can be drawn here with Bauhaus movement, as founder Walter Gropius saw the division between artisan and artist as one of 'divisive class pretention', believing there was 'no essential difference between the artist and artisan' and that the original source of creative design was a solid foundation of technical proficiency (Bauhaus Manifesto).

However, this theoretical blurred line between artist and artisan can be a reality in the production of some crafts. For example, renowned Seto/Mino potter and designated living national treasure Hajime Kato (1900–1968) regularly traversed this line, submitting works of creative "art expression" to the Nitten exhibition, and works that study craft technique to Nihon Dento Kogei Ten (Kida 2010). This suggests a strong link between technical proficiency and artistic expression, and this fluidity between roles as artist and artisan is echoed in the contemporary practices at the Kyoto kiln of Takehiro Kato covered below. Conversely, the case of Takeshi Nishimura's transition from artisan to artist can be seen as a result of the decline in the textile industry that gave rise to his technique.

Despite the functional daily life criteria, the required production values and (artisanship) and lack of economies of scale (cost) mean that the symbolic and hedonic value from these products will greatly outweigh their utilitarian benefits. Indeed, each craft's survival relies on the consumer's perception and belief that they are acquiring far more than a functional bowl, cup, brush, or piece of fabric, and due to the hand-made, historical, place-based, or aesthetic/design related properties, are willing to pay a premium for it.

While new artistic innovations might not meet the classification for "traditional craft", the greater concern is for these crafts to no longer meet the everyday needs of consumers. The dramatic drop in demand over the last decades provides support for such a claim, suggesting that if only in theory, innovation is the only way for craft to maintain this aspect of its "traditional" designation.

10.2.2 Hand or Human Made?

Might cost pressures or advances in technology drive production from hand to machine? In this case, is the line between craft and industrial manufacturing drawn on the basis of technique (when processes change from hand to machine), volume (when production surpasses a critical mass), or organisational structure (when production process shifts from one or two artisans to a highly specialised division of labour)?

In questioning whether anything is actually done "by hand", Pye (1968) raises problematic definitional concerns over partly and fully made-by-hand distinctions, concluding that the distinction between hand and machine-made is 'all but mean-ingless' (Pye 1968: 25), preferring to consider whether the process was applied to deliver *workmanship of risk* or *workmanship of certainty*.

To this end, the romanticised perception of craft as pre-modern and fully hand-made often runs counter to the realities of the workshop floor. But whether tools used are hand or machine operated, the Densan Act leaves to the respective guilds. The definition pragmatically calling for parts that greatly influence the craft's fea-tures to be 'mainly' made by hand (Densan Association 2017), allowing for flexible interpretation—presumably in line with the craft's ethos.

Further, this notion of pre-modern production often assumes the marginalisation and decay of the industries due to new technologies (Adamson 2013). While the sharp decline in these industries in Japan appears to bear out these concerns, when considered as an evolutionary process, technology should—again in theory—only pose a threat to craft if its greatest value came from its functional, utilitarian value rather than its intangible hedonic or symbolic value.

This raises the critical question about innovation in the sector from a marketing perspective: what do artisans and merchants need to change (in both product and communication) in order for people to appreciate the latter intangible, hedonic value?

But would such changes in production disqualify goods from their traditional craft classification? Of critical importance, the designation of a traditional craft does not prevent artisans from manufacturing products outside of the traditional craft framework.

As a blacksmith from Sanjo, Niigata highlights,

> The[traditional craft]designation allows us in the guild to come together to promote our work, but most of the products we make don't fit the criteria of traditional craft so we don't apply the designated Densan Mark to them. If we were to produce everything according to traditional guidelines they would naturally take much longer and the cost would be so high that we could not sell many.

Thus, the traditional craft designation appears to assist in creating and protecting an "authentic" process but also heritage while allowing manufacturers to riff off this in order to create any number of new and original works in different forms and different price points.

10.2.3   Tradition Was Once Modern

When considering if the introduction of new processes or new materials would void a craft's traditional designation, it is first important to place these industries in their historical context.

At the peak of their cultural and economic significance, objects such as *yuzen* kimono, woodblock prints, and lacquerware bowls were in their varying forms, the height of artistic excellence, at the cutting-edge of technology, and/or the most efficient mode of production for daily and household objects.

As *urushi* and *makie* (lacquer) artist Kazami Murose (designated a Living National Treasure in 2008) states 'the classics weren't classics; they were original creations…Those *takamakie* and *hyomon* techniques…were truly original and creative works of the time…they were filled with ideas' (Murose in Kida 2010).

The development of the traditional Japanese umbrella or *wagasa* illustrates how these innovations continually changed the nature of the product, adding successive value for its users until reaching optimum efficiency. As fifth generation *wagasa* master Kotaro Nishibori argues, the addition of wax to waterproof the *washi* paper applied to the umbrella allowed it to evolve from a sun-shading parasol to a shelter from rain. Next, the folding bamboo open/close construction added during the Azuchi-Momoyama period (1573–1600) represented a major innovation of high complexity (Hiyoshiya, n.d.), allowing the portability and storage of a previously unwieldy and cumbersome item. Thus, viewing the *wagasa* not as a historical product but as one with a continual developmental process led Nishibori to adopt the phrase *tradition is continuing innovation*.

This sentiment is echoed in the words of Raku Kakunyu XIV (1918–1980), former master of the eponymous Raku ceramic house, which dates back to the sixteenth century, 'tradition does not mean being bound by the past. It means living in the era you live in, and building the world you believe in' (Raku and Matsubara 2016).

The Nishijin Textile Industry Association highlights the use of computers in the textile design phase, and for some types of textile, the encoding of this on to a 3.5-inch floppy disk—itself an antiquated technology—to assist with the weave of the brocade even when using hand-held shuttles. Indeed, like other craft, technology introduced from Europe during the Meiji period (such as Jacquard looms) were responsible for the revival of Nishijin textile industry. Similarly, *kyo-yaki* not only borrowed from other regional styles throughout its long development, but was again strongly influenced by techniques learned from German ceramists during the same Meiji period (Densan, n.d. a).

Thus, when the Densan Act was enacted in 1974, the 100-year requirement for classification meant that crafts needed to extend to at least 1874—the early Meiji period that saw a major modernization, westernization, and industrialization of Japan's industries, and seismic shifts in the social and cultural fabric. This allowed for craft/kogei that adopted newly modern processes at the time to hence classify as "traditional". In a stark example, Tokyo Antimony, which creates pieces made from metal alloy by casting and plating, designated in 2015 and dates back to the early Meiji period (Densan, n.d. c). Historically many of these pieces have not only benefited from twentieth century techniques but also display a distinctly romantic European aesthetic in spite of their designation as a Japanese traditional craft.

From a marketing perspective, the continued existence of a cultural craft adds to its intangible value: the ability to brand it as an authentic craft with a rich heritage and (if it is a newly designed product) with a modern sensibility, again leading to the creation of hedonic and symbolic value.

10.2.4   Provenance and Organisation

The fifth clause certifies its provenance, inextricably linking it to its place of origin, and allowing registered crafts to act as a quasi-geographical indication (GI). A clear motive of the Densan Act is to support locally-embedded industries and place-branded craft products, in turn lead to the economic development of rural and regional economies (Rausch 2009).

Yet what if some stages of production where shifted to a different region? While the shifting of production to other regions would clearly disqualify the product from using the Densan mark, the definition of "production" is also open for interpretation as is the origin of the traditional materials used in production process.

Pragmatically the Densan Act criteria do not explicitly mandate the provenance of materials—such as *urushi* lacquer, silk thread, or clay for ceramics and porcelain. To do so would be both unsustainable and historically inaccurate. Historical supply chains for materials of various craft in Kyoto, for example, have heavily relied on suppliers from various regions in Japan and overseas. Clay for ceramics cannot be found in Kyoto, and only the barest amount of silk for weaving is grown and spun in Japan. Likewise, only a tiny fraction of natural urushi (lacquer) liquid for example, is now harvested from Japan—approximately 98% being imported from China (MAFF 2017). Even wooden bowls for Kyoto's *kyo-shikki* lacquerware are predominantly hand-turned in Echizen, Fukui Prefecture before being lacquered in Kyoto.

Merchants have historically been the market-makers in many traditional industries, understanding market needs through the demands of buyers, organising disparate specialised productive inputs in textiles and ceramics, and in the case of *butsugu* (Buddhist altar goods), centralising production in-house. The demise of many merchants who have been slow and often unable to respond to market changes has also left many artisans to acquaint themselves with new techniques, materials, and most radically, new markets.

The division of labour has long been an integral aspect of many traditional crafts, despite the romanticized image of a solo craftsman. Specialisation brings technical proficiency and increase performance, and many industries such as textiles show a thinly-sliced division of labour with different functions defining the role each. Nishijin-ori and *kyo-yuzen* kimono—particularly stencil-dyed yuzen (*katazome*)—attest to these highly specialised roles. In katazome, specialised stencil-cutters and dyers who have honed their craft as apprentices operate independently. Below, the case of Nishimura Yuzen Chokoku will demonstrate the struggle of personal reinvention and contemporary application of the industry-specific skills of stencil cutting.

10.2.5 International Interventions

While the above factors focus on supply-side dynamics between tradition and inno-vation, demand-side changes are the driver behind providers striving to understand and meet contemporary market needs.

However, expanding to new markets compels producers to consider whether potential new customers will understand and value their products in the same way that their existing customers do. Thus firms need to both consider whether and how to adapt or re-invent their product offerings for foreign markets, and to determine how to best communicate both the handmade nature of the item and the ethos of its craft to non-Japanese buyers.

As third-generation *oke* (wooden bucket/tub) artisan Shuji Nakagawa mentions,

> The problem is that we Japanese, ourselves, do not fully recognize the value of what we produce here… It was only when the quality and value of my work was acknowledged by many people from abroad that I finally realized how great Japanese traditional technique really was….Establishing ourselves globally depends as much on PR [sic] and design as it does the skill level that produces the work'. (Kyoto Journal 2014)

Likewise, fellow GO ON project and Japan Handmade collaborator, Masataka Hosoo, the 12th generation of Nishijin textile house Hosoo, indicates this firm belief the disparity between product and promotional know-how: '[our] product has no downsides/weaknesses but we didn't have the ability to communicate its strengths in global markets' (DBS 2016). Since then Hosoo have successfully positioned their brand so that their woven textiles decorate the boutiques of Dior and Hermes and feature in various luxury hotels.

Adapting products to foreign markets in not a uniquely modern phenomenon. The boom in Arita (and Imari) porcelain and Satsuma-ware in Europe after the 1867 Paris International Exposition led Sato (1973) to suggest that Arita porcelain, being 'inspired by continental taste…can hardly be considered truly Japanese' (Sato 1973: 10). But the sheer scale of industry decline has driven not just market savvy merchants but artisans to embrace internationalisation in order to survive. A plethora of public-sector programs have emerged to support various aspects of this process. These include national ministries and agencies such as METI, the SME Support office, and JETRO, and initiatives by prefectural and municipal government across the country. In 2018, METI budgeted 3.6 billion yen to subsidise the promotion of regional traditional crafts through local guilds, and 7.0 billion yen for the Densan Association's activities (METI 2017).

The Densan Association, for example, does not just monitor and administer the designated tradition crafts and the associated Densan Mark and provide a retail channel through their Aoyama Square but also actively foster innovation and interna-tional promotion, including through projects such as New Densan and Japan Artisan Material.

One such regional project is Kyoto Contemporary, organised and supported by Kyoto City and directed by *wagasa* master Kotaro Nishibori. While the format changed from its inception in 2013–14 to its final project in 2018–19, its objective is to pair Kyoto artisans and merchants (providers) with foreign designers and international advisors to develop new products to present at a major interior trade show Maison & Objet in Paris each January.

10.3 Cases in Internationalisation of Kyoto Artisans

Using interview and extensive observational data, five cases below reflect how artists, artisans, and merchants have wrestled with tradition, innovation, internationalisation, and survival.

10.3.1 Hiyoshiya

Assuming the role of the fifth-generation master of one of the last *wagasa* (Japanese umbrella) makers in Kyoto, Kotaro Nishibori faced this critical threat to the continuity of the house from the beginning of his tenure. After four generations, his predecessor (and mother-in-law) was considering closing the business. An outsider to the family, the industry, and the city, he agreed to train as a craftsman and head the *wagasa* house so long as he was given free rein to implement radical change. While preserving the traditions of *wagasa* craft and maintaining their existing customer base, Nishibori believed that continuity for the family business and for the craft as a whole could only come from diversifying their orientation and business model, by combining new product development with market development [For a detailed description of the Hiyoshiya's product innovation and diversification, see Lesage and Ronteau (2012)].

Taking the aesthetic and functional properties of a *wagasa* (bamboo, open/close construction, semi-translucent *washi* (paper) covering that allows light to filter through), and working with a succession of Japanese product designers, Hiyoshiya developed the *Kotori*, a bamboo-ribbed cylindrical pendant lamp made from *washi* and that was collapsible just like its *wagasa* inspiration. This collapsibility brings significant utility in terms of storage and shipping, but allowed the aesthetic and ethos of the wagasa into homes, hotels, and restaurants. By varying the shape, colour, and silhouetted patterns, and extending the bamboo ribs allowed for a product line extension to stand-alone floor lamp.

Together with Japanese designer Kazushige Miyake, Nishibori next embarked on an extensive trial and error process of exhibiting prototypes at international design trade shows, based on buyers' observations that the *Kotori* was "too Japanese", ultimately arriving at the *Moto*, a new lampshade rich with the DNA of *wagasa* without using the traditional materials of bamboo and *washi*. However, as Hiyoshiya artisans were unable to make the shades for this product, a suitable contract manufacturer was found in China. While this diverges from the craft's origin in both function, materials, and manufacture location, it provided a modern and less Japanese aesthetic, further diversifying the reach of Hiyoshiya.

On the back of these successes, Nishibori began working with international designers and attracted the attention of luxury European brands. The critical result for Hiyoshiya was that as they developed knowledge and experience, and as sales grew, they were able to use revenue from sales of new products not both cross-subsidise their extant *wagasa* business—effectively sustaining their traditional craft with revenue from their innovations—and also fund further product and market development. Ultimately, Nishibori weighs insights from buyers, distributors, and designers with what he believed the essence of the company and the craft to be, that "tradition is continuing innovation".

Subsequently, Nishibori sought to nurture these skills in other artisans and traders, instilling them with the creative confidence to step outside of the notional boundaries of their craft, the national boundaries of their traditional distribution networks, and to collaborate with international designers. Government sponsored programs (such as Kyoto Contemporary) where he acts as coordinator/director, aim to develop these innovative competencies in local artisans and merchants. Below are four short cases of participants in Kyoto Contemporary and other programs, each reflecting a different perspective on innovation and internationalisation.

10.3.2 Kobori Butsugu

With origins dating back to 1775, *kyo-butsugu* (Kyoto Buddhist altar goods) manufacturer and retailer Kobori is one of the largest manufacturers of Buddhist altars in Kyoto. Demonstrating the centralized design and in-house coordination of specialized labour, Kobori combines all stages of production of Buddhist altars for residential homes (wood carving, lacquering, metalwork, and gilding) in-house through to repairs and refurbishments for some of the largest temples in Japan, such as Higashi-Honganji in Kyoto. Demographic changes such as shrinking population and urban migration have resulted in fewer families willing to maintain family tombs, and little space in their homes for a dedicated ancestral altar. As a result, they have found their traditional markets waning. Focusing on their core values—delivering peace and tranquillity—Kobori has steadily expanded sales into Asian markets.

First participating in the Kyoto Contemporary project in 2016–17, Kobori partnered with Paris-based interior design team Atelier Pelpell, who proposed using Kobori's wood carving, lacquering, and gold leaf gilding expertise to produce high-end artisanal wall tiles for luxury hotels, restaurants, and boutiques. *Urushi* lacquering is a time-consuming process usually applied layer upon layer with time needed between application for the lacquer to set in a dust-free humidity-controlled room. Yet the designers sensed that the cost involved in producing the flawless mirror-finish, while revered in Buddhist altars and lacquerware, could easily be mistaken for mass-produced plastic in Europe—and also added considerably to the cost of the end product. The suggestion to apply just a few layers of lacquer to the wood was at first met with disbelief by the *urushi* craftsman: 'This is no good, it won't work,' indicating that while it could be done, his sense of workmanship and affinity with the essence of his craft required the designers to persuade him to "experiment" through prototyping and that this might allow foreign audiences to better understand his work. The resulting product, *Komyo*, (presented at Maison & Objet in 2017) combined wood carving, lacquer, and gold leaf, and in some special cases, up-cycled wood from temples that Kobori were engaged in repairing. The end result required the artisan to subjugate his usual technique in the name of the finished product, designed to appeal to a market segment the company had previously never imagined.

The following year, Kobori partnered with the same designers again to develop a product that was closer to their core business, resulting in the *Komyo Hiraku*—a small, portable altar for homes that was modern but had the aesthetic hallmarks and design sense of the Komyo tiles. While the Komyo tiles clearly do not fit the description of *kyo-butsugu* (the designated traditional craft) the experience in product and market innovation allowed Kobori to explore new market segments, new consumer trends, and new techniques they had otherwise not thought to employ.

10.3.3 Kumagai

As a large *kyo-yaki* and *kiyomizu-yaki* wholesaler/merchant founded in 1935 and located in the centre of the Kiyomizu-yaki ceramics area, Kumagai Co. Ltd. has built an extensive network of ceramic artists and potters (*kamamoto*) in Kyoto of whose works the company distributes. Highlighting the distinction between ceramic artists and artisans (ceramicists or potters), Kumagai exhibits and distributes collections of artists, whose work bears the artists' name and seal, but their main business involves contracting potters to produce tableware and other items on their wheels and in their kilns without affixing their name or seal.

While this latter activity allows them to engage in new product development, as a merchant, Kumagai do not produce in-house but instead have served as market makers, connecting their network of potters to traditional distributors and retailers such as department stores, specialty retailers, and other wholesalers. The dilemma facing the company is typical of many surviving merchants in the traditional sector, as the wholesale system began to collapse due to its specialized nature and the fall demand for traditional products.

Under the helm of third generation head Takayoshi Kumagai, the company has responded by bolstering its product development prowess and international marketing expertise, first by participating in projects such as Kyoto Contemporary, Neo-Densan, Japanese Artisanal Material, and Contemporary Japanese Design.

Participating in the Kyoto Contemporary project for three years, before "graduating" and shifting to the Neo-Densan Project, the company embarked on regular collaborations with Japanese and international designers that saw them produce eclectically designed bowls and vessels with unique glazes, as well as applying *kyo-yaki* techniques to interior decorative tiles. The form and decoration of many of these new works is decidedly modern and in stark contrast to the often-decorative motifs of *kiyomizu-yaki*. While all the ceramics are thrown and fired in Kyoto, these products do not necessarily bare the *kyo-yaki/kiyomizu-yaki* traditional craft Densan Mark.

As a result, Kumagai created a new subsidiary brand, "=K+" (representing the company name, it's location (Kyoto) and the *kyo-yaki/kiyomizu-yaki* that it produces) specifically to collaborate with designers 'from different cultural backgrounds'. By creating its own brand and product range, Kumagai has shifted from merchant to producer of original goods. Furthermore, realising the skill shortage, they have sought to provide a space to develop young talent by installing a kiln on their premises and a space for painters to carry out *utsushi* reproductions under the supervision of a master artisan. The ability to expand their existing customer base through product and market development is critical not only for Kumagai but for the survival of their local network of artisans.

10.3.4 Takahiro Kato/Joubugama

Ceramicist Takahiro Kato runs a kiln Joubugama in Kyoto's Kiyomizu-yaki area producing hand-thrown, hand-painted, and hand-glazed pieces in small-batch with his small team of artisans. However, Kato's credentials as a ceramic artist are firmly established through his regular solo pieces being exhibited at the national Nitten exhibition (being selected for an award in 2019 for his piece *Waterfall*). Kato believes this dual identity of artisan an artist is natural:

> My work as an artisan is to meet the needs of customers. Not simply just to make something as instructed but to propose suggestions on how it can be made better. My work as an artist is about wholehearted self-expression…that only I can do. These experimental applications of techniques and accidental discoveries feedback to my work as artisan by allowing me to make something that surpasses the expectations of customers.

This insight to such a dual professional identity indicates that the artist/artisan divide is actually likely to be an organisational distinction rather than one of technical prowess. Ultimately his identity as artist allows Kato to budget ample time for experimentation—effectively research and development—that pure artisans may struggle to find.

As the representative of Joubugama, Kato participated in Kyoto Contemporary 2016–17 collaborating with Paris-based design duo AC/AL. Through a process of trial and error where the designers' prototypes were unable to survive the firing process, the team came to focus on Kato's expertise and methodical experimentation with glazing techniques, choosing several two-tone combinations from hundreds of test glazes for their final product: vase *Tomo*. While the item only saw muted success at Maison & Objet, the positive experience of working in this team stimulated Kato to seek out AC/AL again. Yet after just one year in the Neo-Densan project he shelved this project to focus on a new market: providing high-end architectural and building materials such as bathroom vanity basins based on *kyo-yaki* techniques through an additional "brand extension"—Joubu Art.

Kato's clear understanding of how his experimental work as an artist allows him—and his team—to excel as artisans provides an insight not just to the identity of ceramicists but more importantly into the critical role that experimentation and creativity play in a nominally "traditional" sector.

10.3.5 Nishimura Yuzen Chokoku

Kyo-yuzen, a Kyoto-based kimono dying technique registered as a traditional craft in 1976 and broadly includes two specific techniques: hand-painted *yuzen* and stencil-dyed *yuzen*. Yet as changes in consumer preferences, advances in printing technology, and low-cost global outsourcing has left artisans with little opportunity to apply their lifelong trade.

Takeshi Nishimura, a *kyo-yuzen* stencil maker, cuts stencils by hand with his own handmade tools, applying the craft he learned from his father as an apprentice. Yet being responsible for only one stage of production in the value chain of a declining industry, he encouraged his own children to pursue a career elsewhere. 'It would be irresponsible for me to take an apprentice when I know they won't be able to make a living out of it,' says Nishimura, now in his sixties.

His dilemma is characteristic of challenges facing those sectors of the industry that have been highly specialised. As demand for locally-produced kimono has plummeted, technological advances have meant that his precision hand cutting can be efficiently achieved by a machine's blade or laser with less variation, and industrial printers can pattern-dye textiles with much lower cost and faster response time.

Nishimura's goal through Nishimura Yuzen Chokoku is to create a platform that will allow his craft (or art) to continue to the next generation. To do this, he needs not only innovative designs, but new applications outside of the specialized industry that developed around the production of custom-dyed *yuzen* textile for kimono. Yet as a solo artisan, Nishimura faces the high opportunity cost of downing tools for any new product development or market development activity. As such, much of his work outside the *yuzen* space had resulted from fielding requests for product development—such as tumbler inserts and leather iPhone and iPad cases that reveal their carved design when backlit. His carving demonstrations in Firenze, Paris, and Tokyo always draw a crowd who marvel at his technique, yet this rarely converts to sales.

Participating in projects such as Kyoto Contemporary over three years saw him diversify his materials from paper to leather and wood, working with international designers. Through such projects, Nishimura has tirelessly applied his technique to the development of new products such as desk caddy and stationary accessories, a wood sheet candle holder *Komorebi*, and a decorative fan that sought to tie in aspects of *yuzen* production materials. Naturally none of this work classifies as a designated traditional craft, yet his status as one of the few stencil cutters remaining in Kyoto has earned him the accolade "the legend" by those close to him.

Yet the high cost of his time-intensive work has born muted success in the consumer products, and collaborating designers have wrestled with resolving a critical challenge: how to express the handmade nature of Nishimura's work to the extent that buyers will recognise it and be willing to pay a premium. His response has been to refocus his work as an artist not an artisan, which has led to design collaborations in retail spaces and hotel lobbies, and since 2018 collaborate with French visual artists. Yet despite this artistic recognition and his ability to stay busy while the *yuzen* industry continues to shrink, he, like many other artisans, has thus far struggled to reach his goal of creating a lasting platform for the continuation of his craft and art.

10.4 Conclusions

As indicated by the continual decline of traditional crafts, the Densan Act on its own has not slowed the decline. Yet it is difficult to calculate the extent to which firms have proactively engaged in new product development and market development based on these figures alone as these only account for sales in designated traditional craft.

While there are some cases of intrinsically innovative firms in this sector, programs supported by regional governments, led by successful pioneers have allowed access to new creative inputs and international markets.

Importantly, the registering of a traditional craft (*dento kogeihin*) does not prevent certified artisans and manufacturers who produce these works from creating related works outside of the traditional craft goods framework. Works that have changed according to the above processes may not be officially considered "traditional" craft but most are producers accept this reality.

As indicated above, the internationalisation imperative has resulted in varying degrees but nonetheless a significant volume of product innovation. While this may result in a divergence from the codified essence of the craft and possibly a divergence from strict definition of traditional craft, it in allowing more latitude for changes to incorporate outside influences and change production processes and materials, arguably brings the practices back closer to their innovative historical origins.

Indeed, there is an emerging consensus among industry players that tradition and innovation are not merely compatible but rather that the very concept of tradition entails a process of repetitive innovation to reinterpret yesterday's successes to meet today's needs. In this light, efforts to catalyse innovation across the sector in Kyoto are not radical but rather an attempt to return to the tradition of creative receptivity that has characterised the crafts' evolution for a millennium.

References

Adamson, G. (2007). *Thinking through craft*. London: V&A Press.
Adamson, G. (2013). *The invention of craft*. London: V&A Press.

Association for the Promotion of Traditional Craft Industries (Densan Association). (2017). *Traditional crafts of Japan*, Association for the Promotion of Traditional Craft Industries.

Bauhaus Manifesto. (n.d). Manifesto of the Staatliches Bauhaus—Walter Gropius, April 1919. https://bauhausmanifesto.com. Accessed January 19, 2018.

Densan Association. (n.d. a). *Traditional Craft—Kyo-yaki/Kiyomizu-yaki—Notice* (in Japanese) https://kougeihin.jp/craft/0414/#notice.

Densan Association. (n.d. b). *Traditional Craft—Nishijin-ori—Notice* (in Japanese) https://kougeihin.jp/craft/0120/#notice.

Densan Association. (n.d. c). *Traditional Craft—Tokyo Antimony—Notice* (in Japanese) https://kougeihin.jp/craft/070310/#notice.

Densan Association. (2018). *Genjo [Current situation]* (in Japanese) https://kyokai.kougeihin.jp/current-situation/.

Doshisha Business School. (2016). *Dento Sangyou Bunka Bijinesu no miraizu [The future of traditional industries and cultural business]* (in Japanese) Doshisha Business School.

Gore, N. (2004). Craft and innovation: Serious play and the direct experience of the real. *Journal of Architectural Education, 58*(1), 39–44.

Guth, C. M. E. (2010). The multiple modalities of the copy in traditional Japanese crafts. *Journal of Modern Craft, 3*(1), 7–18.

Hiyoshiya. (n.d.). *Wagasa no rekishi/ Kyo-wagasa nitsuite [The history of the Wagasa/About Kyo-Wagasa]* (in Japanese) https://www.wagasa.com/kyowagasa/history/.

Kida. (2010). Traditional art crafts (Dentō Kōgei) in Japan: from reproductions to original works. *The Journal of Modern Craft, 3*(1), 19–35.

Kyoto Journal. (2014). Nakagawa Shuji: Oke Maker—Interview by Steve Beimel. https://kyotojournal.org/conversations/nakagawa-shuji-oke-maker/. Accessed February 3, 2017.

Lesage, X., & Ronteau, S. (2012). Assessing embedded agency of entrepreneurs in context of internationalization and innovation: An exploratory research. *International Business Research, 5*(6), 62–72.

MAFF—Ministry of Agriculture Forestries and Fisheries. (2017). *Nihon no dento bunka o sasaeru "urushi" [Urushi: Supporting Japan's traditional culture]* Rinya Issue No. 129 December 2017.

METI—Ministry of Economy Trade and Investment. (2011). *Dentoteki kogeihin sangyou o meguru genjo to kongo no koshin shisaku [Current situation and future promotional policies for the traditional craft industries]* (in Japanese) Traditional Craft Industries Office, Manufacturing Industries Bureau, METI. February 2011.

METI. (2017). *Dento kogeihin sangyo no genjyo to shinko ni muketa torikumi [Current situation and approach to promoting the traditional craft industries]* (in Japanese) METI Kanto Office, September 2017.

Murata, D. (2015). The Kogei tragedy. *The Journal of Modern Craft, 8*(1), 9–28.

Murayama, Y. (2019). *Heritage cultural and business, Kyoto style: Craftsmanship in the creative economy* (English Edition). Japan Publishing Industry Foundation for Culture.

Pye, D. (1968). The *nature of art and workmanship*. London: Herbert Press (Reprint 2015).

Raku, Y., & Matsubara, R. (2016). *Chawan no naka no uchu [The cosmos in a tea bowl]* (in Japanese) Kodansha.

Rausch. (2009). Japanese rural revitalization: The reality and potential of cultural commodities as local brands. *Japanstudien, 20*(1), 223–245.

Sato, M. (1973). *Kyoto ceramics (Arts of Japan)* (English edition). Art Media Resources.

Sato, D. (2011). *Modern Japanese art and the Meiji state: The politics of beauty* (English Edition). Getty Publications.

Adam Johns is an Associate Professor at Sophia University's Faculty of Economics in Tokyo. Specializing in the international marketing, place branding, and policy of cultural and creative industries, his research has examined branding, product development, and international expansion of Japanese cultural and creative industries such as craft, fashion, and food at the firm, industry, regional, and national level. He has previously held positions at Dōshisha University (Kyoto) and Rikkyō University (Tokyo) and holds an M.A. from Waseda University and a Ph.D. from the Australian National University.

Printed by Printforce, the Netherlands